DE

For Allan, without whे
single mile. With my lo
Roa

(A line from 'Daisy Bell

Life in tandem

Tales of cycling travels

By Jackie Winter

◆————————————◆

Chantries Press, Dorset, UK.

Book Layout © 2014 Createspace.

Cover Image by Jolyon Winter an

Life In Tandem/Jackie Winter. 1s

ISBN 978-1500198466.

CONTENTS

CHAPTER ONE
Can't ride a bike – won't ride a bike

I NEVER learned to ride a bike as a child. I was 26 before I wobbled my way half-a-mile up the road to a country pub. But I've spent the last 35 years pedalling around the countryside ... on a tandem. I still can't ride a bike but that doesn't matter because on the back of a tandem you don't need to.

I've freewheeled downhill at 45 mph – sometimes even with my eyes open – and I've managed to smile on the numerous occasions someone has yelled at my husband: "She's not pedalling at the back!"

I have countless holiday photographs in which only Allan or I appear, always holding the tandem, which takes centre stage as if by right, usually laden with saddlebag and panniers, against a background of sea, mountain or lake.

I really wish I'd kept count but I know I've ridden at least 100,000 miles. However, I can still vividly remember the very first time my bum made contact with a saddle, back in the 1970s.

Allan and I had been married for almost two years, it was a warm Sunday just after Easter and we were enjoying a walk in the Dorset lanes not far from our home, when we spotted a bike heading in our direction. As a true cycling fanatic, Allan's eyes lit up but mine glazed over, glancing instead towards the True Lovers Knot pub, where I was looking forward to my ploughman's lunch.

"It's a tandem." Allan grabbed my hand. "Look, a tandem!"

Whoopee-doo, I thought. Some weird couple on a tandem. Do I have to talk to them?

As they drew closer, Allan became even more excited.

"That looks like Theo," he said. "He sings at the folk club."

They slowed to a halt beside us. Well, they had to. Allan practically leapt out into the road in front of them. The men launched into bike talk immediately. Mysterious stuff about gears, cranks and rear suspension. The girl smiled at me, wryly amused.

"I'm Jess," she said. "I haven't a clue what they're on about either. We're making for the pub. Is it far?"

"Less than half-a-mile," I replied. "We're going there too."

"Tell you what," said Theo, presumably taking pity on my husband's wistful expression. "How about you two cycle to the pub on the tandem and we'll walk there?"

I stared at him. No way was I getting on that thing. I ignored Allan's eager face.

"I'd love to," I lied. "But I'm afraid I can't ride a bike."

Then Jess uttered three extraordinary words. "Neither can I," she said.

So Allan got on the front of the tandem, Theo held it steady and Jess made encouraging noises, while I endeavoured to hoist myself on to the saddle.

"Keep it straight," Theo advised Allan. "It's not like on a solo, when you can lean the bike over. It's important to always keep the tandem upright when setting off."

"Tell Allan when you're ready to go and press down hard on the pedals," Jess told me. "If the bike wobbles, don't panic. It's probably because you're gripping the handlebars too hard, so try to relax. It's all much easier than it sounds, honestly."

"You can reach the pedals OK anyway," Theo said. "You and Jess must be a similar height. Your trainers won't fit into the toe clips but don't worry about that. You'll be all right, as you're not cycling far."

I wasn't worrying about toe clips, whatever *they* might be. I had other things to fret about. Like trying to bend my knees in my tight jeans. Like wondering how on earth I was going to get off the bike without Theo there to hold it. Like that patch of thinning hair at the back of my husband's head, which I'd never noticed before.

I felt safe enough, with Allan's bulk solidly in front of me, and I knew his cycling credentials were second to none, so I wasn't really worried about falling off. But the technique of pedalling was alien to me and I didn't know whether or not to lean when we turned a corner. My trainers were clumsy on the pedals and I couldn't get into a smooth rhythm. A couple of ramblers stopped to watch as we passed and I felt self-conscious, but also oddly pleased with myself.

It wasn't until a long time later that I understood how generous Theo and Jess had been, allowing a total novice like me to wobble even a short distance up the road on the back of their cherished tandem. Fortunately we arrived at the True Lovers Knot without mishap and Allan remained firmly on the bike, one foot planted solidly on the road, while I thankfully slithered off the saddle.

"What do you think?" He looked so thrilled, so hopeful, that I couldn't bear to spoil it.

"It was fun," was the best I could manage and a long way from the whole truth. I was relieved to have the ground beneath my feet again. It was hard to imagine myself ever getting fond of this cycling lark – and did I really want to anyway?

Lunch, on the other hand, was definitely fun and we were soon well on the way to becoming friends. Theo and Jess were married, although they were both still studying. He was in his second year of a PhD and she was at teacher training college. They lived in Cambridge but Theo had grown up in Dorset and they were spending a couple of weeks visiting his parents.

"Can you really not ride a bike?" I asked Jess.

"No, I can't. But Theo persuaded me to give the tandem a try and I absolutely love it."

"Non-cyclists make perfect stokers," said Theo.

"What's a stoker?" I asked.

"The one on the back," he explained. "If you've never ridden a bike, you're far less likely to try to steer or control it. So, are you two thinking of getting a tandem?" He looked expectantly at Allan and Jess looked mischievously at me.

"Well, Jackie took to yours straight away," my husband said, adding, before I could dilute this statement with a few unwelcome nuggets of truth, "I thought she was a natural on the bike. Anyone would think she'd been pedalling around for years."

"She's the right build for cycling," said Theo. "Looked very comfortable on the tandem."

"Far better than me, the first time I had a go," Jess agreed.

I said nothing, concentrating on my last pickled onion. I knew Allan well enough to recognise a bit of crafty flattery but I was enjoying our new friends' praise, while at the same time deploring my gullibility, which I could see was likely to lead me into trouble.

"You don't see many tandems," Allan said. "I can't understand why they're not more popular."

"Their heyday was during the first part of the 20th century," Theo said. "After the Second World War, people aspired to owning cars and that was the start of their decline. But there's been quite a revival recently."

"Do you have a roof rack for your tandem?" Allan asked. "I suppose you've driven down from Cambridge?"

"I can't drive," said Theo. "Neither of us can. We go everywhere by bike and train."

They were in fact a far less conventional couple than us. Vegetarians – less common in the seventies – and most disconcerting of all, in my opinion, they didn't own a TV. I couldn't imagine spending evenings without the company of *The Likely Lads* or *The Two Ronnies*.

Theo and Jess had travelled many miles on their tandem. After they married, during the long summer break from university, they'd cycled all through northern France.

"We camped," Theo said. "French camp sites are great. Much better than British ones."

"How on earth did you carry everything on the bike?" I asked.

"Just panniers and a saddlebag," Theo shrugged. "It's easy to travel light if you want to."

"And you've never resorted to bizarre measures to keep the weight down, have you, love?" Jess grinned. "Tell them about the toothbrushes."

Apparently, after one exhausting day spent grinding up the Normandy hills, Theo had sawn their toothbrushes in half and thrown away the handles, in an attempt to lighten the load.

"Paris was great," Theo said. "We did some tourist stuff."

"Hardly anything," Jess protested. "I'd have loved a boat trip on the Seine but Theo wouldn't leave the bike."

"Too risky," he said. "Especially in a city. Tandems are unusual, so they attract attention. But at least they aren't easy to jump on and make a quick getaway, not like a solo bike."

Later on in the ladies, Jess confided that there were times in France when she wouldn't have cared if the tandem had been stolen.

"So you didn't enjoy the holiday?" I surprised myself by feeling a little disappointed.

"I did, but there weren't enough rest days and 10 weeks is too long to go without a decent loo. Men don't understand how girls feel about these things." Jess smiled at me. "I need an ally."

On our return, we found that a bike ride was being planned for the following weekend. Theo's parents rode a tandem and also had a spare one tucked away in the shed, which apparently 'would be perfect for a beginner like me'. Watching our new friends cycle off, I felt a mixture of excitement and apprehension.

Allan was very bossy when we arrived home, issuing instructions about what 'Real Cyclists' wore, but I took no notice. I had neither the money nor the inclination to buy shorts from the Hebden Cord catalogue he produced. Apparently 'Real Cyclists' were slavish followers of this boring company. Well, I was going to be different.

I had a pair of yellow cord jeans, no longer in the prime of life, which would be perfect. Incredulous, Allan watched me take the scissors to them and start hacking. When I'd finished, I felt rather pleased with my efforts. I'd used the spare material to make padding for the bum, which after even a mile on a bike I realised was essential. Allan's shorts had chamois padding stitched into them, which used to make me snigger – but now I could appreciate the need for some cushioning.

"Not bad," admitted my husband, as I paraded in front of him. "You've certainly got cyclist's legs." I chose to take this as a compliment.

I was so used to thinking of cycling as something which Allan did and I put up with, that I couldn't quite believe what was happening. Did I really want to pedal for miles, getting hot, tired and red in the face? It sounded far too much like *exercise*, not a word that had so far entered my personal vocabulary. And yet that short bike ride to the pub had been exhilarating and I knew I wanted to repeat the experience.

I would never have believed I'd be a cyclist. Not a remotely sporty sort of girl, I'd done my best to avoid all athletic activities at school. I just wanted to read books and the first place I remember walking to on my own was the library. Mum enjoyed cycling and she used to ride to work from Broadstone into Poole before she got married, which was about four miles each way. But I don't remember seeing her on a bike until she was about 50, when a hefty black one made a sudden appearance.

After that, Mum cycled into Winton to do her shopping nearly every day and thoroughly enjoyed her independence from buses and fares. I had a go on her bike once – and rode it straight into a wall. I was my mother's only child and she loved me dearly but she rushed straight to that bike, clucking over it and making sure it was OK, before casting so much as a glance in my direction – and that was only to tell me off.

So when I met Allan and discovered he was a keen cyclist, it wasn't something in his favour. An enthusiasm for bikes was something he shared with his dad, although Arthur also liked motorbikes. When they lived in Yorkshire he'd owned a Norton, which after a few hours spent at the pub, he'd once ridden straight through the house – in at the front door and out at the back.

Allan cycled to work every day, which was a round trip of about 20 miles, and that seemed enough to feed the obsession, so on the whole this hobby was easy enough for me to live with. And it certainly kept him fit – a flat tummy, muscular thighs and nice broad shoulders.

Allan worked for a builder's merchant and I was a library assistant, so neither of us were high earners, but that didn't stop us having big ideas. I was fairly besotted with my Yorkshire lad by now and raised no objection when he set his heart on an elderly white MGB. Even his mum Betty tried to talk some sense into me, cautiously suggesting that perhaps we should be thinking of saving our money and not squandering it on a cash-gobbling sports car.

Betty was absolutely right, as I realised a few months later when due to the first of many expensive breakdowns, I had to buy my own engagement ring. The only positive thing about the MGB was that, for a while at least, it did get Allan off his bike.

We married on 1st June 1974 and spent our honeymoon camping in my husband's beloved Yorkshire Dales. Unfortunately, it rained every day, enveloping the moors in thick wet cloud, which meant I returned to Dorset still sadly ignorant of their beauty.

Our first home was a tiny, middle-terraced cottage in the village of Spetisbury, in north Dorset. The bedroom ceiling was cross stitched with black oak beams, there was an inglenook fireplace in the sitting room and a dormer window at the top of the stairs, which looked out on to the River

Stour at the bottom of the garden. We thought ourselves the luckiest couple in the world.

The car had to live on the road and it sulked by frequently refusing to start on chilly mornings. The owner of the filling station would sometimes take pity on us and help push it, which usually persuaded it to choke into reluctant life. Even after all these years, Allan's expression is wistful when he sees a white MGB. But I just shudder, as the memories surface.

I was looking forward to seeing our new friends again and on the appointed day we drove to Theo's parents' house near Poole. Mr and Mrs Wood had an old Freddie Grubb tandem in their garage, which was coming out of its long retirement just for us. Cyclist and bike builder Freddie Grubb had won two silver medals in the 1912 Stockholm Olympics, which gave an eye-watering clue as to the bike's age.

"Real Cyclists never sell their bikes," Theo's dad told me. "Even when you're proud as punch of a spanking new one, a Real Cyclist can't bear to part with that trusty old friend."

There was that phrase again –a 'Real Cyclist'. Mr Wood was certainly one of those, smartly clad in serviceable Hebden Cord. He and Theo were rather alike. Both had slightly melancholy expressions, alleviated by brown eyes with a tantalising hint of mischief.

"Will you two be all right on that old tandem?" Mrs Wood looked anxious. "It's very heavy."

"Jess and I could ride it," Theo offered. "It's a great bike. Mum, did you know Fred Grubb belonged to the Vegetarian Cycle and Athletic Club?"

"Did he, dear? People couldn't be choosy during the war years. Things are different now."

"We'll probably never get another opportunity to ride a Grubb," Allan said. "I'm looking forward to it. Where shall we go?"

As it was a warm and sunny day, we decided to cycle to the Scott Arms at Kingston, near Corfe Castle. I knew the pub well, as the folk club held regular singing sessions there. I also knew it was at the top of a very steep hill.

"Bit of a climb up to the Scott," I said.

"If you run out of puff, tell Allan you want to get off and walk," Jess told me. "That's what I do and if Theo objects, I put less effort into pedalling and then he soon changes his mind because he has to work a lot harder."

After a bit of adjustment to the height of the saddle, I managed to hoist myself on to Freddie Grubb without much assistance. Three tandems travelling in convoy are a rare sight and several cars slowed down to get a good look. One driver even honked his horn as he passed, which startled me.

"Stop wobbling," Allan instructed and I glared at the back of his head. *Stop wobbling, indeed.* I wanted more of the admiration and encouragement I'd enjoyed last time – or I'd not only stop wobbling, I'd take Jess's advice and slacken off the pedalling, too.

We boarded the ferry from Sandbanks to Studland. Cycling to the front of the long line of motorists queuing for the ferry was very gratifying, as was paying the modest return fare for a pushbike. The attendant looked at us rather doubtfully but tandems obviously didn't figure in his rate of charges, so we paid the same as solo bikes.

Most people were headed for the beaches but we cycled into Studland village and turned off along the road to Corfe Castle. We were in single file most of the time because of passing cars, so weren't able to chat much. Nevertheless, cycling in a small group like this had a companionable feel about it.

The spring sun was warm on my bare legs and I felt pleased with my homemade shorts, which both Jess and her mother-in-law had admired. Jess was wearing a pretty blue headscarf embroidered with white daisies, which tried unsuccessfully to restrain her tangled brown curls.

We'd travelled in this direction many times before in the car but that had been entirely different. On a bike, I almost felt part of the landscape and being at the back of a tandem meant I'd no responsibility for braking or steering, so I could concentrate on simply enjoying the scenery. The hedgerows were golden with primroses and daffodils and an occasional tang of freshly cut grass scented the air. We'd been going downhill for at least a minute and I suddenly realised that right now, I'd sooner be freewheeling along this road than doing anything else in the whole world, even getting stuck into the new Ruth Rendell.

At Corfe Castle we turned towards Kingston and the road soon started to climb steeply. It was hard work and, using some instinct I didn't know I had, I got my head down and put some serious effort into it. I wondered what was going on when Allan pulled out into the middle of the road, then I realised we were passing Mr and Mrs Wood. I felt I should apologise to them, as it seemed such a rude thing to do. They were the 'Real Cyclists' after all. Theo and Jess were still a little way in front of us and hardly slowing down, let alone giving up and walking. I gritted my teeth, kept going and at last we reached the top, with the Scott Arms ahead of us. Breathless, I was pleased to discover I wasn't the only one who needed a few moments to recover.

Theo glanced back. "I see we've left the other two behind."

"Shouldn't we wait for them?" I still felt uncomfortable.

"Getting the drinks in would be a better idea," Theo said. "Mum and Dad always walk up steep hills like that one."

We were sitting in the pub garden, looking at the lunch menu, when his parents arrived. "You kids are young and fit." Mr Wood settled himself in front of his Guinness. "We were like that once."

"Well done, Jackie," his wife said. "You did brilliantly. Are you enjoying yourself?"

I was certainly enjoying myself now, sitting in the sunshine and looking forward to a plateful of Wareham trout, with salad and chips. But as far as that hill was concerned, Theo's parents had my sympathy. However, everyone was looking at me expectantly.

"It was fun," I said, which was the same answer I'd given Allan the previous week at the True Lovers Knot. But this time I found I really meant it.

Mr and Mrs Wood set off for home as soon as they'd finished lunch. Theo's mum wanted to get started on a farewell meal for Theo and Jess, who were returning to Cambridge the next day.

"Do your legs ache, Jackie?" Jess asked.

"Only a bit," I said. "But my bum hurts."

She nodded, sympathetically. "It'll feel even worse when you get going again," she warned. "But it does wear off, after a while."

"You must get your own tandem," Theo urged. "We could go on holiday together."

"That would be great," Allan said. "But perhaps we should buy a second-hand one first and get some miles in, just until we're sure about it. Any ideas?"

Theo recommended Les Simpson Cycles, near Poole, so the following Saturday we headed straight there. It was a popular shop and we had a long wait. Allan didn't mind this because he enjoyed pottering around, mysteriously comparing hub dynamos with bottom bracket dynamos and muttering about gear ratios. I found it excruciatingly boring. After I'd tutted over the crazy price of new bikes, managed to resist the entire range of energy bars, admired the pretty patterns on the kids' water bottles and read the notice-board several times, I'd had enough.

When we finally pinned Les down, Allan explained that we were looking for a cheap, second-hand tandem.

"Well I never." Les looked so pleased, anyone would think we were his favourite niece and nephew. "I've got just the thing for you. You won't be able to believe your luck."

He took us through the shop and into a small space cluttered with bikes in various stages of repair. Allan spotted the tandem at once and stared at it in awe.

"It's a Claud Butler!" he said.

"I knew you'd be thrilled." Les beamed at us.

"What do you think?" Allan asked me, walking round the dusty green bike.

"I don't like the colour," I said and both men cast me a pitying glance.

"This is a genuine Claud," Les said, patiently. "Built in 1948."

That made it older than me. I surveyed the green machine even more doubtfully.

"Do you know who owned it?" I asked, hoping that was an intelligent question.

"A dear old couple who've just moved into the Eventide Homes," Les said. "The last time they rode it was to the Salvation Army hall, where their daughter had laid on a party to celebrate their diamond wedding anniversary. I took the sparkly balloons off the handlebars only yesterday."

I looked at him suspiciously but Les's face bore the guileless expression of an elderly teddy bear. Allan wasn't really listening.

"A pity it hasn't got the decorative lugs Claud Butler's famous for," he said, speaking in some sort of foreign language, which only Les understood.

"Ah yes." He nodded regretfully. "But then, of course, it would be much more expensive."

It turned out that the dear old couple's tandem would cost us £60. With mortgage interest rates at 13%, we didn't have much spare cash and this was a lot of money.

"Have a ride," Les urged. "Take it up the road. You can't fail to fall in love with it."

Allan was keen to have a go on Claud, so Les took us round the corner to a quiet side road.

"I'll leave you to it. Best get back to the shop." Smiling, he waved us off and we cycled slowly up the road. I felt uncomfortable and soon realised why.

"This saddle is as hard as a rock," I told Allan, wriggling around a bit.

"Stop wriggling. It'll have felt as comfy as a sofa cushion to that old lady."

"Do you mean her bum was tough as old boots?"

"Probably," he admitted. "But Real Cyclists won't be parted from their saddles. I've had my Brooks Professional since I was 15. It's real leather. Maybe I'll treat you to one for Christmas."

Silly me. I'd been hoping for some Aqua Manda perfume.

Back at the shop, Les gave Claud a quick polish and asked: "Are you riding it home?"

"We live in Spetisbury," I told him. "That's miles away."

"Ten, maybe 12. Nothing much. Not a nice ride, though," he conceded.

It turned out that Allan would have to drive me home and then come back for the tandem.

"I think it'll fit in the car," he said. "If I open the sun roof."

"Chance of a shower later on," Les said, looking doubtfully up at the sky. Ten minutes later it started tipping down.

It was still raining when Allan dropped me off at home but nothing could stop him going back for that tandem. A couple of hours later I opened the door to my rather damp husband, wheeling a bike loosely draped in a layer of plastic sheeting. He stood on the step, looking at me expectantly.

"Let us in then," he said, clearly in high spirits.

"Where's it going to live?" I suddenly realised we hadn't discussed this and as the house was middle-terraced, there was no side entrance.

"In the back garden. I'll make a proper cover tomorrow but it's OK for the time being. Let us in, out of the rain."

"You're not wheeling it across the sitting room," I protested. "My dad bought us this carpet and I don't want mucky wet tyre tracks all over it."

Then I remembered Allan's dad riding his motorbike through the house. Could history be about to repeat itself? Was this some manly Yorkshire ritual, passed down from father to son? I folded my arms and positioned all seven stone of myself squarely in front of husband and bike.

"I'll carry it," Allan said, patiently. "Open the back door."

Ten minutes later we were drinking tea and admiring Claud, who was leaning against the fence underneath his plastic overcoat.

"I'm really looking forward to our first bike ride," Allan said. "The weather forecast is pretty good for tomorrow. Where shall we go?"

We were keen to show off the tandem, so it was a toss-up between cycling to my mother's house or his parents. In the end Mum won because she lived a little closer, but it was still a long way for our first ride on Claud and although we took as many minor roads as possible, there was quite a lot of traffic.

When Mum opened the door, I immediately noticed the hideous cycling shorts she was wearing but it was still a surprise when she started cooing over Claud, calling him the most splendid bike she'd ever seen and what a beautiful shade of green. Even if he wanted to, there was no way Allan could have turned down her eager request to go for a ride.

It was at least an hour later before they returned, by which time my mother's credit rating with Allan had soared and I had a sneaky suspicion she put more effort into her pedalling than I did.

"She never complained about the saddle once," Allan teased, as we cycled home.

"I'm not surprised," I said. "Those shorts were so thick she wouldn't have felt a thing."

"They looked like vintage Hebden Cord to me," Allan mused. "Fancy your mum being a Real Cyclist. I wonder if she'd let you borrow them?"

My friends were surprised and amused when I told them about the tandem. They couldn't believe I enjoyed going for bike rides and some thought I was only doing it to please Allan.

"Does he threaten to go off cycling on his own and leave you behind?" Jan asked. She was my best friend but her marriage had lasted all of six months and she took a cynical view of wedded bliss. "I know Allan's not bad looking and that soft Yorkshire accent is really sexy but stick up for yourself, girl. Come out with me and have some fun."

"I enjoy cycling," I said. "I like seeing the countryside from the back of a tandem, instead of through a car window. I like the satisfaction of climbing to the top of a hill and whizzing down the other side."

"You like having aching legs and a sore bum?" Jan asked.

"I'm a lot fitter than I used to be," I said. "And my bum will toughen up. Eventually."

This was rather a sore point, as it were. Apparently the condition is a common one, especially among novice cyclists and is called being Saddle Sore. There are various remedies for it, a good saddle being most important. Allan swore by his Brooks Professional but because they were very expensive, I wasted much time and cash on hopeless substitutes. The first saddle I bought was a fairly wide, padded one. It felt lovely when I first sat on it but the comfortable feeling didn't last long.

"It's friction, not pressure, that's the problem," Allan told me, in his wise old cyclist voice. "You need a good leather saddle and a pair of Hebden Cord shorts."

I sighed. The whole subject was indeed a total pain in the arse.

TOP TANDEM TRIVIA

Dan Albone built the first tandem in 1886, with his friend, Arthur James Wilson. Born in Biggleswade, Bedfordshire, in 1860, Dan excelled at cycling, accumulating 180 awards and prizes, even though he died when only in his mid-40s. He built a penny farthing all by himself, when he was just 13, and went on to invent other bikes, including the Postman's Parcel Carrier. Apparently he was a good-natured chap, known among his friends as Smiling Dan.

CHAPTER TWO
Bitten to bits and not enough knickers

L IVING so far apart didn't make it easy to plan a holiday with Theo and Jess and the phone bill was hefty that quarter. We'd agreed on Yorkshire, mainly because Allan was desperate to give the Dales another chance. We were disappointed to discover that Claud wasn't equipped to take panniers, so how could we carry a tent and everything we'd need for two weeks camping? The problem was solved when Theo and Jess offered to lend us their other tandem. It seemed that once this obsession really got a grip, one tandem just wasn't enough.

We bought a very small lightweight tent, a sleeping bag, two panniers and a front bag. Slowly, I began to realise just how little I could take with me. No moisturiser, only sun protection cream; no hairdryer, only a small comb; no perfume, only deodorant; no sleeping mat, only the hard ground. I phoned Jess and listened in horror to the voice of experience.

"Only five T-shirts," she advised, "and seven pairs of knickers. Socks are very important, especially if it rains, so take as many as possible. You'll need waterproofs, a warm jumper and one towel between the two of you. It'll get a bit smelly, I'm afraid."

I reflected that it wasn't just our towel which would be smelly – and long before the end of a fortnight.

"Only seven pairs of knickers!" I squeaked.

"You turn them inside out on the second day," Jess explained. "That way you can make them last for two weeks. We tried paper pants once but they disintegrated."

"What about normal clothes for going to the pub in the evening?" I asked, though I doubted whether four whiffy cyclists would be made welcome anywhere.

"Depends how isolated the camp site is," was her unpromising reply. "Farmers' fields tend to be remote. And we're often knackered after cycling all day and go to bed early. But take something, just in case."

Rebelliously, I packed one of my favourite dresses and a pair of flip-flops. Allan and I had different ideas about what ranked as essential items.

"You can't take books," he said after catching me hiding the latest James Herriot inside a T-shirt.

"His books are set in the Dales," I protested. "It's research. I'll never survive a fortnight without anything to read."

"Theo's bound to buy a newspaper. You can read that."

Somehow I doubted whether clever Theo, with his First in Politics, would share my lowbrow taste in journalism. Belatedly, I was beginning to wonder what sort of holiday I'd let myself in for.

On a Saturday morning at the end of June 1976, the rising sun found us ready for the off. We drove to Jess and Theo's house in Cambridge, left our car there and we all cycled to the station to catch the London train and then a connection to Harrogate. It felt strange, riding a borrowed tandem. Already I was missing the comfortable familiarity of Claud.

Safely on the Harrogate train at last with only seconds to spare, and with the bikes in the guard's van, we sank into our seats and started to relax. I was so busy chatting that I didn't notice how quiet Allan was. Then Jess produced a packet of sandwiches she'd made that morning and suddenly I realised I was ravenous.

"Cheese and chutney or tuna and mayonnaise?" she asked. Allan went very pale, muttered something, pushed his way into the aisle and rushed towards the toilets.

"What's wrong with him?" they asked but I didn't know. He'd seemed fine earlier on. In silence, we all looked hungrily at our lunch.

"I think it would be OK," Jess said. "So long as we save him some."

"We'd better be quick," Theo said. "Before he gets back and the sight of us scoffing makes him want to throw up again."

Allan returned about ten minutes later, by which time, pleasantly replete, we were innocently admiring the scenery.

"I got in a panic when it looked as if we might miss the train," poor Allan admitted. "It was all a bit stomach-churning."

"When you feel better," Jess said kindly, "there's two cheese and chutney left."

"Thanks." Allan shuddered and we quickly changed the subject.

It was late afternoon when we reached Harrogate and we were all tired after our early start. Fortunately we'd planned to camp at Knaresborough, just three miles away. Theo already had a map of the area and it didn't take long to decide on the quietest route, avoiding main roads.

As a child, Allan had often camped at Knaresborough with his family and before that his dad used to cycle there from Barnsley with friends and camp overnight. He even did this during the war years because as a coal miner he was never conscripted. Arthur hid an old tent in an abandoned barn just outside the town and he and his friends were most upset when one day they found the tent had been stolen and they were forced to spend a chilly night, sleeping beneath the stars.

That first night in Yorkshire, we were in our sleeping bags by 9pm before it was even properly dark. We'd no pillows, of course, so we made do with folded jumpers. This was my first experience of basic camping and I was surprised and relieved to find the tent quite cosy. There weren't many other campers, so the site was quiet and sleep came quickly.

It gets light appalling early in the summer, far earlier than we realise when there's double glazing and thick curtains between us and the outside world. The birds are up for it – one and all, vociferously thrilled to welcome another day – and the dawn chorus begins with a few tiny chirrups at around 4am, expanding within minutes into the full orchestra. When I was a more hardened camper, I managed to shut out most of this joyful row, except on a few occasions when we shared our field with a herd of cows. Even a shattered cyclist can't sleep through a cacophony of early-morning mooing and trilling.

It was around 6am when I pushed my way out of the tent, obediently wearing yesterday's knickers inside out, as per Jess's instructions. In fact, all my clothes had been worn the previous day and I wasn't very happy about it. Another thing I wasn't thrilled about was a fairly urgent need to renew my acquaintance with the concrete toilet block I'd visited briefly the previous night. The floor had looked unpleasantly damp and there weren't any hooks for a towel or sponge bag. Naturally there was no loo roll.

I had the place to myself, which was good because I was very self-conscious, due to mild but persistent acne that had pursued me into my

20s. Thankfully my skin looked fairly calm, so I didn't need the concealer I'd managed to smuggle past Allan's strip search while we were packing.

I went back to the tent, noticing that the camp shop didn't open until 9.30, so the chances of buying breakfast looked remote. Once more, however, Jess had come up trumps and I found a bowlful of muesli waiting for me. No milk though, only water.

"We might as well make an early start." Allan, obviously feeling fighting fit again, was on his second bowl of muesli. He'd already got most of our stuff packed into the panniers. "We've decided to head for Pateley Bridge," he said. "It's only about 13 miles, so we'll be there long before lunchtime."

"Never mind lunch," Jess said. "Where are we stopping for coffee? Muesli and water won't keep our energy levels up for long."

I could see Jess and I were going to be kindred spirits. Once on the bike, Allan had a regrettable tendency to get his head down and keep going.

"We could have a look around Knaresborough before we set off," Theo suggested. "Isn't there a famous cave there?"

Mother Shipton's Cave is possibly the oldest visitor attraction in the UK, dating from 1630. Old Ma Shipton, a renowned 17th century soothsayer, is said to have been born in the legendary cave. But it's mainly the adjacent Petrifying Well which people find most intriguing. The water in the well has such a high natural mineral content that it can turn objects into stone and there is always an assortment of household items, slowly petrifying in the surging water. The museum has a shoe donated for petrification by Queen Mary, a lace parasol turned to stone in the 1890s, a handbag belonging to Agatha Christie and a petrified top hat, which visitors can try on.

Somewhat reluctantly, because he'd been there as a child, Allan agreed to visit the cave. But as it turned out we were far too early, unless we wanted to hang around for almost two hours because it was still only 8.15 on a Sunday morning.

We were all in high spirits as we set off to Pateley Bridge. It looked set to be a beautiful sunny day and was already getting quite hot.

"I've heard there's going to be a heatwave," Jess said. "With temperatures in the 80s and 90s."

searing sun. I put more suncream on my face and arms but feared it was already too late. I could feel my skin beginning to burn.

"You do look a bit red," Jess confirmed. "I think I've caught it too."

Her nose was very slightly pink. She tanned fairly easily, as did Theo and Allan, but I always burned and never went brown.

"A broken block sounds dreadful," I said. "What's happened?"

"I'm not absolutely sure but I know it's all to do with the gears. It means the free wheel is knackered."

"So you'll have to keep pedalling, even going downhill?" I was puzzled.

"Something like that." Jess sighed.

"Will the boys be able to fix it?" I asked.

"They might be able to do something temporary but we'll need a new block, and goodness knows where the nearest bike shop is."

We were silent for a few minutes, taking in the scenery. It was quiet and very still. Dry stone walls between peaceful green meadows continued their way into the barren moorland, zig-zagging through sheep-nibbled scrubby grass, towards the horizon. All that could be heard was the distant sound of bleating. Full of Parkin and hot tea, I was feeling pleasantly sleepy. But just as my eyes began to close, Allan plonked himself down beside us. Theo was still crouched despondently beside his tandem.

"We've shortened the chain," Allan told Jess. "You can cycle now but only using one gear. And you won't be able to freewheel. With any luck we'll make it to Appletreewick. There's a camp site there."

"How far away?" Jess sounded sleepy too and slightly apprehensive.

"About 10 miles."

"Oh well," she shrugged, "I suppose we've got all day."

Which was fortunate, as from then on progress was slow, especially as Theo and Jess were forced to walk the steep downhill stretches, as well as the uphill ones. We either walked with them, or cycled slowly and waited for them to catch up. Greenhow Hill was a long trudge under pitiless sun and there were three sections where the ascent was about one in six. We had neither the breath nor the inclination to chat and, anyway, Theo was sunk in deepest gloom. We passed signs to the Stump Cross Caverns, which were discovered in 1860 by miners looking for lead seams. But we were troubled cyclists, not carefree tourists, and without even a glance in the direction of the caves, we plodded ever onwards.

The little village of Appletreewick is as attractive as its name suggests, although we weren't in the best frame of mind that evening to appreciate its charm. At the camp site we put our tents up straightaway, still not saying much. At least we didn't have to forage for supper, as we had the Pateley Bridge lady's bacon and egg pie. Allan and I enjoyed ours but we felt sorry for Theo and Jess, who were picking out all the bits of bacon. We thought about going to the pub but in the end decided on another early night.

After breakfast, the men set off to Skipton on our tandem, as there was a good bike shop there. It would be a round trip of about 25 miles, so all being well they might be back in the early afternoon.

"I've been reading the guidebook," I told Jess, "and there are some famous gardens near here. Shall we take a look?"

"Good idea," she agreed. "Hanging around the camp site all day would be too dreary. And we can wear our ordinary clothes for a treat."

We took our money with us but left everything else inside the tents. Jess was used to this but to me it felt like leaving home and not locking up.

I felt a bit more like a normal person in my thin cotton dress and flip-flops. I was beginning to get used to people staring at us when we were on the tandems but it would be good to behave like a regular holidaymaker for a few hours. Once again the sun was blazing down and we both plastered on the suncream, though I feared it was already too late to salvage my face. I'd stopped worrying about spots – the redness from those was mingling in nicely with the sunburn.

Parcevall Hall Gardens were relatively quiet but the heat was overwhelming and we were soon thankful to find a seat in the shade, with wonderful views over Wharfdale. Jess knew a lot about plants and said she enjoyed gardening almost as much as cycling.

"One day, when we have kids and I'm home more," she said, "I'm going to grow all our own vegetables. Are you thinking about babies yet?"

I wasn't. I knew my mum would love to be a grandmother and I was her only hope, but fortunately she never pestered me, unlike my dad – but he was easily fobbed off. My father had remarried and was living in domestic bliss with my stepmother, whom he adored.

"I can't stop working," I said. "We need the money."

"We're always broke too," Jess said. "But I definitely want kids."

"I bet the first thing you do for the Terrible Twos is to buy them a telly," I told her.

It was time for lunch, so we made our way to the cafe and while we waited for our toasted sandwiches, I picked up a leaflet about the gardens. Although I enjoyed chatting to Jess, I couldn't resist the chance of something to read and Parcevall Hall had an interesting history.

The gardens had been planted by Sir William Milner and were fairly well established shortly before the start of the Second World War. Sir William sounded very grand, being the 8th Baronet of Nun Appleton, near York, but apparently he was a shy man, preferring the company of plants to people. At 6ft 7ins, he was known as a gentle giant. I read the leaflet three times, some of it aloud to Jess. After buying a pint of milk from the tea shop lady, we set off back to the camp site. Because of the heat, the milk was well past its best long before breakfast, but at least we managed several cups of tea that afternoon.

We'd been back at the camp site for less than an hour when the men returned, proudly brandishing a new block. Theo and Jess's tandem was soon back in working order and we were all in the mood to celebrate. The luxury of tea with real milk soon palled and didn't exactly count as pushing the boat out, even accompanied by a melting chocolate digestive, so we decided to search out a pie and a pint in Appletreewick.

We were surprised to find two pubs in the village, but it was easy to make a choice when we discovered that one was entirely non-smoking. None of us had ever allowed a fag to stain our lips so we confidently assumed we would feel comfortable with like-minded people. But no sooner through the door, we hesitated. Frowning, we breathed in the unpolluted air and dubiously assessed the clientele. They were all so much older than us! They didn't seem to be having much fun and the barman looked miserable and rather cross.

We didn't even bother checking the menu. Heads down and with one accord, we scuttled out and made for the other pub round the corner. Despite the annoyance of emerging at the end of the evening reeking of tobacco, somehow we felt much more at ease eating our supper surrounded by a bit of cheerful fug. Much as we liked Appletreewick, it was time to move on and the following day we intended making for Hawes, a small town further north.

We woke early as usual and packed the tents away after our breakfast of muesli and water, followed by the remainder of the stuck-together chocolate biscuits. Theo was a bit of a devil with biscuits. When we bought a packet, he squirreled it away in the front bag of their tandem and kept having a nibble as we cycled along. By the time the rest of us got to them, there were only a few crumbs left. I exaggerate, but not a lot.

That day Allan and I wore identical T-shirts, which had come free with a bottle of Brut aftershave. They were shiny white Bri-Nylon with the Brut logo printed centre stage. This was the second of the five T-shirts I'd brought with me, so it was something of a red-letter day. However, we hadn't been cycling for long before I realised we'd made a big mistake.

It was 9.30am, the sun was blazing down and it was all set to be another scorcher. It's hard to describe how uncomfortable I felt in that T-shirt. The material didn't absorb sweat at all and I just carried on getting hotter and hotter inside it. I think I might as well have been wearing a black plastic bin liner. I kept getting a whiff of Allan – a mix of BO flavoured with some sort of toxic chemical – and knew I smelt just as bad. We stopped at Kettlewell for a cup of coffee and a look at the map but not before Allan and I made a beeline for the toilets, clutching fresh T-shirts and avoiding Theo and Jess's relieved expressions. We flung those Brut ones straight into the bin.

"You should join the Tandem Club," Jess said. "They sell clothing, including rather nice cotton T-shirts. We're saving ours up for week two of the holiday."

I bought the Daily Express but could tell by his face that Theo's craving for fresh reading material was even greater than mine, so I let him have first look at it. Tomorrow it would be his turn to buy a paper and that would probably be my introduction to The Guardian. I picked up the guidebook, first to flap it around in a vain attempt to cool my burning face, before reading up about the villages en route.

"Hubberholme has one of the country's few remaining candle auctions," I informed the others. "What are candle auctions? I've never heard of them."

"I have." Theo looked up from Rupert Bear, possibly the only bit of the Daily Express he was enjoying. "They were quite common before the end of the 18th century. Lots of things were sold by candle auction, even ships."

"These days, the only ones left deal with land tenure," I quoted from the guidebook.

"What else does it say?" Theo abandoned the newspaper.

"A field called Poor Pasture is auctioned every year in January," I read. "It all happens at The George Inn, which used to be the rectory, and the vicar still acts as auctioneer. Whoever's bidding when the candle goes out gets the field for another year."

"Perhaps we could have lunch at The George," Jess suggested. "It's not far."

The thought of food and a long cold drink perked me up, struggling as I was to recover from the debilitating Brut experience.

The tiny hamlet of Hubberholme probably contained more sheep than people and the pub was quiet that Tuesday lunchtime. Almost straightaway, Allan noticed a lit candle on the counter. My instinct was to recoil from the unwelcome scrap of warmth but he was curious.

"Is it something to do with the candle auction?" he asked the barmaid.

"That's right." With a sigh, she launched into her own imitation of a guidebook, for probably the umpteenth time. "This pub used to be the rectory and the vicar, being a hospitable sort of chap, would put a lighted candle on his kitchen windowsill when he was home, as a signal to his parishioners that he wouldn't mind a bit of company. We keep up the tradition for similar reasons."

"So what happens these days at the candle auction?" Allan asked.

The barmaid sat down, waving a menu in front of her flushed face. "It's always at the beginning of January, when it's often really cold with lots of snow," she said wistfully. "The vicar plays at being an auctioneer and any farmers who want the field keep bidding until the candle goes out and there's a winner. That's it really. Do you want to order? The curried parsnip soup's off."

Before leaving Hubberholme we had a look inside the 12th century church, partly because we thought it would be lovely and cool inside but mainly because Theo wanted to go on a mouse hunt. The pews and choir stalls were the work of Robert Thompson, a Yorkshire furniture maker who was famous for carving small mice on everything he made.

"He had the idea after chatting to a customer, who complained about being as poor as a church mouse," Theo explained, prowling around the pews. "Look, here's one!"

Jess and I left the men counting mice and found a shady spot near the bikes. The views across the dale were beautiful, with the River Wharf drifting between meadows bisected by dry stone walls. Grazing sheep were dotted white in the distance and a couple of walkers trudged slowly up the hill.

"They must be so hot. At least we get a bit of cooler air when we're freewheeling." Jess leaned back, closing her eyes. "It's gorgeous here. Does Allan ever mention moving back north?"

"Sometimes, but I'm not keen. People would make fun of my snobby southern accent."

"Eeeh by gum, our lass," Jess said. "Tha'd soon be talking reet. There's nowt to it."

"What are you two giggling about?" Theo sat down beside us. "Allan's still looking for mice. I've counted more than him but he won't give up."

"Tell him there's at least 20 more," Jess suggested. "We're happy here."

But we had to move on, if we were to reach Hawes in time to do some food shopping. It was only about 10 miles but hard going along Fleet Moss, especially under the relentless sun and with heavily-laden bikes. It was a long haul, climbing to about one in four at its steepest.

Conversation petered out and we walked most of the way, pushing the tandems. In theory, we girls could choose whether to help our husbands push, or lag a few feet behind and have a natter. As Jess was the more experienced stoker, I tended to let her take the lead in making this decision. The men generally trudged uncomplainingly uphill, silent and stoical, but when the going got tough, Jess would call out to Theo: "Do you want a push, love?" He usually nodded and then I'd lend a hand with our tandem too.

Allan had been looking forward to cycling over Fleet Moss and he didn't seem particularly deterred by either the heat or the gradient. He even had enough spare breath to admire the wild, beautiful landscape and swiftly flowing river, only a few feet away from the melting tarmac beneath our wheels.

"I want my ashes scattered here," he told me. "Please don't let me finish up in Dorset."

"He's determined to find his way back to Yorkshire one way or another," Jess said and poor Allan looked quite hurt when we both started laughing. He'd been deadly serious.

After struggling up Fleet Moss we were looking forward to a freewheel into Gayle and finally Hawes. Just before the descent, we met an older couple on a tandem. The woman seemed nervous and was warning her husband against going too fast and telling him to be careful. We chatted briefly and then parted company, thinking we'd seen the last of them.

Tandems really get a move on going downhill, especially when laden with camping gear, and this descent was all too swift and the speed would possibly have been terrifying, had it not been for the sheer relief of cooler air on our burning faces.

Almost at the bottom, I looked back and was surprised to see the older couple racing along just behind us. They stopped briefly to say cheerio and the broad smile on the man's face was positively ecstatic. Allan reckoned he'd shed 10 years in two minutes but I expect his wife was relieved to see the back of four reckless youngsters.

We decided to shop for supper before finding the camp site. Hot, tired, hungry and the tiniest bit irritable, we trailed around the supermarket, slowly realising that this was not going to be easy. With only two small primus stoves and a couple of billy cans for cooking, we all had to share the same meal, which needed to be quick, simple and definitely not sausages. Theo and Jess were vegetarians mainly because they didn't like meat, so fortunately they were happy to eat fish, otherwise our choice would have been almost impossibly limited. Even so, the only ingredients we could agree on were fish fingers and boil-in-the-bag rice.

The camp site was bordered by trees and a river, which at first we thought was very pleasant, but both seemed to attract flies and mosquitoes, which became a menace during the evening. They pestered us while we were cooking, to such an extent that we eventually ate supper huddled under the inadequate shelter of our cycling capes. As usual, it was early to bed because we were so tired, but during the night I kept waking up to have a good scratch.

I was looking forward to the following day, when we would cycle to the tiny village of Keld, where holidaymakers were once woken by a bugler, before trekking to nearby waterfalls for an early-morning wash.

TOP TANDEM TIP

It only costs £10 a year to belong to the Tandem Club, which has around 4,000 members. You will receive a bi-monthly magazine and access to advice from people who are passionate about riding tandems. **www.tandem-club.org.uk**

CHAPTER THREE
Whingeing wives and long cashmere socks

IN the morning we were all counting our bites but I was way ahead of the others, with 22 itchy red lumps. What with sunburn, insect bites and the aforementioned spots, I wasn't looking my best. Jess was blessed with beautiful clear skin, now softly and prettily sun-kissed. The men boasted ridiculous cyclists' tans. From knees to ankles and from elbows to wrists, they were a toasty golden brown, while the rest of their bodies looked as if they'd spent a few months incarcerated in an underground cave. That's what Allan looked like, anyway – I can't honestly speak for Theo.

The sun was late appearing and we decided to make an early start. We bought a substantial wedge of Wensleydale cheese and a nutty granary loaf for our lunch. Very reluctantly, we agreed against buying butter because it would melt and make a nasty mess. With some trepidation, Allan and I watched Theo put the bread in their front bag, temptingly within nibbling range. We'd treated ourselves to apple pie for afters, which was squirrelled away in our saddlebag, so at least we could take revenge if necessary. In Yorkshire, this pudding is sometimes served with a slice of Wensleydale, hence the saying that 'an apple pie without the cheese is like a kiss without the squeeze'.

As we headed out of Hawes towards Buttertubs Pass, the sun came out and we all groaned. Fortunately that day we were travelling light, without the camping gear, but the extreme heat was becoming difficult to cope with. The name Buttertubs comes from the large limestone potholes, up to 60ft deep, where farmers stored their butter on hot summer days, to keep it cool while they visited the local markets. So unlike us, those enterprising Yorkshire lads had found a way of lunching on a thickly buttered butty, in defiance of sweltering weather.

The road was steep, with sharp hairpin bends. It was hard going and we got off and pushed the bikes, stopping to look at the impressive potholes and admiring the wonderful views across Swaledale, with moorland stretching for endless miles into the pitiless blue skyline. Jeremy Clarkson describes this as England's one and only truly spectacular road. I am reminded of him, when I recall the frizzy-haired motorist who screeched past in his souped-up Ford Capri, lowering his window to yell: "She's not pedalling at the back!"

We descended swiftly into Muker but didn't linger there, mainly because I was keen to carry on to nearby Keld. I'd been reading about the history of HF Holidays, previously known as the Holiday Fellowship, and this tiny village figured intriguingly and rather romantically.

The Keld Literary Institute is now incorporated into the Village Resource Centre but at the dawn of the 20th century, it was the chosen destination for the Holiday Fellowship's youngest and most intrepid followers. Physical fitness and enthusiasm for the simple life were key requirements for every member of the fledgling association, but the Keld experience challenged these attributes to the limit.

In search of their bed and board, visitors had to walk eight miles from Hawes, over the Buttertubs pass, while their luggage was transported by cart. Some were accommodated under the leaking roof of Keld's old ruined post office, while others slept in cottages which had been bought and sparsely furnished by the Holiday Fellowship. Food was cooked and eaten in the Literary Institute, using very basic facilities. An evening meal could be as humble as a big tureen of soup on the kitchen table, with guests expected to help themselves and do the washing-up afterwards.

A bugler woke everyone at 7.30 each morning, summoning them to enjoy/endure a pre-breakfast bathe. The men trekked to the waterfall above Keld, while the women washed in another fall closer to the village. This was an era in which people trembled before the stern spectre of their widowed Queen and anxious parents expressed fears about improper behaviour in this remote Yorkshire hideaway. So despite attracting huge visitor numbers, the unique Keld experiment survived for just three short summers.

We managed to find a shady spot beneath some trees to eat our lunch and Allan pointed out the signpost to Catrake Force.

"That was probably the waterfall where the men went to have a wash. It's about half-a-mile away."

"And to think I complain about camp site toilets," I said. "At least they're in the same field."

"And there's some privacy," Jess agreed. "I bet those chaps managed to find a spot where they could see the ladies stripping off in the lower waterfall."

Theo hacked away at what was left of the bread, then happily immersed himself in the pages of The Guardian. I scratched the bites on my legs and covered them with a disgusting concoction of antihistamine cream and sun lotion.

"It was 92 degrees at Wimbledon yesterday," Theo said. "Spectators fainted in the heat and tennis balls were bursting."

"How's Chris Evert getting on?" I enquired and he turned to the back page.

"Through to the next round. She's wearing a pretty dress but her hair's limp with sweat."

"How about Nastase?" Jess was cutting up the cheese. "I like him, he's fun."

"All the ladies seem to like him," Theo said. "But I don't think it's just because of his sense of humour."

"When his credit card was stolen, he said he didn't report it to the police because the thief was spending less than his wife did." I enjoyed reading the Daily Express gossip about Nastase and hoped he'd beat the brilliant but sombre Bjorn Borg.

Allan was studying the map. He didn't mind the heat and wasn't happy about our low mileage.

"I think we should go up Tan Hill," he said. "The pub there is England's highest inn."

"But it's so hot," I whinged. "And we've not got much water left in our bottles."

"I suppose we could think about cycling at night," Theo suggested. "When it's cooler."

"And when all the cafes are closed," Jess pointed out. "We'd never get any sleep on camp sites during the daytime, and think how hot it would be in the tents!"

In the end we trudged up over Tan Hill, past the high and lonely pub, which was sadly closed, and on to Reeth, where we thankfully spent an hour, melting over tea and cake in the cafe of the recently-opened Swaledale Folk Museum. It was wonderful to be out of the blistering sun. Then it was on to Askrigg and finally back into Hawes. This had been the longest ride of the holiday so far and we were all tired and very, very hot. Once again, in the supermarket we dithered over what to cook for dinner. In the end, we settled for boil-in-the-bag cod fillets in parsley sauce, accompanied by tinned sweetcorn and carrots.

In the showers, there were signs warning campers that unless we all conserved water, there was a real chance of standpipes very soon. As it was, warmish water trickled reluctantly and my money was gone before I'd got all the shampoo rinsed out of my hair. I trailed back to the tent with Jess, feeling slightly miserable and not much looking forward to my plate of boiled cod. I cheered up a bit when I found that Theo had gone back into Hawes and returned with a bottle of cold white wine and a strawberry cheesecake.

"Supper seemed too much like something from a Holiday Fellowship nightmare." Allan put a sweaty arm round me and looked upset when I recoiled. Jess frowned at her husband.

"Great idea," she said. "But why only one bottle?"

"Booze and bikes don't mix that well," Theo reminded her.

"If we're going to do it, we might as well do it properly. You're not usually a cheapskate."

"Talk about ungrateful," Theo muttered. "I'm off for a shower, and so is Allan. It's less than half-a-mile to the shops, if you're that keen."

Trudging along the main road, Jess and I indulged in a good old moan.

"They don't realise how lucky they are," she said. "How many other girls would call this a holiday? Sleeping on the hard ground, in a tent so small you can't even stand up in it and then after an exhausting day cycling we have to endure a lukewarm shower, a smelly towel and one bottle of Blue Nun between the four of us."

I'd never heard her complain before and although I knew it was just because of tiredness and the overwhelming heat, I was happy to join in.

"I'd give anything for a long soak in the bath, with rose-scented soap and huge fluffy towels. I never thought the day would come when a clean pair of knickers would be a big treat."

"My friends go on holiday to places where they sit beside swimming pools and waiters bring drinks on trays," Jess said. "None of them has to walk miles to buy their own booze."

"Allan wouldn't let me bring a book." This was still my biggest grudge.

"Theo made me leave my knitting behind."

"Knitting!" I didn't even know how to knit.

"Well, I enjoy it," Jess said. "It's my way of relaxing. And I'm in the middle of knitting a very pretty scarf."

I couldn't help thinking a scarf was the very last thing she needed in boiling hot Yorkshire but I said nothing. I was feeling sorry for myself too.

We hitched a lift back to the camp site, carrying a bag containing insect repellent and two bottles of Lambrusco. The men's faces managed to convey a perplexing mixture of repentance, guilt and wounded feelings, but supper was ready and there were even a few daisies stuck into an empty wine bottle. An empty Blue Nun bottle.

While polishing off the wine, and no doubt grumbling about wifely disloyalty, Theo and Allan had been looking at maps and trying to decide where we should head for next.

"We thought it would be good to explore the North York Moors," Allan said. "And go to the coast. Whitby and Robin Hood's Bay are both really nice."

"A swim in the sea would be great," Jess said, topping up her glass for the third time.

"You'll sink if you drink any more of that." Theo made a grab for the bottle she'd been guarding and drained it fast. "We thought somewhere near Richmond tomorrow and then on to Helmsley. We can go to Rievaulx Abbey. It sounds fantastic."

"Never mind 12th century Cistercian ruins," Allan said. "Tell them the best thing about Helmsley."

"Oh, yes." Theo grinned. "You girls don't have to wait for the sea before going for a dip. There's an open-air pool at Helmsley."

The following morning, we all felt rather fragile but we couldn't leave Hawes without seeing Hardraw Force, England's highest unbroken waterfall. The only access is through the bar of the Green Dragon Inn, after which it's just a short walk to the waterfall, which cascades from a height of 100ft and must normally present a magnificent sight. However, due to the many weeks of dry weather, we were treated to more of a tremulous trickle than a torrential torrent. This was the first of several waterfalls we visited in Yorkshire and they were all equally disappointing, that drought-cursed year.

Cycling with heavily-laden bikes was hard work as usual, especially in the relentless heat, and we thankfully stopped for tea and cakes in the small village of Askrigg. Everyone knows the warming effects of a welcome pot of tea in cold weather but only Real Cyclists understand its refreshing qualities, when temperatures are soaring into the high 80s. It's more thirst-quenching than a cold drink, even one rattling with ice cubes.

A few people were sitting outside the cafe, sweltering in the sunshine, but we made a beeline for the relative coolness on offer inside. Theo immersed himself in his Guardian, while I began reading the guidebook.

"Askrigg was famous for its knitting in the 18th century," I told Jess. "Lots of villagers were skilled at hand knitting, men as well as women."

"Theo can knit," she said, and Allan looked up from his brandy fruit cake.

"That's what too much spare time and no telly does for you," he said.

But Theo took no notice, pointing to the front page of The Guardian, on which was a picture of a bone-dry Welsh reservoir.

"Looks like standpipes are definitely on their way," he said. "There's a new car sticker which says 'Save Water, Bath With A Friend'."

"A bath would be such bliss" I said. "I'd consider sharing it with just about anybody."

"The Government is telling us to make do with five inches of water," Theo said. "So that hardly leaves enough room for your big toe, let alone a friend."

Reluctantly we walked back into the bright sunshine, where a couple of young lads were giving our bikes the once-over. They watched in smirking silence until we began to ride away, whereupon one of them suddenly shouted out the words "Can You Ride Tandem?" while his pal cracked up laughing.

"What did they say?" Jess asked and Theo looked equally bewildered.

"It's a TV advert," I said. "Of course, you've never seen it."

"For PG Tips," Allan explained. "There's a bunch of chimps cycling in the Tour de France and one of them says that to a female chimp he fancies. It's a chat-up line."

"It's a bloody stupid line," Theo snapped.

Stupid, infuriating, ridiculous, exasperating, maddening, inane, idiotic ... over the following weeks, months and years we used every one of those adjectives to describe the question which was hurled at us again and again. Of course we could ride tandem, what else did people think we were doing? It was almost enough to make us abandon The Cup That Cheers but we compromised by transferring our allegiance to Tetleys.

We'd decided to camp near Richmond, which should have been well within reach, were it not for the scalding sun, which was even melting the roads along which we toiled and forming lumps of sticky tarmac, which attached themselves to our tyres. My legs and Jess's were scarlet with painful sunburn, which didn't make for comfortable cycling. On the outskirts of Bolton Castle, we collapsed in a patch of shade and heated up some dried vegetable soup mix on one of the primus stoves. Gradually, we convinced ourselves we might manage a few more miles after all.

Richmond, when we finally arrived there, provided a bizarre solution to mine and Jess's scorched legs. We were pushing the bikes along its main street, lined with a craft market which was just beginning to pack up for the day, when something on one of the stalls caught Allan's attention.

"What do you think of those?" he murmured.

"Long woollen socks?" I giggled. "Haven't they noticed the temperature's soaring towards the 90s? No wonder they've not sold."

"They look beautifully soft. Hand knitted, I expect. And they're so long, I should think they'd pull up well above your knees."

Jess was starting to take an interest now.

"They could be cashmere," she said. "Let's have a proper look."

The stall owner was a middle-aged man, understandably not modelling his own knitwear but sensibly dressed in shorts and T-shirt.

"Can I help?" he asked, with absolutely no hint of a Yorkshire accent.

"These socks are lovely," Jess said, gently stroking one.

"They're 70% cashmere," he told her. "But no takers today, which is why there's such a good reduction. I've sold everything except the socks and egg cosies. They're half-price too."

"I think we'll pass on the egg cosies," Jess said. "But those socks are just what Jackie and I need to protect our legs from sunburn."

"Won't they itch?" I asked, and the stall holder gave me a pained look.

"Of course not. And you'll have an enviable fashion accessory. The ones with yellow daisies would look good with your shorts."

I saw the disappointment on Jess's face and guessed she'd lost her heart to those.

"You have them," I told her, picking up a pair delicately striped with palest blue. "I like these best, they're gorgeous."

"Where are you from?" Allan asked the stall owner while Jess and I sorted out payment.

"London. I came to Yorkshire on holiday 20 years ago and fell in love with the Dales. Couldn't wait to sell up and move here for good."

"No problems settling in?" Allan gave me a sideways glance and the stall holder laughed.

"Richmond is a lot friendlier than London," he said.

"Don't people call you a snobby southerner?" I asked.

"There's a bit of good natured teasing, that's all. It was more the knitting that took people by surprise."

"You knitted these socks yourself?" Theo looked at Allan triumphantly.

"Sure. Knitting's my passion and normally there's plenty of demand for woollen clothing up here."

An old lady began showing an interest in the egg cosies, so we said goodbye and moved off. Allan glanced back, thoughtfully.

"I bet he's another one with no telly," he said.

Charming though Richmond was, we only camped there for one night because we were desperate to dunk our boiling bodies in the North Sea as soon as possible. It was too far to cycle there in one day but Helmsley, with that tantalising outdoor swimming pool, was just about within reach. Next morning the weather was more humid than sunny, which made cycling slightly easier. Rather reluctantly, Jess and I decided not to wear our new designer knitwear straightaway but to give our scorched legs a chance to recover, before the sun's talons swooped on them once again.

We were soon back into sheep country, playing the familiar game of thwarting those panicky ones who seemed determined to hurl themselves under our wheels. Black masked faces stared at us and the occasional youngster ran bleating to its mother. In the distance we heard plaintive birdsong, which Allan excitedly believed to be the cry of a curlew.

While we were eating our picnic lunch the sun came out, whereupon Jess and I pulled on our cashmere socks. The wool felt wonderfully soft and it was good not to have the sticky feel of suncream on our legs.

We'd made good progress and reached a campsite on the edge of Helmsley by mid-afternoon. We hastily pitched our tents, with none of the customary banter, laughter or complaints. We were four sweaty cyclists united in a single aim – finding that open-air swimming pool and flinging our hot, grubby bodies into its blissful depths.

The pool did not disappoint and neither did the cafe we found afterwards, which sold ice-cream sodas in six different flavours. Cool for the first time in days, we wandered around, prepared to be thoroughly charmed by every aspect of this small market town. Now the starting point for the 110-mile Cleveland Way, it was hard to imagine that Helmsley had once been more famous for rowdy drinkers than respectable walkers. But so I was informed by my trusty guidebook and, as ever, I was keen to share information.

"Helmsley was a successful weaving centre in the 17th century," I told them.

"Is this leading us back to knitting?" Allan asked.

"No, those weavers were rough, tough Yorkshire men," I said. "Hardened drinkers who liked a night out boozing and singing. Often followed by fist fights in the market square."

"They sound like the founders of traditional folk music," Theo remarked, happily opening his Guardian. He'd hardly been able to believe his luck at finding one for sale so late in the day. I'd stopped bothering with the Daily Express and fancied I was developing a taste for more intellectual journalism. Now I was more familiar with current affairs, I enjoyed listening to Theo going into one of his rants over a controversial editorial opinion piece.

We stood outside The Black Swan Hotel and tried not to feel intimidated by its appearance of relaxed opulence.

"I had a pint in there once," Allan said. "It was my cousin's stag night and we sampled every pub in Helmsley."

"Let's eat at The Black Swan tonight," Jess suggested. "We deserve a treat."

"And it would save us having to make the usual difficult choice between boil-in-the-bag cod or fish fingers," Theo agreed.

Back at the camp site, Jess and I changed into our crumpled finery and I treated myself to a clean pair of knickers and applied a layer of concealer to help tone down my red nose and cheeks. In hungry high spirits, we went back into town and made straight for The Black Swan, where we set out to spoil ourselves. We all had avocado with prawns to start with, then Allan and I ordered coq-au-vin, while Theo and Jess had trout, studded with almonds and surrounded by chips. They shared the chips generously, which was probably the point at which I crowned them my dearest friends. Mind you, we had downed the best part of one bottle of Liebfraumilch and another of Mateus Rose by then.

The finale to this feast was generous slices of Black Forest gateau, accompanied by a bill for £17.50p. Since this was more or less the equivalent of half-a-week's wages, we all sobered up smartly. The impassive waiter stood patiently by, while Jess and I rummaged in our purses and muttered anxiously to each other about giving a tip and whether we had the nerve not to. When Jess handed over the exact amount, the waiter politely accepted the brimming handful of notes and coins and glided smoothly away.

We all loved Helmsley, not because of its charming houses and the streets with their enticing little shops, delightful as these were. No, it was the lure of the open-air swimming pool which ensnared us, shortening our rides so we could soak for hours in that cool water at the end of each sweltering afternoon. Then we'd prolong the spoiling process by testing yet another flavour of ice-cream soda. We did manage to visit Rievaulx Abbey, but since that was only three miles up the road, it didn't detract too much from time spent sloshing in the pool or spooning up ice-cream.

But then the men began to get twitchy and started talking beguilingly about Whitby, Robin Hood's Bay and the wonderfully chilly waves of the North Sea. So we packed our stuff into the panniers, Jess and I donned our woolly socks and we bid Helmsley a reluctant farewell.

There was a long ride ahead of us but we intended to camp that night with the scent of the sea drifting into our tents. We cycled through Kirkybymoorside, resisting the lure of coffee and cake, and out onto the long, winding stretches of quiet road leading us into the heart of the North York Moors National Park.

We were all pretty fit by now and managing to cope a little better with the extreme heat, which that day was more intense than ever. But towards the middle of the afternoon, grim determination was about all that kept us going and no-one had energy to spare for conversation. Theo eventually broke the heat-soaked silence when, after glancing at his map, he announced that we were approaching the small village of Great Fryup and its neighbour, the even smaller village of Little Fryup. We were to discover the following day that we struggled through the Fryups on the hottest day ever recorded in Britain, when the temperature climbed to 96.6 degrees.

It was early evening when we finally reached Robin Hood's Bay, by which time we were in no condition to appreciate its considerable charms. Wearily, we hammered the tent pegs into rock-hard ground at the first camp site we found with the required sea view, before trudging to the showers, where I winced when the water thudded on to my scorched skin. Luckily, a nearby greasy spoon was still open and we feasted on scampi and chips served in baskets.

Afterwards, sitting outside the tents and drinking coffee which only Allan had the energy to make, we all complained about sunburn, exhaustion and the indescribable torment of being saddle-sore.

"I think it's time for bed," Allan said. "It must be at least 8.30."

"I need to look at our tandem before we go anywhere tomorrow," Theo said. "It's been making a rattling noise."

"I haven't heard anything." Jess frowned. "You know you usually regret fiddling with the bike, unless there's definitely something wrong."

"I'll look at it before breakfast," Theo said. "It'll only take five minutes."

TOP TANDEM TIP

If you already ride a solo bike, then when you sit on the back of a tandem for the first time, you will probably instinctively attempt to steer. Try putting your hands on your partner's waist as you cycle along, until you can resist the urge.

CHAPTER FOUR

Ear trumpets, tough Yorkshire women and a lost ring

DESPITE our early night, it was only when the tent became unpleasantly hot, due to the by now loathed and dreaded sun, that Allan and I crawled out onto the scorched, brown grass. We found Theo frowning down at his tandem, while Jess silently poured muesli into bowls. Sensing marital discord, I offered to go to the shop for milk and she promptly decided to go with me.

"Theo likes nothing better than tinkering with the bike," she said. "I never heard any rattling noise yesterday."

"At least we're not planning on cycling far," I said. "No further than the beach, I hope."

"You don't know Theo very well yet," Jess warned me. "He'll be perfectly happy spending the morning at the camp site, with the tandem in bits all around him."

I thought she must be exaggerating but on our return from the shop, I realised her fears were justified. With a puzzled but helpful expression, my husband was eating muesli and watching Theo get covered in oil, while he stripped down their tandem.

"He thinks it's something to do with the bottom bracket," Allan said and Jess sighed.

Half-an-hour later and impatient to dip our toes in the waves of the North Sea, we all surveyed Theo warily. Contrary to Jess's assertions, his was not the demeanour of a man enjoying himself. On bended knees and with his nose barely an inch from the frazzled grass, he was hunting feverishly for a small nut, which apparently formed an integral part of the chain wheel. His temper matched the weather, as both were fast approaching boiling-point.

"Shall we help look?" Allan offered. "Or go to the beach and you follow later?"

Theo's reply was fairly inarticulate but Jess interpreted it as meaning that to give our friendship a fair chance of survival, we would be wise to go to the beach and remain there until either darkness fell or he managed to lay his oily hands on that elusive little nut.

Robin Hood's Bay is a pretty jumble of steep and twisting narrow streets, leading down to rock pools and a sandy beach. We parked ourselves close to the sea and immediately stripped down to our swimming costumes. Our peculiar cyclists' tans triggered several smirks and curious stares.

"Should one of us stay here with the stuff?" I dithered.

"You're such a worrier," Jess chided. "Who's going to bother pinching our sweaty T-shirts? And we only brought enough money for ice-creams. Come on!"

Grabbing my hand, she pulled me towards the sea and seconds later we were thoroughly and gaspingly wet.

"Poor old Theo," said Allan, his hair streaming water as he emerged from yet another blissful dunking. "I wonder if he's found that nut yet?"

Quite a long time later, and still pleasantly damp, we treated ourselves to ice-creams from a kiosk. Jess and I chose Little John Juicy Raspberry, while Allan decided on Friar Tuck Triple Chocolate.

"Are you going to educate us about this place?" Jess asked when we were settled on a pleasantly shady bench. "I presume you've brought the guidebook with you?"

Well, of course I had and this was the paranoid reason for my reluctance to lose sight of our belongings. My insatiable reading compulsion had to be satisfied by a share of The Guardian and this one precious book.

We gobbled our ice-creams in the few seconds before they melted and I turned happily to the relevant page.

"Why's it called it Robin Hood's Bay?" Allan asked.

"Perhaps Richard Greene was born here," Jess suggested.

"You're not supposed to know about TV programmes," I said.

"I haven't always lived a telly-free existence. When I was 13, I fantasised every Saturday afternoon about being Maid Marion."

"Me too," I said and Allan shuffled impatiently.

"Get on with it," he said.

"It's a bit of a letdown," I admitted. "There's not a scrap of evidence to suggest Robin Hood ever came here."

"Better not tell that ice-cream seller," Jess said.

"But in the 18th century, this was the busiest smuggling community for miles around," I told them. "Everyone was at it: fishermen, farmers, gentry and even the clergy. They all got very bolshie when the excise men paid a visit. The women would pour boiling water on them from upstairs windows."

"What's that about Press Gangs?" Allan was trying to read over my shoulder and I pushed him off.

"I was getting to that, and there's more about tough Yorkshire women. When a Press Gang was spotted on its way to the village, the wives used to beat a drum to warn their men folk, who were working in the fields or fishing."

"It's always women who take the lead," Jess said with satisfaction. "I wonder how Theo's getting on?"

Apprehensively, we made our way back to the camp site, where to our relief we found Theo sprawled beside the tent, reading The Guardian.

"Sorry about earlier on," he said.

"Did it take you ages to find the beastly nut?" Jess sat down and hugged him.

"Only all morning. I'd rather not talk about it, if you don't mind. The bike's OK now, anyway. Shall we cycle into Whitby this afternoon? It's not far."

"Let's leave it until tomorrow," Jess suggested. "I'd like to have a proper look around Robin Hood's Bay and I want to sample the Sheriff of Nottingham Nutty Fudge ice-cream."

I thought that was a much better idea and even Allan raised no objections. So we idled the afternoon away and revisited the greasy spoon later on, where we ate the most delicious fried cod any of us had ever tasted. It hardly seemed possible that this fish could be any relation to those greyish white rectangles lurking in our boil-in-the-bag meals.

Next day we were all keen to make the most of what little remained of our holiday. We decided to cycle to Whitby and spend a leisurely few hours exploring the town, before packing up the tents the following day and making our way to Scarborough. From there, we would travel to York by train and visit the city's annual cycle rally, before beginning the long rail journey back south.

The tireless sun was beating down before we'd even finished breakfast but it was only about eight miles to Whitby and we were looking forward to the day ahead, not least to a substantial lunch in one of the town's renowned fish and chip restaurants. There was no separating Jess and me from our long socks, even though they were by now well overdue for a good wash. In fact, following a rather spirited discussion with Allan, mine now spent their nights outside the tent, tied to the tandem's handlebars.

At Whitby, we left the bikes padlocked to some railings on the harbour front while we strolled beside the water and bickered amiably about how to prioritise our day. As usual, I was ready with suggestions plucked from my trusty guidebook.

"Obviously we must go the abbey," I announced. "Via St Mary's Church, although it's a bit of a trek up there."

"It's 199 steps," Theo contributed. "I want to look inside the church – apparently there's a three-decker pulpit."

We turned towards the abbey and the long haul up those steps in the boiling sunshine. Thankfully there were several benches on the way, which Jess and I were happy to make use of but which the men loftily ignored. Left to ourselves, we chatted and admired the fabulous views, so by the time we caught them up, they'd already had a look around the church.

"There are two ear trumpets fixed to the back of the pulpit, which belonged to a deaf vicar's wife in the 19th century," Theo told us.

"A devoted wife," Allan added. "I bet she raced up those steps, not like some."

"If you two were that slow on the bikes," Theo complained, "we'd still be at Pateley Bridge."

"Yes, come on girls," Allan grinned. "It's about time you pulled your socks up."

"How long have you been rehearsing that one?" Jess said.

"Some of the pews have the words *For Strangers Only* carved on them," Theo mused. "I can't decide if that's welcoming or not."

"Bram Stoker used this as a setting for one of the spookiest scenes in Dracula," I said, looking around the graveyard. "He spent six years in Whitby. Several famous people have lived here, actually. Frank Sutcliffe was a very successful Victorian photographer and he hardly ever left Whitby, even for a few days."

"Captain Cook must be the town's most famous resident," Theo said. "He was born here in 1728. I remember that from a question on University Challenge, when I was still at school."

"Maybe we should get a telly," Jess suggested. "And just watch the edifying stuff."

"I'm not sure if I could trust you to keep away from Coronation Street," Theo said.

"I like Crossroads best," I said, and Allan groaned.

"We fit supper in around watching that," he said.

"I have to make do with The Archers, on the radio." Jess sighed.

"Oh, I like that too." I hadn't known Jess was an Archers addict. "Wasn't it dreadful when Dan shot Joe Grundy's dog Jacko because he thought he'd been worrying sheep?"

"You don't like dogs," Allan said. "I'd have thought you'd be cheering him on. Anyway, that's enough about soaps. Let's have a proper look around the abbey."

Afterwards, we walked back into town and wandered around the shops for a while. Jess and I were rather taken with Whitby jet jewellery, especially some of the ear-rings, but the ones we liked best were far too expensive.

"Whitby jet really took off in Victorian times," I said. "Necklaces and ear-rings were fashionable accessories for women to wear with mourning clothes."

"Jet was the only jewellery the Queen would allow at court, after Albert died," Theo said.

"Black's not really my colour," Jess decided, turning her back on the tempting display. "How about those fish and chips? I'm starving."

Continuing the patriotic mood, we decided to eat at The Royal Fisheries. Even though it was mid-afternoon the place was packed, which had to be a good sign. Luckily for us, a table next to the wide-open window had just been vacated but it was very hot in the restaurant and noisy overhead fans were working full-blast. It was hard to imagine how excruciating kitchen work must be, in temperatures of 100 degrees and more. We all agreed this would be our main meal of the day and we shouldn't stint. An hour later, stuffed full of battered haddock, chips, bread and butter, pea fritters and pickled eggs, we walked very, very slowly back to the harbour.

"I hope the tandems have been nicked," Jess whispered to me. "Then we could catch a bus back to the camp site. The thought of cycling anywhere is a horrible reminder that eating that second pea fritter was a very risky thing to do."

"Both the tandems are yours, remember," I murmured. "Think how upset Theo would be."

"What I'd like," she mused, "is for the bikes to have been pinched for a bit of a laugh and left undamaged, somewhere not far away and brought back to the campsite in a police van, by a Dixon of Dock Green-type copper, who just happens to live in Robin Hood's Bay."

Needless to say, our tandems were still safely attached to the railings, with neither thieves nor policemen in sight. Fortunately, Theo and Allan, both of whom had enjoyed extra large portions of chips washed down by shandy, were eyeing the bikes with minimal enthusiasm.

"Whitby's such a beautiful place," Theo said, leading the way to a shady bench. "It would be a shame to rush off. It could be years before we come here again."

"Years," Allan agreed, putting an arm around me. "Years and years."

Desultory chat soon ebbed away entirely, as all we could think about was our bursting bellies. The next hour or so passed in a pleasant blur as we dozed gently, every now and again jerked awake by the sound of laughter or passing conversation.

It was early evening before we got on our bikes and cycled back to Robin Hood's Bay, where we sat outside the tents, drinking tea and watching the distant sun sink closer to the still waters of the North Sea.

"Our last day tomorrow," Theo said, voicing what we were all probably thinking.

"We've had a great holiday." Jess leaned against him and he stroked her hair.

"It's not quite over yet," I protested.

"Tomorrow's going to be a long day." Allan pulled me to my feet. "Better get those socks off and tie them to the handlebars for the very last time."

But we left the tents unzipped for at least another hour, watching the rosy sky turn deepest crimson and listening to the faintest lap of wave against rock and the distant, clamorous shriek of gulls, swooping over the rippling sea.

We made an early start the following morning and were in Scarborough before midday. We went straight to the station, hoping there was a regular service to York. Luckily, the next train was due at 1pm and the journey took just under an hour. It was strange to be travelling by train once more, watching the countryside race past so swiftly and effortlessly, very different from the 8mph we averaged when cycling.

We had a difficult choice to make between exploring the city and spending as much time as possible looking around the huge and prestigious York Cycle Rally, before travelling home the following day. Theo was worried that the camp site at the show might already be full, so it seemed best not to allow ourselves to be sidetracked by tea shops – or indeed any other type of shop. Rather to mine and Jess's disappointment, we cycled straight to the racecourse, which hosted the annual event.

Allan was determined to look for an aunt and uncle, whom it seemed were regular visitors. He was convinced they would be there, even though he'd not seen them for at least a decade.

"It's an enormous site," Theo warned. "We might not find them."

"I'll recognise their caravan," Allan said confidently. "They come here every year. Uncle Arthur used to cycle with my dad before we moved to Dorset."

Fortunately, as our tents were so small we had no trouble finding a space to camp. The place was swarming with Real Cyclists, some of them dressed in smart Hebden Cord, despite the excruciating heat, and there was an incredible range of bikes to be seen. Loads of tandems, several triplets, a few penny farthings, a couple of recumbents and lots of trailer bikes, suitable for every stage of childhood. Plenty of parents were obviously determined that nothing was going to stop them cycling and even tiny babies were tucked neatly into little carriers.

Jess and I were in urgent need of the ladies, so we arranged to catch up with the boys at the trade stands in the biggest marquee. Then we would try to hunt down Uncle Arthur and Auntie Ruth, which I feared would be a daunting task, in view of the endless rows of seemingly identical caravans.

The toilets were cleaner than I'd expected, considering how many people there were. I was so busy nattering to Jess that we were almost at the trade stands before I happened to glance down at my left hand.

"Oh no!" My voice trembled and my legs were trying to join in. I grabbed Jess's arm. "I've left my engagement ring on the wash basin!"

"What?" She stared at me in horror. "Did you take it off? I mean, why on earth would you take your ring off?"

But I'd already turned round and was running back towards the toilets. Maybe it would still be there. Maybe a miracle was happening right this second and no-one had used that wash basin. Oh, please, please, please let it still be there. My gorgeous, beautiful opal, which people had warned me meant bad luck unless it was my birthstone, which it wasn't. But it hadn't been unlucky, even if I had paid for it myself. I loved Allan, I loved our life together and I loved that ring. I'd never realised before quite how much I loved it. Please, please, let it still be there.

It wasn't, of course. I burst into anguished tears and Jess put her arms around me and tried to talk soothingly and sensibly.

"We'll go straight to the lost property desk," she said. "Some kind lady has probably handed it in already."

"Do you think so?" I whispered. "Do you really think so?"

I grabbed that flicker of hope with both hands and held on tight. If I'd lost my ring, every happy memory of this holiday would always be tainted with sadness.

There was a queue at lost property. A very slow moving one, under the ferocious glare of the afternoon sun. It took ages before it was our turn and then, when I opened my mouth to speak, to my horror I started sobbing again.

"My friend left her engagement ring in the toilets about 15 minutes ago," Jess told the startled lost property lady. "It's an opal. Has anyone handed it in?"

To my incredulous relief, the woman smiled at me. The smile of someone who knew there were honest people in the world. People who wouldn't dream of helping themselves to something that didn't belong to them. I slid the ring back on my finger and held it there so tightly that it hurt.

"Who was she?" I asked. "I'd like to say thank-you."

"No idea, love. She just said where she'd found it and that was it, she'd gone."

When we eventually tracked them down, our men folk looked quite relieved.

"Where on earth have you been?" Allan asked. "We were getting worried. What's happened?"

I looked at his dear, anxious face and my eyes filled with tears once more.

"Don't cry again," Jess begged. "Please don't."

"But why did you take it off?" Allan asked, after he'd heard the whole story.

"I usually do when I wash my hands at home," I said. "To stop soap clogging it up. But never when I'm out anywhere. It must have been an absent-minded moment."

"Poor you." He hugged me. "You look exhausted, and so does Jess. How about a nice cup of tea?"

"A stiff gin and tonic would be better," Jess said. "But I suppose I'll settle for tea."

After we'd established for the umpteenth time that I was both a very lucky girl and a very foolish one and confirmed that the whole experience restored your confidence in the intrinsic goodness of human nature, Allan suggested we start trawling through the hundreds of caravans.

Theo and Jess agreed, albeit rather wearily, and I could see they thought this would be a wild goose chase. However, lady luck was still with us, as after only about 10 minutes Allan triumphantly hailed his Auntie Ruth and Uncle Arthur, quietly sitting outside their Sprite Alpine, drinking tea and doing a crossword. They were surprised but pleased to see us and confirmed Allan's assertion that they came to York every year and hadn't missed a show since 1946.

"Our Mollie's here too," said Auntie Ruth. "She'll be back soon, she's just gone for a shower."

This elicited the sorry tale of my engagement ring, which in turn led to an explanation of their absence from our wedding. Something to do with an annual 24-hour time trial organised by Uncle Arthur's cycling club, which no Real Cyclist would dream of missing. A royal summons to Princess Anne's wedding would almost certainly have received the same response.

On Mollie's return, Auntie Ruth put the kettle on and cut generous slices of brandy-laced fruitcake. When we mentioned that we were catching the 5am train to London the following morning, she insisted that they set their alarm for 4am, so they could wake us up in plenty of time to cycle to the station.

"It's no trouble, lad," she told Allan. "Your mam would play pop with me if I let you miss that train."

"Aye, it's no trouble," Uncle Arthur echoed. "Happen it'll be me she kicks out of bed at crack of dawn, anyway."

But it was Mollie who shone an unwelcome torch on our sleepy faces in the early hours of Sunday morning. Bleary-eyed, we thanked her and she slipped away, leaving us to start taking the tents down as silently as possible. It was eerie in the moonlit field, with seemingly only the four of us awake and quietly busy, in the midst of that slumbering canvas city. In fact, the racecourse was a restless place, even at that early hour. As we hurried along the edge of the pleasantly chilly camp site, we heard a baby's sudden cry and the slim outline of a young woman, moving swiftly to soothe and rock.

A dog trotted purposefully alongside us without a glance, intent on his own concerns. An old man emerged from the toilets, smoking a roll-up and carrying a transistor radio. He half raised a hand in greeting and hesitated, as if to speak but deciding better of it.

At last we reached the busy road leading to the city, where traffic never ceased and brightly-lit lorries raced towards and past us, lighting up the sign ahead which directed us to York Station, one-and-a-half miles away. This was it, then. The last lap of our heat-soaked 1976 holiday.

A little over an hour later and with the tandems safely ensconced in the guard's van, we settled into our seats and wistfully watched the Yorkshire landscape rapidly disappearing from view. There hadn't been much choice in the station buffet and breakfast comprised cheese and chutney sandwiches, reminiscent of those made by Jess on our outward journey.

"When I was a kid, at the end of a holiday we told each other our high points and low points," Theo said. "Come on, Allan. You first."

"Lowest point was being ill on the very first day." Allan scowled at his sandwich. "And too many boil-in-the-bag cod suppers. High points are the swimming pool at Helmsley and Auntie Ruth's Dundee cake."

"My lowest point came when we broke our block," Jess said. "Helmsley pool is definitely a high point and swimming in the sea at Robin Hood's Bay comes second."

"Breaking the block was bad," Theo agreed, "but spending most of the day searching for that blasted nut was equally dire. Fish and chips at Whitby were a high point but I suspect we're all going to put Helmsley pool at the top of that list."

"Not me," I said. "Losing my ring was the lowest point and getting it back was the highest."

"How about Most Unforgettable Memory?" Jess suggested and that set us all off.

"The heat." We were agreed on that one.

"Trying to make seven pairs of knickers last a fortnight." Me.

"People shouting 'Can You Ride Tandem?'" Theo.

"Cycling through the Dale of Fryup in 96 degrees." Allan.

"Our posh meal in The Black Swan Hotel." Me.

"Wearing our long cashmere socks." Jess.

"Those pongy Brut T-shirts you and Allan wore for a whole morning was quite a test of friendship," Theo said. "But we seem to have survived. I can't imagine going on holiday without you now."

It was just what I'd been hoping to hear. I smiled at my husband and two best friends in the whole world.

"So, where shall we go next year?" I asked.

TOP TANDEM TIP

Even a second-hand tandem is an expensive purchase and it's often a good idea to try before you buy. At 'The Tandem Experience', Pete and Sara Bird provide a range of opportunities for the fledging tandemer, which vary from a fun day out in Shropshire to a guided holiday in France. Pete and Sara teach basic skills and offer expert advice and enthusiastic encouragement. All practical aspects of tandem riding are explained and demonstrated. www.tandeming.co.uk. There are many other places offering a range of similar opportunities.

CHAPTER FIVE

John Barleycorn, Bob Jackson and The Wessex Road Club

IT was hard getting used to normal life back home in Dorset. I wasn't happy at work because I didn't like my boss and Allan tried to cheer me up with a surprise present. He picked me up from the library one day and when I started to moan as usual, I could tell he wasn't really paying attention. There was a little smile on his face. When I opened our front door, I was startled by a sudden scuttling noise.

"What was that?" I demanded.

"Damn," Allan muttered. "He was asleep on the sofa when I left and I gave him strict instructions to stay put."

"Who?" I was peering behind the sofa and could just make out a shivering ginger fluff ball.

"A kitten!" I squeaked. "Where did it come from?"

"Mum found him for us. I know you like cats and I thought it would take your mind off work." Allan was trying to tempt the little chap out by trailing a piece of ribbon slowly along the carpet. He eventually succeeded and I immediately lost my heart to the ginger scrap, even though he kept retreating to his safe place behind the sofa and wouldn't sit on my lap, however much I coaxed.

Allan's mum phoned to see how the kitten was settling in.

"He's gorgeous," I said. "But he's a real scaredy cat."

"Give him time," she said. "A bit of love and kindness and he'll be bossing the pair of you around in no time. Has he got a name yet?"

We'd decided on Barley, short for John Barleycorn, one of Allan's favourite folk songs, sung by Fairport Convention.

Betty was right. Barley was far from timid and made himself at home very quickly. We fussed around, worrying that he'd be lonely and cold, on his own all day. We left a paraffin heater on for him day and night in the kitchen. It smelt horrible and must have been a fire hazard. It took us several months to discover that Barley had won the devotion of Mr and Mrs Radley next door and spent Monday to Friday curled up in front of their fire and eating the choicest titbits from their midday meal. They loved him but forced themselves to shoo him out every day at teatime, so he'd be at home to greet us, like a loyal and dutiful cat.

Allan was tireless in his quest to enrich my life and compensate for work getting me down. At least, that was one reason he gave a few weeks later, when he decided we needed a new tandem.

"But what's wrong with Claud?" I asked, lying on the sofa reading my book, with Barley purring loudly on my lap, while Allan paced around our small sitting room.

"Nothing, nothing. Well, it's an old bike." He sat down beside me. "And we're not doing much cycling, are we?"

"We get out on Sundays," I said.

"Usually only for an afternoon ride, which isn't much. Think how fit we were a couple of months ago when we came back from Yorkshire. Where's all that gone?"

"Real life gets in the way," I said. "Work and stuff."

Allan interrupted me hastily, before I could launch into that particular topic.

"Theo and Jess belong to a cycling club," he said. "Maybe we should think about doing that. But to keep up with a bunch of Real Cyclists we'd need a new, lightweight tandem."

"How much will one of those cost?" I stroked the kitten's velvety ears and his purr deepened to a rumble.

"I looked at some frames at the York cycle show and I reckon on about £1,000."

"What!" I shrieked, causing Barley to leap off my lap and disappear behind the sofa. "This house only cost £8,750!"

"We'll have to start saving. Obviously it'll take a while."

I suddenly had a brainwave. I looked sideways at my husband. This was my chance to find out which of his two passions meant most to him.

"You know what takes most of our money, don't you?" I said.

"Cat food and paraffin?" Allan was trying to wheedle an affronted Barley out from his bolt-hole.

I took a deep breath. "Your MGB," I told him.

He went very still and decided to leave Barley where he was.

"We've got to have a car," he said.

"Not necessarily. We could cycle to work. You drop me off and then carry on to Parkstone. That'd keep us fit and, after all, it's the sort of thing Theo and Jess do."

"They don't live in a village and neither of them drives."

"I wasn't expecting you to make excuses. Are we Real Cyclists or not?" I demanded.

"Have you thought this through?" he said. "It would mean cycling everywhere. To your mum's and my parents. Every time we go to see friends. Are you sure you're enough of a Real Cyclist for that?"

"Of course." I wasn't at all sure really but I had a huge incentive.

"How much would we get for the MGB?" I asked.

Not as much as I'd hoped, was the disappointing answer, once Allan had finally brought himself to put his beloved motor up for sale. I did feel a little sorry for my husband, when he watched his car being driven away by a paunchy chap in corduroy bell-bottoms, who was clearly indulging a midlife crisis. But really I was thankful to see the last of our money-gobbling motor and we were now £300 closer to buying a new tandem. If we saved really hard, we'd have enough money by the following Easter.

There were certainly times when I fervently wished for four wheels rather than two, especially on cold, wet mornings when I was faced with cycling eight miles to work. Most people thought we were mad. The real worry was that we were in danger of turning cycling into a chore, rather than a pleasure.

Proof of this presented itself one day, when I started chatting to a very pleasant woman called Ruth, who was queuing behind me at the post office and I mentioned my soaking wet ride into work that morning. It turned out her husband was recently retired and had begun the task of resurrecting the Wessex Road Club, a cycling club which boasted many members during the post-war years but had since sunk into a decline.

"You and Allan are just the sort of fit young people Jack's trying to encourage out on the Sunday rides. They're a nice group but we badly need more members."

I sidestepped Ruth's warm smile. I was always ready for a break from cycling at the weekend, however I guessed Allan would almost certainly be interested in this Wessex Road Club. But only if someone was silly enough to mention it.

"We're saving up for a new tandem," I said. "Maybe next summer things will be different."

Ruth looked disappointed but she was too nice to pressure me.

Being without a car certainly wasn't doing our social life any good. I re-read the Jalna books by Mazo de la Roche and secretly fell in love with Renny, all over again. Allan became addicted to *The Sweeney* and we both sat glued to *The Good Life* and *Porridge*.

But Friday night at the folk club was sacrosanct for Allan and we had to find a way of accommodating that. He and his mate John sang together and both were excellent guitarists. I didn't often go to the club now, preferring to spend the evening in the company of John's wife Pat and a bottle of Cinzano. They lived about 10 miles away, near Wimborne, and we decided we could easily cycle there after our tea, then the men would go to Bournemouth in John's car, while Pat and I enjoyed ourselves chatting, drinking and eating biscuits. On the return of our musical duo, we'd cycle back home.

But as wise old Theo had said on holiday, booze and bikes aren't a happy combination. Our husbands didn't get back from the folk club until after 11pm, which left Pat and I with several hours in which to scoff and swig. We didn't intend to drink all the Cinzano but it does go down well, diluted with lemonade and accompanied by shortbread biscuits. And when you're busy chatting and laughing at *Are You Being Served?* it's surprising how quickly the bottle empties. Allan, wisely anticipating the possibility of having to cycle home hindered by an inebriated stoker, had only drunk one pint of shandy. We arrived back in Spetisbury at half-past midnight, exhausted and barely on speaking terms. After that, I limited my Cinzano evenings with Pat to every third week when I had Saturday off, which meant Allan and I could both have a long lie in. He was happy to cycle to John's house on his own bike, although it did mean he was late home.

When I worked at the Lansdowne library, I had lots of company and because many of the girls were my sort of age, we had fun together. I used to meet Jan at the Wimpy Bar on my half-day for cheeseburgers and chips and a good old gossip. But Jan had remarried and moved away to Bristol and I feared our friendship was on the wane. Now I spent my days with a woman I didn't like and all my free time with my husband, whom I loved of course – but you can have too much of any good thing. It seemed that only Barley's antics could coax a smile to my face.

But shortly before Christmas things began looking up. Allan was unexpectedly given promotion at work and with the new job came a company car. That bog-standard little Ford Popular Plus was the best Christmas present either of us could wish for. Now that I wasn't cycling to work, I had more enthusiasm for a Sunday bike ride and our bank account was looking gratifyingly healthy. My boss was jealous of our good fortune and didn't try to hide it.

"You'd better enjoy that car while it lasts," she said darkly. "And I hope you're going to start ironing your husband's shirts, now he's so important."

I'd made the mistake of telling her that I hated ironing and did as little as possible, which resulted in a wardrobe full of un-ironed shirts. In vain did I try to explain that I was only following my mother-in-law's instructions, imparted in her kitchen before we were married.

"Watch me, lass," Betty had said, deftly dumping one of Allan's shirts on the ironing board but with no intention of showing it to the iron. "You smooth it out like this, fold it like this, and there you are – ironed! He always pulls the sleeves up and wears a waistcoat, so ironing his shirts is a waste of time. I've never done it and there's no need for you to."

Up until then, I'd been happy to follow her example but perhaps now was the time to mend my ways, especially as I was keen to facilitate my husband's progress up the career ladder.

Allan celebrated his promotion by placing an order with Bob Jackson, a Leeds bike builder, for a custom-built tandem frame, which should be ready for us in early March.

"We'll buy everything else we need from Les Simpson," Allan said. "Only the best. No expense spared. Then we can start looking for a club to ride with on Sundays."

"I've already found one," I told him. "It's called the Wessex Road Club and I think they meet in Blandford."

"Definitely worth looking into," Allan agreed. "But I think we'll wait until we've got our new bike and you're kitted out in some Hebden Cord shorts and proper cycling shoes. Then I'll be married to a Real Cyclist at last."

I knew he was right. Reluctant though I was to bin my homemade shorts, they didn't have much life left in them and my feet were getting cold and wet rather too often these days. So I chose a pair of boring brown shorts from the boring brown catalogue and stumped up a vast sum for some sensible, leather cycling shoes. Both items proved excellent value for money as they were extremely comfortable and I wore them for the best part of a decade.

Our excitement mounted as the day we would take possession of our new tandem drew closer. Les Simpson offered us £55 for Claud, which was only a fiver less than we'd paid for him the previous year. We struggled over whether or not to part with him.

"Real Cyclists never sell their bikes," I reminded Allan, not that he needed any reminder. He'd adhered to the golden rule all his life.

"We could use the money," he pointed out. "And we haven't got room for two tandems."

"Claud is such a patient, sweet-natured bike," I coaxed. "He's never taken advantage of having to put up with a complete beginner like me."

Naturally, such foolish sentimentality failed to soften Allan's stony heart, but he did agree to keep Claud for a little while longer.

On Saturday, 12th March 1977, we drove to Poole station to meet the London train. Bob Jackson was sending the frame by rail from Leeds and we were anxious about its safe arrival, especially as it would have been shunted around in London. The train arrived promptly and the platform was immediately engulfed with passengers.

Despite trying to position ourselves close to where we expected the guard's van to be, we were nowhere near it and struggled along the busy platform, straining to see that exciting package. At last we had a glimpse of a small heap of parcels, tantalisingly obscured from view by hurrying passengers. But as we drew closer, it became obvious that none of them was big enough to be our new tandem. At that moment, a whistle shrieked and the train began to pull away.

"Maybe it's still in the guard's van," I gabbled. "The next stop's Bournemouth. We could head the train off. Quick, let's get back to the car!"

"No, look." Allan grabbed my arm. "There it is!"

He pointed a few yards up the platform, where a porter had just heaved a bike-shaped package on top of a trolley laden with other parcels. Somehow, in the crush, neither of us had seen it. Ten minutes later, after doing the paperwork, we had our new pride and joy safely in the car, en route to its new home.

Surrounded by brown paper and corrugated cardboard, we spent all evening admiring the new occupant of 2 Jasmine Cottages. Allan didn't turn on the TV and I never even glanced in the direction of my book, even though I'd reached a very exciting part of The Thorn Birds. Barley entered into the excitement by getting his paws covered in parcel tape and chasing scraps of packaging around the sitting room.

The frame was matt black with 'Bob Jackson' picked out in gold lettering. Allan began fitting Bob's accoutrements.

"What's special about this lot, then?" I asked. "Apart from the fact that everything cost a fortune."

"The frame's made from Reynolds 531 double-butted tubing," he said. "So it's strong but also light. And we've got Mavic cantilever brakes and a TA chainset, not to mention GB handlebars. Now, where's this bike going to live?"

Once again we had neglected to resolve this very important question. Claud spent his off-duty hours beneath plastic sheeting in the back garden but we couldn't possibly expect Bob to put up with such humble accommodation.

"Nothing else for it." I took a deep breath. "He'll have to stay in here. Actually he looks rather nice there, in front of the fireplace."

"He does, doesn't he?" Allan agreed. "But I've a feeling he might outstay his welcome in our sitting room."

"Let's put a greenhouse in the back garden," I suggested. "Bob could live in there and we can grow tomatoes round him."

"Good idea," Allan agreed. "We'll keep him in the sitting room until then. I'm really looking forward to our first ride tomorrow, with the Wessex Road Club."

As per Ruth's instructions, we arrived in the car park at Blandford just before 9.30am. We'd felt like royalty, cycling from Spetisbury, and quite thought there should have been cheering from those we passed en route. But the admiring response we received from the handful of cyclists already gathered was most gratifying and banished any initial awkwardness immediately. Jack was a tall man, recently retired, with a kindly expression on his weather-beaten face. His wife had told him about us and he couldn't have been more welcoming. Apparently Ruth didn't go out with the Wessex Road Club, preferring to ride with a more leisurely group called the Thursday Potterers.

"This is John and his son Mark," Jack said, introducing us to a chap somewhere in his late 30s and a lad of about 14.

"Fantastic bike," John said. "Is that Reynolds 531 double-butted?"

"Strong but light." Jack nodded. "You can't do better than Reynolds 531. And those brakes look like Mavic cantilever. My word, you must be proud of that tandem."

"We're particularly pleased with the TA chainset," I told them, much to my husband's surprise, if the bemused expression on his face was anything to go by.

We were joined by Chris and Luke, young lads who both lived nearby, and then by Percy, who was probably around Jack's age, although there the similarity ended. The youngsters shared jokes and Mars bars and began kicking a battered Pepsi can around the car park. Percy started talking earnestly to Jack, without giving us or Bob much more than a cursory glance, which made me feel indignantly slighted on behalf of our posh new tandem.

"Percy cycled down from London recently," John told us. "He's spending a few weeks in Dorset, visiting his sister and researching family history. See how clean and shiny his bike is? It's always like that. He hates cycling anywhere muddy."

"Where are we going today?" Allan asked.

"Cerne Abbas," John told him. "Jack's leading, so we're bound to have a good ride with a tea stop this afternoon. We take turns leading rides. It's me next week."

"Time we were off." Jack had peeled himself away from Percy. "I doubt if anyone else will arrive now."

It was warm for early March and the sun had won its initial battle with a few threatening clouds. Jack led us away from the town centre and on to a road through the Bryanston Estate, but almost immediately we left the main path and followed a track alongside the River Stour. This was narrow and climbed fairly steeply in places, so I was quite relieved when we joined the road once more, passing Bryanston School on our left and eventually reaching the village of Durweston. Here Jack stopped, to make sure all his ducklings were keeping up.

"All right so far?" he asked us.

"The track was great," Allan said. "I didn't even know it existed."

"That's the beauty of cycling with a club," Jack explained "You get the benefit of local knowledge. I expect we'll learn a thing or two from you as well. You got trouble, Percy?"

Percy was off his bike and dabbing at some spokes with a handkerchief.

"A few splashes of mud," he said. "I wouldn't have taken that track at all, if it had been any wetter underfoot."

John caught my eye and grinned but Jack appeared not to hear Percy's tiny hint of reproof. He was slightly deaf, a defect which worked to his advantage on occasions. Off again, we kept going until we were on the outskirts of Hazelbury Bryan, when a small terrier, barking and growling, suddenly rushed from its garden and practically flung itself under our wheels. I squealed and we wobbled alarmingly before Allan managed to stop safely. I was so relieved Bob hadn't hit the deck that I temporarily forgot my fear of dogs, which was perhaps why this one decided to attack my ankles, whereupon I started squealing again.

"Get off, you little sod!" John was suddenly at my side, brandishing his pump. The terrier had second thoughts and scooted off, continuing to snarl fiercely, once safely back in its own front garden. After making sure I was OK, Jack suggested a quick elevenses break while we all calmed down. Everyone had their own story to tell about being chased by dogs while cycling and it was generally agreed that over-indulgent or careless owners were usually to blame.

After that bit of excitement we carried on along peaceful lanes, eventually reaching the little village of Minterne Magna, where the Digby and Churchill families were lords of the manor for almost 400 years. The first Sir Winston Churchill lived there in the 17th century and was apparently a very superstitious man.

On the basis of having been born and baptised on Friday, he decided it was his lucky day and ensured that he married and was even knighted on a Friday. He was also convinced he would die on that day but, disappointingly, the exact date of his death is not recorded.

What is known is that his eldest son John, who became the first Duke of Marlborough, was enraged when Sir Winston left Minterne House to his little brother Charles, leaving him to make do with Blenheim Palace. The house is closed to the public but the gardens are open and consist of over a mile of walks among a chain of small lakes, waterfalls and streams.

I'd learned all this stuff while doing a six-month stint in the local history section of the reference library. Percy knew a bit too but not as much as he thought he did.

"Thomas Hardy used Minterne as a setting for Far From the Madding Crowd," he told us.

"Actually, it was his setting for The Woodlanders," I corrected him. "But Minterne was used when filming scenes for the movie of Far From The Madding Crowd. I expect that's what you're thinking about."

"I doubt it," Percy sniffed. "I never watch film adaptations of books I've enjoyed. I find they always disappoint."

Since I wasn't a Hardy fan and my acquaintance with his novels was limited to the first 50 pages of *Tess Of The d'Urbervilles*, I thought I'd better back off, especially as Percy's expression implied that for someone who couldn't even ride a bike, I had altogether too much to say for myself.

Jack took us along a lane through the hamlet of Up Cerne. This was a brief detour from our route, for the simple and admirable reason that the setting is so beautiful, with its tiny chalk stream bordering the grounds of a 17th century manor house. Then it was straight into Cerne Abbas for our picnic lunch.

Cerne is best known for a club-wielding giant – brazenly male and arrogantly naked – carved into the hillside. It is not known how many centuries ago this 180ft tall figure was created, though there is much speculation. The first written reference was found in church accounts dated 1694, which casts some doubt on the conventional view of the giant as a great emblem of ancient spirituality, originating from prehistoric or Roman times.

His status as a symbol of fertility has never failed to fascinate. The fact that he is now fenced off may have some connection with the grassy slopes around his massive body becoming bald and scrubby, after many decades of having his reputation put to the test by both courting and childless couples.

We spent a leisurely hour leaning against the church wall in the early spring sunshine, eating our sandwiches and chatting. Eventually we left Cerne via Piddle Lane, which soon turned into a long and steep climb. Allan and I had to get off and walk, while all the others overtook us. I wasn't used to this, since with Theo and Jess we'd been pretty well matched.

"I don't like it," I told Allan. "What's wrong? Why's it so much easier for them?"

"Tandems are always slower than solo bikes on hills," he said. "It'll be a different story when we're freewheeling and on the flat too, if we get some momentum going."

"First chance we get, we've got to show them," I muttered. "Especially Percy. Did you see that superior look he gave us as he went past?"

My wounded feelings were soothed on the subsequent downhill, when Allan really let the bike go, and we quickly took the lead, passing everyone including Percy, who I loftily ignored as we swept past.

Mid-afternoon we stopped at the tea rooms in Milton Abbas. This village is famous for being demolished in the 18th century by Joseph Damer, lord of the manor at that time, simply because he disliked its proximity to his own mansion home adjacent to the abbey. Capability Brown was commissioned to build a new village half-a-mile away, to which Damer relocated those residents who had not already found themselves alternative accommodation. Most of the old village is now under the lake and only a single original cottage survives. One obstinate tenant refused to move and was flooded out by Damer. This heroic villager later won his case in court but by then his home was irretrievably lost.

We relaxed and chatted over tea and scones, only preparing to leave when the waitress plonked the itemised bill down on the table. I noticed that John was being asked to pay 50p more than Allan and me, despite having also ordered a pot of tea for two. He was puzzled when I pointed this out and queried it with the waitress. She looked baffled for a few seconds, then realisation seemed to dawn. Lifting the lid of John and Mark's teapot, she peered inside.

"Thought so," she said triumphantly. "You had an extra teabag."

This struck us all as so funny that we were still laughing about it as we cycled out of the village. Even Percy had a smile on his face. Back at Blandford, we went our separate ways and Jack gave us a list of rides for the following few weeks. Next Sunday we were off to Alvediston, via Sixpenny Handley. Despite its delightful name, Sixpenny Handley had once been described as the ugliest village in Dorset – and I was curious to see if it warranted such cruel treatment.

TOP TANDEM TRIVIA

The early tandems were known as 'courting tandems'. They placed the female rider in the front saddle, so she could admire the scenery during the ride, while the man pedalled away at the back and took control of all steering and braking.

CHAPTER SIX

Flo's lemon drizzle and a three-holer toilet

I HAD an interview for the job of clerical officer at Poole library on Monday and was very nervous. Joy Wilkins, the secretary, welcomed me with a warm smile. "I'm sure you have an excellent chance, Jackie," she told me. "You're by far the most experienced candidate."

To my relief the interview went well and just before lunch I was told the job was mine.

"Are we celebrating?" Allan asked, as he drove us home.

"No expense spared." I produced a packet of cat treats from my bag.

"Yummy," he said. "Rabbit flavour, my favourite. Or maybe we could go to the pub?"

The week sped past and Sunday dawned, dark clouds gathering overhead. This time the Wessex Road Club members were all meeting at Witchampton. John, who was leading the ride, surveyed the sky doubtfully.

"Alvediston may be too far," he said. "Especially if it comes on to rain."

"Which looks likely," Jack nodded. "That'll be why Percy's not here. Doesn't want to get his bike splashed."

Chris grinned. "Alvediston does sound like Hell Of A Distance," he said, which made us all smile.

We set off and were approaching Gussage St Andrew when a fairly oldish chap on a definitely oldish bike suddenly appeared alongside us, seemingly out of nowhere.

"Hello Fred," Jack said. "Decided to join us?"

"Thought I'd see if I could catch you up," the new fellow said. "I've left the car a couple of miles away."

We realised over the following months that Fred was a bit of a maverick, who often wasn't to be seen for months on end. He never set off from Blandford with the rest of us and generally disappeared in the afternoon, sometimes without so much as a cheerio.

"I've not seen you two before. Nice tandem." Fred cycled next to us but it was me he starting talking to. "Don't you get fed up with looking at the back of your husband's head?"

He winked at me and I couldn't help but smile.

"So what do you do when you're not cycling?" he asked.

"I work in the library," I told him. "I'm just about to start a job at Poole."

"I'm a member of Poole library," he said. "I'll look out for you next time I'm there."

"You won't see me. It's an office job in admin."

"Admin! Admin, eh?" For some reason this tickled Fred. "So you won't be faced with awkward customers like me?"

There was something appealing about that mischievous face, with the pouched blue eyes, and I wondered if he was lonely.

"Any reason you don't want to work behind the counter?" he asked and I tried to look mournful.

"They only want the pretty ones on show," I said and this really amused him.

"I'll ask for you one of these days," Fred promised.

And sure enough, a couple of months later a befuddled library assistant hunted me down in the stationery cupboard, where I was having a good old natter with Joy. She said someone was asking to see the admin girl called Jackie, who had to be kept hidden out of sight.

"Shall I tell him you're at lunch?" she offered.

"I'll tell him," Joy said. "I'm not having anyone being nasty about my mate Jackie."

I tried to explain the curious phenomenon of Fred but Joy had gone and I left her to it. Apparently the wily old man was quick to assume a dotty but endearing persona and my soft-hearted friend was soon sitting with him, in a comfortable corner of the lending library, listening to his life story.

After that, on the rare occasions Fred rode with the club, he'd ask wistfully after Joy and bemoan the fact that she too was admin and never to be seen behind the counter, despite being – as he kept telling me – as pretty as a picture.

But back to our ride. Rain was still threatening and it was cool, so we decided to cut the ride short and eat our lunch at Tollard Royal. Alvediston and Sixpenny Handley would have to wait until another day.

"We'll stop for tea in Wimborne St Giles," John told us. "We try to fit as many rides as possible around afternoon tea in the village hall. Fantastic cakes. You're in for a treat."

The St Giles W.I. members took turns baking cakes and buttering bread every Sunday afternoon from March until September, raising money for charity. We joined the queue of people waiting to make their choice from trestle tables laden with teatime treats. Following the good old-fashioned rule of delayed gratification, the sandwiches had been laid out first and no-one was rude enough to push past those and dive greedily into the cake. There was a modest range of fillings: egg and cress, meat paste, corned beef, sardine and tomato.

The cakes were making everyone drool with anticipation. Each poised in the centre of its own paper doily, on a china plate and carefully labelled. Maud's cherry loaf dwarfed by Eileen's ginger stout cake, Polly's coffee and walnut perched neatly beside Betty's Dorset apple cake. Mary Jane's sultana delight spilt golden crumbs on to Aggie's butterfly cakes. Flo's lemon drizzle leaned gently towards Lily's Victorian sponge and Edith's rock buns kept a respectful distance from Hettie's chocolate marble cake. Dot's pineapple upside-down concoction was inexplicably dumped between plates of wonky scones and pretty little pottery dishes, heaped with clotted cream and strawberry jam.

"Flo's lemon drizzle is always marvellous." Jack told me. He was clutching a gold-rimmed dinner plate holding one small sardine and tomato sandwich, so leaving plenty of room for the main event. "Better watch out for that Victoria sponge, it could be a bit dry."

Anxiously, I watched the lemon drizzle cake begin to disappear as the queue moved slowly forward. Jack was obviously not Flo's only admirer.

We sat at a wobbly card table, its shabby green baize almost concealed by a soft lace tablecloth, faintly yellow in its creases. Allan and I had been given our tea in a Poole Pottery teapot, covered with a knitted blue and white striped tea cosy, while John and Mark's came in a sturdy china pot decorated with fat pink roses. The tea cups were thin bone china, there was a silver teaspoon in the dish of strawberry jam and a fish knife in the butter dish.

Allan had managed to secure the very last of the lemon drizzle, which he shared with me. We also went halves with slices of coffee and walnut sponge and Dorset apple cake smothered with clotted cream.

After finishing our wonderful tea, we all huddled glumly in the porch, watching the skies darken and rain begin to teem down with growing determination.

"We'd better go our separate ways," Jack said. "And just concentrate on getting home as quickly as possible. At least we've got some hot tea inside us. You can't do better than a pot of Wimborne St Giles good strong brew."

"Would you two like to lead next week?" John asked us. "It's supposed to be me again but you might like to have a go."

"Great," Allan said and I could see he was already planning the route.

We were very wet when we finally arrived home and this was the first time I had frowned on Bob's presence in our sitting room. He leaned against the fireplace with both wheels planted on thick wads of newspaper, handlebars dripping dismally on to the carpet.

"I'll get a greenhouse sorted out over Easter," Allan promised. "I won't have time before then. I think we'll cycle to Wardour next week. Everyone's bound to enjoy that."

"Wardour's in Wiltshire," I said. "Must be a round trip of 60 miles. Much too far if the weather's like this."

But the following Sunday morning nine cyclists gathered at Blandford in warm sunshine and high spirits.

"Old Wardour Castle," Jack said. "I haven't been there for years. It'll be a great day out. I see you're taking it seriously, Jackie." He nodded towards my saddle, with a mischievous smile.

In my quest to avoid the major expense of a Brook's leather saddle, I was stubbornly throwing good money after bad, much to Allan's despair. So far, I'd tried a cheap wide saddle, a cheap narrow saddle, saddles made of foam and gel, a mattress saddle and a sprung saddle, none of which proved comfortable for more than a few hours. Today I'd covered a padded saddle with a thick furry beret, which I'd found in a charity shop. It felt fine and I was ignoring all the smirks.

With Allan and I in the lead, we set off promptly at 9.30. We cycled through Tarrant Monkton and then along the Salisbury road for a couple of miles before turning off towards Chettle, a small village with fascinating history. Since the mid 19th century, every farm, cottage and acre of land has been owned and controlled by the Bourke family. Yet this medieval state of affairs seems to please everyone. Tenants pay modest rents for their very attractive thatched cottages and there is a rich social life to be enjoyed, with a thriving shop and village hall.

Not one property in Chettle has been turned into a holiday home and anyone showing a tendency to treat their cottage as a weekend retreat runs the very real risk of eviction. The Bourke family exercise what has been described as a benevolent feudalism, which benefits all concerned. They are choosy about their tenants and don't offer a home to anyone whose reasons for wanting to live in the village fail to meet their criteria. Precedence is given to those who work in the Chettle timberyard, the Chettle farms, the village shop or the Castleman Hotel, all of which are owned by the Bourkes. Priority then goes to anyone whose parents or grandparents lived in the village. Because rents are so affordable, there is a healthy mix of young and old and everybody is encouraged to play their part in keeping the community alive and flourishing.

After stopping briefly for elevenses at Tollard Royal, we cycled through the villages of Donhead St Mary and Donhead St Andrew. Then we continued almost into Semley, before turning off on to a narrow lane, which after less than a mile led us finally to old Wardour Castle. With the waters of a secluded lake practically lapping at its crumbling ramparts and surrounded by peaceful Wiltshire fields, the setting could scarcely be more picturesque or romantic. But as tired and hungry cyclists, at first we were oblivious to the charm of anything except the picnic lunches waiting in our saddlebags. We settled down on a grassy bank with our backs to the castle ruins and, for a few minutes, the only sounds to be heard were the rustling of crisp packets and cracking of hard-boiled eggs.

"There can't be a better way than this to spend Sunday," said Jack, as he leaned back and signed happily, full of Ruth's chicken salad sandwiches and homemade fruit cake. "It's a pity we don't have time to look around the castle."

"Do you know much about its history?" Allan asked. But Percy chipped in before Jack could answer. He'd obviously been doing his homework and didn't intend getting any facts wrong this week.

"It was built for the Lovell family in the 14th century, more as a stylish home than a fortified castle," he told us. "But they lost it during the Wars of the Roses and eventually Sir Matthew Arundell bought it in 1570 and did a lot of renovations."

Percy paused, but if he hoped for eager questions he was disappointed.

"I think I saw an ice-cream van beside the entrance," John said. "Anyone interested?"

Watching his audience rapidly shrink to Jack, Allan and me, Percy looked annoyed.

"Carry on," Jack said. "What happened during the Civil War?"

"The castle fell to Cromwell's men and was practically demolished," Percy said, sulkily. "Lady Arundell put up a brave fight but her husband was away on the King's business and she'd been left with only a few soldiers."

"Poor old duck," I said. "I'd love an ice-cream. Strawberry would be nice." I smiled at Allan and he stood up. "Anyone else?" he asked.

Jack put in an order for vanilla but tight-lipped Percy applied himself to a Kit Kat and lapsed into wounded silence.

We were all enjoying our ice-creams when Jack made his unique contribution to the store of Wardour-related facts.

"A three-holer was installed when the castle was first built," he told us.

"A three-holer?" John looked puzzled. "What's that?"

"A toilet built for the convenience of three people all bursting to go at the same time," Jack said.

The lads thought this was very funny and wanted to know if there were any remains still to be seen or, even better, tried out.

"Of course not," Percy snapped. "I don't know what Christmas cracker you got that from, Jack. It certainly wasn't mentioned in any of the books I borrowed from the library."

Maybe not but I reckon in years to come, the only thing any of us will be able to remember about the castle's history was Jack's decidedly dodgy assertion that it had once been home to a three-holer.

It was time to leave Wardour and we led the way along a track through quiet woods on to the Ansty road, where we soon turned off towards

Berwick St John, on the border of Wiltshire and Dorset. It was a long haul out of this village and Allan and I had to relinquish pole position to those riding solo bikes. A thin stream in a concrete culvert ran along the edge of the narrow road and Mark decided to try riding through it. John called out a warning but it was too late and his son fell off into the slimy, greenish water. He was wet and probably smelly but unhurt, except for his wounded pride, and we didn't feel guilty about using his misfortune as a chance to get back into the lead.

Tandems don't negotiate rough ground well and Allan and I walked most of the track along Win Green, the highest point on Cranborne Chase, with beautiful views in all directions, from the Isle of Wight to a hazy outline of the Quantock hills, 80 miles away in distant Somerset. We all stopped for a breather at the very highest point, beside the clump of beech trees growing on a Bronze Age bowl barrow.

"I love it here," Jack said. "If I had to choose a favourite place in Dorset, this would be it. The ground's a bit bumpy, though. Are all the bikes OK?"

"Mark's rear mudguard looks a bit loose." Allan went over and took a closer look. "That needs tightening up, otherwise you'll be going arse over tit."

For just a second, there was a stunned silence, then each young face lit up with glee and they all fell about laughing.

"Arse over tit!" For at least the next 15 minutes, they refused to let it drop. "Mark's going arse over tit!"

Eventually things calmed down and we carried on into Ashmore, where we were lucky enough to discover afternoon teas being served in a cottage garden. Allan and I found ourselves sitting at a table with only Percy for company. We were enjoying the weak spring sunshine when a young woman with bare feet, an assortment of silver ankle bracelets and toenails painted with scarlet ladybirds came to take our order.

"There's scones with jam and cream," she said. "And buttered tea cakes. I don't remember seeing you lot in the village before. Are you local?"

"Blandford and thereabouts," Percy told her. "I do enjoy cycling through Ashmore. Such a peaceful, quiet village."

"There's more goes on here than you'd think," she said. "Strange things, some of them. You'd be surprised."

And with a tinkle of ankle bracelets, she went off with our order.

"What strange things does she mean?" I was intrigued.

When ladybird girl returned she had a chap with her, helping to carry the trays laden with pots of tea, scones and teacakes.

"I hope you don't mind us asking what strange happenings you were referring to," Percy said, with a charming smile which I'd certainly never seen him bestow on anyone before. "As something of an amateur historian, I'm most curious."

Smarmy old devil, I thought, but even I hoped his attempts at friendliness would persuade her to tell us more. But no such luck.

"I just meant Ashmore's not the dull little village people sometimes think." Putting down a plate of scones, she glanced quickly at the chap, whose face bore an expression of scowling martyrdom.

"No shenanigans, then?" Percy carried on, with jovial heavy-handedness.

"It's not The Archers, you know," retorted ladybird girl. "Why don't you go back to the Grand Prix, love," she suggested to her dour companion. "I can manage now."

He disappeared with alacrity and she relaxed, leaning against the table and smiling down at an affronted Percy.

"You should come back to Ashmore in a few weeks time," she told him. "On the Friday closest to June 21st, the longest day of the year."

"Why, what happens then?" Allan asked.

"Something called the Filly Loo. In the evening the villagers gather beside the pond to dance and have fun. Well, most of us do. Miseries like my hubby stay away – and good riddance."

"What else happens?" Percy seemed to have recovered from being snubbed.

"Lots." Ladybird girl absentmindedly helped herself to a scone and licked the cream slowly.

"A procession, followed by more dancing and eventually it starts to get dark."

"Then what?" Percy asked eagerly.

"There's another procession, torchlit this time, and we all wear fancy dress." Her voice grew husky. "It's almost impossible to recognise people, dressed up as Maid Marion or Robin Hood. Everyone holds hands and dances round the pond to soft, hypnotic music."

"How does it end?" Even my pragmatic Yorkshire husband was looking enthralled.

"We all go home." Briskly, ladybird girl began clattering plates together. "Eventually," she added, with the briefest of winks at Percy.

"What did you reckon to all that?" I asked Allan back at the bike.

"I reckon she ate one of our scones, which we've paid for," he said and I was pleased to see he was back to his usual northern self. "She'll not get many tips if she does that too often."

The day came to a most satisfactory conclusion when we were on the homeward stretch and whizzing down a long hill. The tandem was freewheeling but everyone else had to pedal hard to keep up with us. Suddenly Allan turned round and shouted to the others: "Beat you to the Blandford sign!"

We put a spurt on and not one of them stood the ghost of a chance, taken by surprise like that. Bob tore past the sign at 30mph and carried his riders victoriously home.

TOP TANDEM TIP

When going uphill, the stoker needs to know when the front rider intends changing gear, so she/he can briefly slacken off the pedalling, while the gear engages. Then it's straight back to putting in the same amount of effort as before. It all needs to be done smoothly, which will soon become second nature. When stopping at junctions, the stoker can keep both feet on the pedals. The front rider takes one foot off the pedal and places it on the ground, prior to pushing off again.

CHAPTER SEVEN
Racing, ridiculously long rides and shaved legs

E cycled with the Wessex Road Club every Sunday and went on some seriously long rides. Often we'd set off from Blandford at 9am and not get home until nearly 7pm. My friends at work used to ask where we'd been but were often no wiser when I told them.

"Where's Cadbury Castle?" Joy asked. "I've never heard of it."

"It's not far from Compton Pauncefoot," I said.

"And where's that, when it's at home?"

"In Somerset. Percy punctured just before we got there. He was cross because he prides himself on his bike always being in perfect nick."

"I should think you were too shattered to look around the castle. Is it still owned by Cadbury's?"

Sometimes it was hard to tell if Joy was serious. She had a mischievous sense of humour. She'd caught me out on April Fool's Day by ringing my extension number and telling me to look out of the window because there was a naked man on the roundabout.

"It's a hill fort near the town of South Cadbury," I told her. "It may have some connection to King Arthur but no-one's sure about that. It made quite a nice picnic spot."

"How many miles did you clock up?" Kate asked.

We were drinking our coffee in Joy's office, keeping a watchful eye out for the boss, Miss Elder.

"Eighty-two," I said, hardly knowing whether to be proud or apologetic. I was pretty sure quite a few people thought I was completely mad. Not Kate though. We were the best of friends.

"You must be completely mad," she said and Joy, my other best mate, nodded in agreement.

"Why didn't you just drive to Cadbury Castle, if you wanted to go there so badly?" she asked.

"It's the cycle ride that matters," I tried to explain. "The destination is often just somewhere to eat lunch."

"You and Allan must be fit as fiddles," Joy marvelled.

"She's fit to drop every Monday morning," Kate said. "It takes her until Wednesday to get over the weekend."

"I remember those days," Joy sighed. "Not that it had anything to do with cycling, so far as I was concerned."

"But I bet you learned to ride a bike when you were a kid," Kate said. "Jackie's only ever been on a tandem."

Only my very closest friends knew this embarrassing fact. I kept it quiet, partly because it was beginning to seem quite ridiculous.

"People like me make the best tandem partners," I defended myself. "Because I don't try to control the bike. But that doesn't mean I can take it easy. Allan would soon notice if I wasn't putting enough effort in."

But even my cycling friends thought I ought to be riding solo. Jack kept encouraging me to give it a try.

"Don't you find it annoying when people assume you just sit there and take it easy?" he said. "You have to work just as hard as anyone else. You're a Real Cyclist, there's no doubt about it."

"I'd like Jackie to learn to ride a bike," Allan agreed. "But I do think a tandem is good for couples because it makes you keep together. It can't be much fun when the bloke's always having to wait for his wife to catch up."

"What makes you think it would be that way round?" Jack enquired.

I loved Jack. If he'd been 20 years younger, I'd have fought Ruth for him. He once showed us a photograph of his younger self, taken about 20 years earlier, when he must have been in his early 40s.

"You don't look any different," I told him because he really didn't, or not much anyway, and he laughed.

"I think the next 20 years might make a difference," he said.

A few months later, during the weekend of the Queen's Silver Jubilee in June 1977, we met Richard and Annabelle, who lived two doors away from us. We hit it off straight away and were good friends for many years. An evening spent in their company would always send me home still giggling, while I tottered unsteadily up our garden path. Living so close meant no driving and consequently no limit on alcohol intake. Our cycling compulsion was a mystery to these two but they were always willing to help out in any bike-related crisis, usually involving mechanical breakdown and the need for rescue.

When Allan had to go away on a work-related training weekend, the fact that I couldn't ride a bike might have forced me to spend a housebound couple of days, although I was secretly rather looking forward to putting my feet up and doing nothing more strenuous than reading the latest Dick Francis and eating chocolate biscuits.

But I couldn't help being flattered when several fit young fellows began jostling for the privilege of taking my husband's place on Bob. Well, 15-year-old Chris said he wouldn't mind giving it a go.

It seemed very strange, spending hours looking at the back of a head which wasn't Allan's and it took quite a while before we managed to get the pedalling really smooth. I was bounced around rather painfully once, when Chris swerved to avoid a nasty pothole, and another time I lurched forward when he braked suddenly.

I was worried that he might find this tandeming lark really hard work and tell the others he felt sorry for Allan, having to lug that wife of his around, week after week. So I wore myself out, putting 100% effort in all the time and rather wishing I'd stayed at home, tucked up on the sofa with Barley and Dick Francis.

But after an hour or so, we began to get used to each other and things settled down. While we were chatting over lunch, it became clear that cycling meant more to Chris than anything else in life and he rather assumed I would feel the same.

"You don't want children, do you?" he said, with a shudder. "I mean, just think about it. Kids would be the end of cycling."

It would certainly change my life in a way I wasn't yet ready for. I was only 28 – I could put off any decision for ages yet.

After lunch, Chris and I were feeling pleased with our unexpected compatibility and rather fit too, so consequently we spent a lot of time at the front, immediately behind Percy. I guessed Chris was keen to beat the others in a sprint to at least one village sign, the way Allan and I often did. But my husband was an experienced tandem rider now and knew just the right signs to aim for. The approach road needed to be flat, or better still slightly downhill, then the tandem could easily beat all the solos in that final sprint.

Even with a promising village sign temptingly on the horizon, Chris wasn't quite skilled enough to identify the strategic moment to really put a sudden spurt on and take the rest of the group by surprise. I sympathised with his disappointment but felt quietly proud of Bob for being loyal to Allan and not revealing the secrets of tandem technique to a young whippersnapper, even a nice one like Chris.

I'd enjoyed the day and boasted to Joy and Kate that I'd been cycling with my toy boy. Although, to be honest, I did rather imply that Chris was on the point of going to university, instead of in the first year of his O-levels.

When I was introduced to racing, I discovered an aspect of cycling that I didn't like one bit. Allan used to enjoy time trials in Barnsley and he was competitive by nature. Although I knew he possessed this trait, there hadn't been much opportunity for it to flourish recently and I was dismayed when it suddenly surfaced after the Wessex Road Club began to organise 10 and 25-mile time trials.

Jack must have dug deep into his address books and spent hours catching up with old pals. Droves of former club members appeared out of the woodwork, ready to spend evenings and early mornings marshalling and doing duty as timekeepers. They were all dressed as Real Cyclists, even if they'd driven there.

I hated everything about cycle racing. I hated how seriously Allan took each event – the preparation, the anxiety, the post-mortem afterwards, the determination to do better next time, the way he measured himself against others and the disappointment of being beaten. But what I hated more than anything was when he shaved his legs. Apparently it's all to do with aerodynamics. All I can say is that losing a few wisps of body hair didn't make him go any faster. What it did mean was that his legs felt horrible next to mine in bed, both when they were bald and, even worse, when the bristles began to grow back.

I don't know who talked me into having a go at the racing lark. Jack, probably. I was always putty in the gnarled hands of that old charmer. So somehow, one Tuesday evening in May, after a hard day at work sorting out 15 boxes of returned non-fiction binding, I found myself in a lay-by near Bere Regis, shaking with nerves.

Allan was all hyped up, hissing last-minute instructions and then saying not to worry, we were only doing it for fun. Well, cycle racing is many things – but fun it is not. My idea of spending an enjoyable evening was sitting on the sofa with Barley on my lap, a Kit Kat in one hand and a book in the other. Full of spag bol, or maybe shepherd's pie. Something substantial and stomach-lining. Not a miserable banana sandwich, with the promise of something better later on.

And not standing in the silent company of half-a-dozen chaps, who I normally thought of as friends but who were now rivals we were desperate to beat. Not that you were supposed to think of it like that. Dear me, no. The aim was always to improve on your own Personal Best. That was what Allan told me, so why did it upset him so much when youngsters achieved better times than him?

We all went off at one-minute intervals and then it was hammering along as fast as you could up the road towards Wareham, round the roundabout and back again. We were tearing along so swiftly that it came as quite a shock when Luke, who had started two minutes after us, came whizzing past. What a cheek, I thought! A kid like that, overtaking us! Panting, I tried to force more effort into my tired legs – but to no avail.

Suddenly it was all over and we didn't have much to crow about. Apparently anything under 24 minutes is a pretty good time. We'd managed 27 minutes and 13 seconds. Disgraceful. Not the slowest that evening but fairly disgraceful all the same. And I had a nasty feeling that as the whole 10 miles had all been on the flat, on a tandem we should have had an advantage over solo bikes. I cycled home with aching legs, hoping we'd be back in time to watch *Porridge*, then at least I'd have salvaged something from what scraps of the evening were left.

A few weeks later, when the memory had dimmed slightly, Allan persuaded me to attempt a 25-mile event, which turned out to be my racing swansong. It started at 6am, so we had to get up at 5am in the shivery dawn and drive to The Baker's Arms, near Poole.

It was a cool and windy June morning, not great conditions for cycling. I'd heard that you couldn't hold your head up afterwards if you failed to beat the hour, although allowances would be made for your first few attempts. We managed one hour, one minute and 11 seconds. That was the feeble result for which we'd wrecked a perfectly good Sunday. However, there was plenty of day left, it still being only 9am.

But my thoughts were firmly focused on how soon I could sit down in front of a plateful of fried eggs on fried bread, rashers of bacon and a couple of sausages, followed by a lazy day doing nothing very much. Bob had now taken up residence in his own greenhouse in the back garden and, at that moment, I never wanted to set eyes on him again. One hour, one minute and 11 seconds. How could any self-respecting tandem live with the shame of that?

But although I may have ditched racing myself, I wasn't able to avoid all involvement. There was plenty of marshalling to be done, especially at the longer events, like 25 and 50-mile time trials. I met Wessex Road Club members I hadn't known existed because they weren't interested in touring, only racing. The best riders the club had in the late 1970s and early 1980s were Pete Goodings and Willie Kirkland. I'd stand for hours on many a roundabout, with frozen feet or incipient sunburn, my arm stuck out to the left or right, directing riders.

"Dig in, Pete!" I'd shriek, and he would sometimes reward me with a smile or a quick nod. Willie never did. I used to moan to Allan about this but he was on Willie's side and couldn't understand why any rider would waste a single second's worth of energy acknowledging marshals. Both the 25s and the 50s started at the crack of dawn but the 50s were much more demanding because they sometimes took up almost the entire day.

My longest ride ever took place on Sunday, 22nd April 1979. This was the Dorset Coast 200km (124 miles) Randonnee, organised by the Wessex division of the Cyclists' Touring Club. It was only the second time this event had taken place in Dorset, inspired from the founding of Audax UK, an association established in 1976 with the aim of encouraging long-distance cycling in Britain.

There must have been several hundred riders, all setting off from different checkpoints around the county. We'd spent the previous night at Allan's parents' house in Hamworthy, so we were close to the start, and met up with a crowd of other riders, setting off from Sandbanks ferry at 8am.

The air felt cool but the weather forecast was for a pleasant day, with some sunshine. I felt shivery with nerves, excitement and the buzz of being with dozens of other cyclists, although I wished we could see someone we knew. A few riders were travelling very light, seemingly with no extra clothing and little in the way of tools.

After the ferry crossing, a group of these hard men went straight into the lead and soon streaked away out of sight. Those chaps were noses down and concentrating solely on completing as fast a time as possible. They never looked to right or left and were oblivious to the pretty Dorset countryside.

As we approached Corfe, flimsy layers of thin cloud gradually dispersed, revealing the lofty castle ruins steeped in pale spring sunshine. It was still early and we cycled along the quiet street, unseen by all but a few worshippers making their way to a church service, none of whom thankfully ruined the peaceful moment with an unholy yell of "Can you ride tandem?"

Neither did we see nor hear any of the castle's resident unkindness of ravens, ancient brooding occupants of the magnificently crumbled walls. Although generally considered birds of ill omen, in medieval times most villagers believed that the castle would soon fall if its ravens ever forsook the battlements. According to legend, that ominous day arrived early in 1638, when each of the huge birds took flight in one dense black cloud, leaving the unprotected village at the mercy of its enemies. Sure enough, eight years later Cromwell's men successfully laid siege to Corfe Castle, practically destroying it.

Walking up the steepest part of Creech Hill, we were overtaken by many solo bikes but consoled ourselves with the certain knowledge that we would whizz past most of them at some point on a downhill stretch.

But after East Lulworth, heading for Weymouth, we suddenly realised something was wrong with the bike and the whole day was put in jeopardy. I stood miserably on the grass verge, while dozens of cyclists swept past us.

"The chain's broken." Allan looked up from the tandem, a streak of oil on his unhappy face.

"Can you fix it?" But a despairing glance gave me my answer.

"No chance. We need a rivet extractor, and I haven't brought mine with us."

"Why ever not?" I couldn't hold back the querulous demand.

"Because I wasn't expecting this to happen! Because we can't carry every single dratted tool on every single dratted ride!"

We glared at each other and at that moment a cyclist on the most extraordinarily beautiful machine I'd ever seen slid to a halt beside us. His bike was painted in shades of palest pink, sliding into deepest purple, and there was lots of shiny, wavy chrome work on the frame.

"Trouble?" he asked, giving Bob a speedy once over before nodding sagely.

"Broken your chain. You need a rivet extractor."

"I don't suppose..?" Allan hardly dared speak the words.

Our rescuer, who turned out to be called Dan Best, looked modestly pleased with himself.

"Never go anywhere without it," he said. "Now, let's see what we can do."

Five minutes later, the rivet extractor had done its work, our chain was again in one piece and we were cycling alongside Dan, who had earned our undying gratitude and become a friend for life. But, regrettably, a friend who soon revealed himself anxious to leave us behind as soon as possible.

"I'm on duty," he said, mysteriously. "No time to waste. Good luck."

Sadly we watched Dan speed away into the distance, his incredible bike soon a dim speck on the horizon.

"On duty?" I said. "What did he mean? I wanted to invite him round for dinner. Or at least put him on my Christmas card list. His bike was amazing. All those curly bits and intricate, wavy lettering."

"A Curly Hetchins," Allan said, reverentially. "There aren't many of them around. Perhaps we'll see him again at Weymouth."

This was the first check-in point, where we had our Audax cards stamped by one of the official timekeepers. It was almost 11am and we'd completed 33 miles. We sat outside the hall in the sunshine, drinking coffee and eating home-made ginger cake, all supplied at very reasonable cost by the organisers. Events like these take months of preparation and dozens of tireless helpers. We soon set off again, bemoaning the fact that we still hadn't met up with anyone we knew, let alone renewed our acquaintance with Dan Best.

The going was getting tough. Up over Abbotsbury Hill, with fantastic views of Chesil Beach, spoilt only by successive cyclists overtaking us as we trudged along, pushing Bob. Then into the village of Burton Bradstock and we were still about 10 miles away from Lyme Regis, which was the next check-in point and approximate half-way mark. We ate our lunch – a few untidy cheese and tomato sandwiches, hastily thrown together at 6am – in a quiet spot away from the road, with a distant view of the sea. Allan had his eye on the time and didn't want to stop for long, so it was hard to relax – but I did my best.

"It's so peaceful." I leaned back, closing my eyes. "The bluebells will be out soon and then it'll be even more wonderful up here."

"Bulbarrow Hill is the best place for bluebells," Allan said. "Perhaps we'll have a club run up there next month. Come on, time to go."

The West Dorset hills hadn't finished with us yet and it was on the outskirts of Lyme Regis, when we were once again pushing the bike rather than riding it, that we at last saw a familiar face.

"Taking it easy?" It was young Luke, looking meaner and keener than he ever did on Sunday club runs. I was pleased to see him and ready for a natter about how the ride was going. He told us he'd had two punctures already.

"That's why I'm so far behind," he said. "I'd planned on being at Lyme half-an-hour ago."

Oh dear, I thought. Someone else set on burning up the miles and with no time to chat.

"The second time I punctured, another cyclist stopped and gave me a repair patch," Luke said. "One of the new sort that work quickly. I've read about them in the CTC magazine."

"Me too," Allan agreed. "They're quite pricey. What a nice chap."

"He had a nice bike too," Luke said. "A Curly Hetchins. I'm off. Might see you later."

And he was gone, without a backward glance and clearly with no expectation of seeing us again, any time before next Sunday.

At last we reached the Lyme Regis check-in point, where we had our cards stamped for the second time. It was 2pm and we were just over half-way through the ride. I was feeling surprisingly good.

"It'll catch up with you soon, love. Get these inside you." A plump woman, wearing a pair of faded Hebden Cords, handed me a cup of tea and two buttered scones. "I used to be mad keen on cycling," she added. "But then the kids arrived and I lost interest. You'll be the same, I expect."

Smiling, she turned away and I sipped my tea thoughtfully.

"What are you looking so pensive about?" Allan had just returned from the gents.

"I was thinking about babies," I said and he recoiled, dropping his scone, buttered side down.

"What's brought this on?" he stuttered. "The cottage is barely big enough for us and the cat, let alone a baby. Surely you're not serious?"

"That scone will be fine if you scrape the butter off," I snapped. "There's been a dog sniffing around but don't let that worry you."

I stamped off to the ladies, furiously blinking away a few inexplicable tears. I didn't want babies either – or not yet, anyway. At least I was pretty sure I didn't.

A brooding silence reigned for the next few miles but at Beaminster we met up with someone whose company was guaranteed to raise our spirits. There was Jack, sitting on a bench with his thermos beside him and his eyes closed, quietly basking in the afternoon sunshine. At last, someone who'd spare five minutes for a chat.

"I'm just about to go," he said, after we'd hailed him joyfully. "You're doing well, Jackie. It's a tough ride on a tandem, with all these hills. You should feel proud of yourself."

"I'm certainly proud of her." Allan put an arm around me. "There aren't many other girls out riding and I think we're the only tandem."

Jack looked from me to Allan and back again. He was pretty perceptive and up to then he'd only seen my husband's pragmatic Yorkshire side, so he must have wondered what was going on.

"You can only do this sort of ride if you're really fit," he said. "Which means giving cycling high priority – and that's not always easy."

"I like your hat." My husband's appetite for reflective talk was on the wane. "I've never seen you wearing that before."

"This is my racing hat. It's 40 years old." Jack straightened his red woollen cap. "I always used to beat the hour wearing this hat."

"But you're not racing against the clock today?" I asked, accepting a couple of Spangles from the packet he proffered.

"No, I leave all that to the youngsters now. I'm just enjoying this wonderful countryside. Dorset's the most beautiful county of the lot, bar none."

I think he could see Allan gearing up to defend his beloved Yorkshire because Jack quickly got to his feet, and after wishing us well, off he rode at a surprisingly nippy pace for someone who wasn't much bothered.

We didn't hang around for long either and were soon back on the tandem and leaving Beaminster behind us – but not before Allan spotted a sign to nearby Mapperton.

"There's a village called Mapperton not far from Spetisbury," he said. "Perhaps we're closer to home than we realised."

"The one near us is tiny," I said. "But no-one lives here at all, except the people at the manor house. That's open to the public, and the garden too."

"I'm so lucky being married to a library girl," Allan teased me. "What else do you know?"

Quite a bit, as it happened. One of the readers at Poole library was a Dorset historian, who had asked for information about Mapperton. Among other things, I knew that the house had been built during the reign of Henry VIII by a nobleman, who was granted special permission to wear his hat in the royal presence because of a gruesome skin disease which disfigured his head.

"The plague decimated the village in 1582," I told Allan. "At the spot where Dead Man's Lane branches off towards Netherbury, there's a sycamore tree, otherwise known as a Posy Tree. Funeral processions went down that lane to Netherbury churchyard to bury their dead, and the mourners carried posies of sweet-smelling herbs to mask the smell of putrefaction."

"Nice. Why weren't they buried in Mapperton churchyard?"

"Because the ground there was shallow and rock hard. Netherbury became a lot less neighbourly when the Black Death arrived. A group of men armed with staves threatened the first plague victim's cortege and wouldn't let them pass. They had to dig a common grave outside the village, and just about everyone in Mapperton ended up in it eventually."

"Perhaps we'll drive here one day and have a look around the house and gardens," Allan suggested. "We could bring your mum. Is there still a Posy Tree?"

"Yes, but not the original one. Mum would enjoy that, it's a lovely idea." I hugged him and for a few seconds he held me very close.

It was late afternoon when we arrived at Dorchester, by which time I was well and truly wilting – and there was 28 miles still to do. Neither of us could face more tea and cakes at the check-in point, so we treated ourselves to cheeseburgers and fresh coffee at the Wimpy Bar. Eating the hot food took up valuable time but it did us good and once my bum had reluctantly and wincingly renewed its acquaintance with the saddle, we were off again.

On the outskirts of Wareham, we met up with a group of cyclists and exchanged a few exhausted pleasantries. The human contact helped wake me up a bit and I felt livelier. Gradually, conversation trickled to a halt and the pace increased until we were fairly speeding along. It soon became obvious that one of the men was determined to burn off the rest of us and Allan was equally determined to show him what a tandem could do, especially when there were no real hills in the way to slow us down. He timed it perfectly.

We stuck steadily on the chap's wheel for ages until, on a straight stretch of road about half-a-mile from Poole, we pulled ahead and I could see from his contorted features as we passed that he didn't have an ounce of energy left. I felt an unfamiliar and fiendish glee in our triumph and was too full of adrenalin to ease up. It was almost dark by now and we continued going hell for leather in shattered silence, until the final check-in point loomed into view and suddenly it was all over.

"Well done." The Poole timekeeper stamped our scruffy cards, sweat-stained proof that we had cycled 200km in 12 hours and nine minutes. "You two don't look in bad nick. Not like some I've seen."

"Are there many riders still out there?" Allan asked.

"A fair few. Some will have given up, of course. We'll wait here until ten o'clock and then go home. It's been a long day for all of us, whether or not we've been on our bikes."

"I suppose Dan Best came through ages ago," Allan said. "The chap on the Curly Hetchins."

"Not you as well! People keep asking about him. I suppose you're going to tell me if it wasn't for Dan Best, your ride would have been scuppered?"

"That's right." Allan looked bewildered. "Our chain broke and he repaired it. Has he helped many other riders?"

"The man must have a saddlebag the size of a suitcase. He's dished out energy bars, paracetamol, Kit Kats, two scotch eggs and a corned beef sandwich. He's handed over two spare jumpers, a pair of socks and a five pound note. Not to mention parting with half-a-dozen puncture repair patches."

"So has he been through yet?" Allan persisted.

"Never set eyes on the bloke." The timekeeper sounded quite aggrieved. "And neither has anyone at any of the other check-in points." He looked wistful. "I'd really love to see that Curly Hetchins. Still, I expect I'll bump into them both one of these days."

"Maybe not until you need a helping hand," I murmured, but he'd already turned away.

Suddenly the day was catching up with me and I wasn't sure I could even manage to cycle the next couple of miles to Allan's parents' house. But somehow I did it and even kept my eyes open long enough to eat Betty's roast chicken with all the trimmings, which she'd kept warm for us. Arthur drove us home at 9.30 and as we limped up the garden path we heard Mr and Mrs Radley's front door quietly open and close. Sure enough, a spoilt ginger puss, tummy full of his own chicken dinner, pushed through the hedge to greet us.

You've been gone flipping ages, his reproachful purrs seemed to say but fortunately I'm not a cat to bear grudges and to prove it, I'll give you both a nice long game of chase the ping-pong ball. Barley soon got fed up, listening to our self-pitying excuses and banged out of his cat flap, not even hanging around to sneeze into the heaps of frothy, lavender-scented bubbles cascading over the edge of the bath Allan ran for me. I promptly fell asleep in the lovely hot water and had to be helped upstairs to bed.

At 7am the alarm went off and apart from a couple of initial groans as he lowered his legs to the floor, Allan seemed much the same as usual.

"Do you want a cup of tea?" he asked.

"Tea, toast, marmalade and a massage please," I replied, making no move to get out of bed. "I'm not going to work. Every single bit of me aches. In fact, I'm in total agony."

"Miss Elder won't like that," Allan said.

He was right. When I phoned the library I was lucky enough to speak to Joy, who commiserated with me but rang back later to say Miss Elder had been very sniffy, saying that because my pain was self-inflicted, I wasn't really entitled to paid sick leave.

"She thinks you should take a day's holiday," Joy explained. "But don't worry, with any luck she'll have forgotten about it by tomorrow."

Rather to my surprise, after a day spent doing nothing more strenuous than stroking Barley, I was fit enough to return to work, where on opening my office door I discovered Joy and Kate holding either end of a paper banner, inscribed *HOW'S YOUR BUM, CHUM?*

Possibly the most ridiculous time trial of all was the Christmas Day Ten. I have to confess that it was suggested by Allan and me, presumably at some point in early spring, when the day itself was a long way off. I struggle to think why it should ever have seemed like a good idea.

Christmas Day was always frantic for us, without the added complication of a cycling event. Tradition dictated that my dad and stepmother Gwen would come round in the morning, bearing presents and a big bottle of Harvey's Bristol Cream. But they never stayed very long because they had to cook lunch for Gwen's mum. After eating our own turkey dinner with one eye on the clock, Allan and I visited his parents, where there was always a houseful, before spending what remained of the day with my mum and grandmother. These attempts to please everybody no doubt resulted in pleasing no-one very much and certainly exhausted us. So trying to fit a bike ride into this packed schedule was sheer madness.

Dad and Gwen were the first people to be upset. We suggested they came round on Christmas Eve instead, which didn't suit them at all. They wouldn't have minded so much if we'd come up with a respectable excuse but being sidelined in favour of a bike ride did not go down well. Then it dawned on us that cooking a turkey and riding the tandem at the same time was fairly impossible, so Allan asked his mum Betty if we could go there for lunch. The faintest of sighs seemed to accompany her assurance that we'd be very welcome, which, since she already had 10 people to cater for, was understandable.

I felt certain she was wondering why we didn't go to my mother's for lunch. The problem here was poor mum's cooking, which sadly stood no chance of competing with Betty's. Eating tea there was bad enough, since we were always more or less force fed huge slices of Miss Wilkinson's Christmas cake.

Miss W was my mother's best friend, although for some reason in all the years of their acquaintance they'd never used each other's first names. Miss W had a kind and generous heart and knowing that mum disliked cooking, every Christmas she lovingly baked her a festive cake. Unfortunately, her cakes were truly dreadful. Sawdust dry, crumbly, only a few raisins and cherries, no booze, far too much icing and covered in hundreds and thousands, Smarties and little coloured jellies.

And this year, after gorging on my mother-in-law's festive meal, which was bound to include Yorkshire pudding, it was highly likely we'd only be able to manage the tiniest sliver of Miss W's cake. But we'd only have a temporary reprieve because Mum would still be bringing it out at Easter.

We decided to add to the stress of the Christmas Day Ten by specifying fancy dress and then letting the side down ourselves by going as tramps, which meant not much different from usual. Jack arrived as a scarecrow and Fred turned up as Noddy, his neck swathed in a yellow scarf with red spots and a blue hat with a bell perched on his bald old head. I think the main reason he'd come was to give me a Christmas card for Joy, which he made me promise to give her as soon as possible, with his very best love.

Percy arrived wearing a policeman's helmet and sporting a sinister pair of handcuffs. John was Dennis the Menace in a red and black striped jumper and crazy black wig. Luke – alias a surgeon in a white coat covered with splashes of red paint, washing-up gloves, a transparent shower cap and carrying a Stanley knife – was one of the few youngsters to compete, and consequently a very convincing winner. After presenting Luke with his prize of a chocolate reindeer riding a penny farthing, we cycled home as fast as possible, to begin the task of mollifying our families and promising never to spend Christmas morning in such a daft way, ever again.

TOP TANDEM TRIVIA

English songwriter Harry Dacre took his bicycle with him when he visited America in 1892 and was furious when U.S. Customs made him pay import duty on it. A friend told Dacre he was lucky that it was not a "bicycle built for two" because then he would have had to pay double duty. Dacre was so taken with this phrase that he wrote the song 'Daisy Bell', with its well-known chorus "Daisy, Daisy, give me your answer do". London music-hall singer Katie Lawrence made it popular in the

UK. It was first recorded in 1893 by the American singer Dan W. Quinn, whose version topped the charts for nine weeks. In the film '2001: A Space Odyssey' the computer HAL 9000 sings 'Daisy Bell', as the astronaut Dave Bowman disconnects him.

CHAPTER EIGHT
The importance of rain bonnets and the value of True Grit

1981 did not start well for us. Allan's mother was diagnosed with breast cancer and the prognosis did not look good. And there was more heartbreak in store. Mrs Radley had told me how much she worried about Barley being killed on the busy road, a fate which she'd seen befall countless other cats.

"But I think he's going to be all right, Jackie," she'd said. "Barley's streetwise. I've never seen him on the other side of the road, despite the lure of that old railway line, with its mice and rabbits. Eric was only saying the other day that Barley's too crafty to get caught out."

It was a wet Tuesday in mid-February and Allan and I were at work. On our return home, our neighbours' front door quietly opened as usual – but no ginger streak came hurtling out to meet us. Instead, Mr Radley beckoned us across and imparted the heart-breaking news. His wife was sitting beside the fire, which she didn't seem to realise had shrivelled to a few smouldering embers. On the hearthrug, covered in a thin green towel, lay a still and pitifully small bundle of damp and dirty orange fur.

"The driver didn't even stop." Mr Radley's face twisted in grief-stricken rage. "Just left him there in the gutter. The postman brought him here."

"Jim the postie." Mrs Radley nodded. "Jim liked Barley. Always gave him a stroke and pulled his ears. I told him off for doing that. Cats don't like having their ears pulled, I told him."

"Barley didn't seem to mind." Her husband cleared his throat. "He was a good-natured cat. Used to have the devil in him sometimes, mind."

They stood in the doorway watching as we made the wretched walk home, with Allan carrying our poor cat, still wrapped in his friends' towel and slightly warm from their fire.

This was my first experience of death and it was hard to come to terms with the loss of Barley. Our house was so quiet without him, my lap so cold and empty, and that ugly paraffin heater a constant reminder of what we'd lost.

"Maybe we should think about moving," Allan said. "We've been here nearly eight years. The cottage must have increased in value and it would be nice to live somewhere bigger."

"Down a quiet little lane where cats would be safe," I agreed. "And spring's on its way. That's the ideal time to move house."

And so it was that six months later, we loaded the tandems and our few bits of furniture into Richard's old green van and headed for The Chantries in Winterborne Zelston, a village only five miles from Spetisbury. In comparison with 2 Jasmine Cottages, our new abode was huge. Standing in a garden comprising two-thirds of an acre, it had three bedrooms, bathroom, toilet and cloakroom, kitchen, sitting room, dining room and a study. And there were two sheds and a garage, so plenty of room for both Bob and Claud.

"I never thought we'd have friends who lived in a house with a study." Richard took a breather from trying to persuade our four-poster bed to negotiate the narrow stairs. "Will you still laugh at my vulgar jokes and get cheerfully drunk, or will you both join the PCC and become pillars of the local community?"

"You jumped ship first," I reminded him. "Since you and Annabelle moved to Blandford and had Tom, we haven't been getting drunk together nearly as often."

"Well, you two certainly aren't getting any closer to starting a family," Richard said. "The mortgage on this place must be crippling you."

It was true. We'd let our hearts rule our heads when we bought The Chantries and at £41,000 the asking price was teetering at the very pinnacle of what we could afford. But with a mortgage interest rate already at 14.4%, at least it surely couldn't climb much higher.

Occasionally I felt a bit panicky, realising I'd shipwrecked my options for probably the best part of a decade, but mostly I was just excited about our new house, which we lost no time in filling with cats. Jasmine,

Farthing and Basil made a speedy appearance and lived long and happy lives at The Chantries. But lives at least a decade shorter than our fourth cat, Thing. Long after the others ended up under their respective apple trees, Thing just kept on going. He was an old cat for more years than most cats manage to stay alive and stone deaf for at least half of them. We adored him and were boastfully proud of his longevity.

After finishing his PhD, Theo had been offered a job in an American university, so there would be no more cycling holidays with him and Jess until they returned to the UK. We were practically destitute anyway, after our move, and spent most of the summer decorating. I insisted on a few hours off on July 29th, when Diana Spencer married Prince Charles. Even Allan put down his paintbrush for a few minutes and watched her climb carefully out of that glass coach, dragging a rather creased and crumpled 25ft-long train behind her.

Despite the out-of-control meringue she had chosen to wear, with its huge puff sleeves, Diana looked so enchantingly beautiful that I found myself blinking away a few sentimental tears, which turned into a giggle when she made a delightful dog's breakfast of her royal husband's four Christian names.

We decided to celebrate my 31st birthday with a tandem ride to Lulworth Lake, one of our favourite destinations. We packed the saddlebag with sandwiches and a half bottle of fizz. Although the roads in this direction were always busy, especially in August, we were pretty sure we'd have the lake to ourselves.

The route is a bit complicated and involves a fairly long trek across several fields, pushing the tandem. There are footpath signs but it's easy to go wrong. Lulworth Castle was built in the early 17th century as a hunting lodge and developed into a splendid country house, surrounded by 12,000 acres of parkland. The estate is owned by the Weld family and the lake was built in the 18th century by Joseph Weld, apparently to test his yacht models.

There's a picturesque castellated folly built into the lake, which on our first visit we fully expected to find locked and barred to intruders. At its bracken-encrusted entrance looms a hefty and rather forbidding gate, giving the appearance of being firmly locked. On each visit we approached warily, hardly daring to believe that the gate would yet again yield to our first tentative shove and feeling an illicit thrill of pleasure when entry was permitted.

The folly consists of a circular room with a big plain fireplace, in which there is usually a few ashes, an unwanted reminder that we are not – as we naively choose to believe – the only people to have discovered this place. But on that hot and sunny day, we were more interested in laying out my birthday feast on the low, thick stone walls jutting out over the lake.

A family of ducks swam busily towards some reed beds on the furthest shore and suddenly a big fish leaped clear of the water, only a foot or so away from us. I jumped and Allan laughed, putting his arms around me as I leaned over the parapet, searching for a final glimpse, as it disappeared among the reeds.

It was dreamily quiet, the only sound an occasional splash of water against stone. For a sliver of time, this peaceful place transformed into our sanctuary. Its sheltering walls towered towards the heavens and that sturdy gate swung shut, a key turning in its rusty lock. We were alone and no-one would find us, the sun caressed our heat-soaked skin, there was champagne to share and memories to nurture.

On our way home we were cycling along a quiet lane near Wool when eagle-eyed Allan spotted a leather wallet lying in the ditch. We stopped to investigate and found it contained a £20 note and a couple of tenners. There was also a receipt from a camp site near Wareham, dated the previous day and made out to John Barnes, who lived in Frome.

Fancying ourselves in the role of bearers of fantastic news, we vowed to reunite a doubtless distraught Mr Barnes with his cash. I'd begun reading Colin Dexter's books and was addicted to the exploits of Inspector Morse, so I felt well qualified to play detective, although, as Allan said, hopefully we wouldn't encounter any murderers.

Wareham wasn't far out of our way and it was still only mid-afternoon, so we cycled to the camp site, which turned out to be much bigger than we'd anticipated.

"How on earth..." I said, slowly. "Do we find him?"

"What would Morse do?" Allan asked.

"He'd go to the bar and make Lewis buy him a pint of beer. He said alcohol helped him to think."

"Then perhaps it's that champagne we've drunk, which is telling me the obvious solution is to find reception and tell someone we're looking for John Barnes," Allan suggested.

"That's a bit tame," I complained. "Let's just have a look around first."

It's hard to stay unobtrusive while pushing a tandem, especially as I was wearing my long Yorkshire socks, so we soon attracted curious glances. Before long, a middle-aged woman, who'd been sitting outside her tent in the sunshine, came up and asked if she could help.

"We want to find a man called John Barnes," I told her and she frowned, looking a tad wary.

"He lives in Frome," Allan added, helpfully.

"Why are you looking for him?" she asked.

"We have some information which will interest him," I said and her frown deepened. "What sort of information?"

"We'd prefer to reveal that to Mr Barnes," I told her, getting into my stride, whereupon Allan sensibly intervened.

"We've found something which belongs to him," he said and her frown suddenly transformed into a delighted smile.

"His wallet!" she said. "Have you found his wallet?"

I was about to request some proof that she knew John Barnes and hadn't just made a wild and lucky guess, but Allan had heard enough.

"Spotted it lying by the side of the road," he told her. "It would be nice to give it to him personally."

"John's my son," she said. "He and his dad are out on John's motorbike right now, looking for that wallet. He must have dropped it this morning, when he went for a ride before lunch. We've been here all week but John only arrived yesterday."

Without more ado, Allan produced the wallet and the woman's eyes filled with tears.

"My lad will be so grateful," she said. "That's all his holiday spending money."

We cycled home with her thanks ringing in our ears and a warm glow of pride in our tummies. But we were both sorry not to have handed the wallet over to the man himself.

"After all, she might have been an opportunist," I said. "Read the situation cleverly, manipulated us and cleverly bagged herself a nice £40 for the weekend."

"Jackie, that poor woman isn't a villain, she's his mother!"

"That's what she said, and I admit she seemed genuine, but maybe we were too gullible."

"How would you have felt if you'd been put through the third degree when you lost your ring at the York cycle rally? Not allowed to have it back until you'd proved it fitted and maybe even asked to show the correctly shaped pale area on your finger?"

That certainly shut me up and I was further defeated a few days later, when a heartfelt letter of thanks from John Barnes arrived in the post. However, as I murmured to an incredulous Allan, that really could have been any old villain's signature ...

Shortly after moving to The Chantries, I realised I could no longer put off learning to drive. One day, Allan was unable to pick me up from work and I was faced with a complicated bus journey home. I explained the situation to an unsympathetic Miss Elder, who reluctantly agreed that I could use a few hours flexi-time.

"So what are you going to do?" Kate asked.

It was our coffee break and we were hiding in the stationery cupboard, eating cream buns.

"I'm catching a bus which leaves Poole at two o'clock," I said. "I'll get off at Bloxworth."

"But you don't live in Bloxworth," Joy reminded me, helpfully.

"Good point," I agreed. "Which is why I'll be walking from there to Zelston."

"How far?" Kate asked.

"Three miles, more probably."

"No problem for you," Joy said. "You're so fit, with all that cycling."

"There must be at least a mile of the A31," Kate said. "Aren't people always getting killed along that stretch of road?"

"Yes, but they're usually motorists," I told her.

"Probably because sensible pedestrians keep well clear. Jackie, you must learn to drive."

Even soft-hearted Joy thought the time had come for a few home truths.

"It's odd enough not being able to ride a bike," she said. "What is this aversion you have to taking to the road unaided?"

"OK, OK," I muttered. "I'll think about it."

"I wonder if you'll be so keen to go on tandem rides after you've passed your test," Kate mused. "The freedom of the road will take on a whole new meaning."

"Abandoning the tandem might be grounds for divorce," Joy warned. "Allan would probably cite unreasonable behaviour."

"I hope you've brought an umbrella," Kate said. "The forecast is dreadful."

"Jackie doesn't need a brolly, as long as she's remembered her rain-mate," Joy said and my two so-called friends started giggling.

The rain-mate, or rain bonnet, is a very sensible piece of head gear for the female cyclist. Its best feature is its transparency, which means that unlike a hood integrally attached to any sort of wet weather jacket, it does not obstruct the wearer's vision. The fact that simply tying that knot beneath the chin automatically pitchforks even a youngish woman straight into the pensioner bracket shouldn't be regarded as any sort of deterrent.

Not long ago, I'd made the mistake of telling Joy that I needed a new rain-mate and she kindly wrapped a cheery, red spotted one in pretty paper and gave it to me as an extra birthday present. She insisted that I model it, whereupon Kate sneakily produced her camera and immortalised the moment. I took it in good part, even when I discovered a blown-up version of the photo pinned to the staff room noticeboard.

For once the weather forecast was right and at lunch time it started raining. When I stepped off the bus in Bloxworth, it was still hammering down and the roads were awash. The lanes were soggy enough but while walking along the A31 I was repeatedly drenched, as car after car swept past. By the time I sloshed my way into Zelston, my mind was made up. I was going to learn to drive. It took me almost two years and I probably only passed on my third attempt by following my instructor's advice and asking my GP for a mild tranquiliser.

That winter, after several weeks of soaking wet weather, we finally managed to get out for a bike ride one Saturday, even though the country roads were still muddily flooded. Just outside Wimborne St Giles, we came upon a chap standing beside the ditch and surveying his bike, which was in that upside-down position unpleasantly familiar to all cyclists. He looked for all the world like a Real Cyclist, until we drew up beside him and spotted the helpless, panicky expression on his face.

"Punctured?" Allan enquired and the young man nodded.

"Have you got repair patches?" He nodded again.

"Left your pump at home?" Allan laughed. "We did that once. Doesn't it make you feel stupid?"

Something was certainly making this cyclist feel stupid, judging by his pinkly embarrassed face – but it wasn't a lapse of memory. After muttering something incomprehensible, he admitted that he'd never mended a puncture before and didn't have a clue how to set about it.

"Have you brought a spare inner tube with you?" Allan asked.

He had certainly come equipped with one of those but the technique needed to fit the little blighter was pretty much a mystery.

While I shared a Kit Kat with the mortified chap – who turned out to be Kevin from Witchampton – Allan fitted a new inner tube and also mended the puncture in the damaged one, explaining at every stage what he was doing. After showering us with heartfelt thanks, Kevin cycled off and we resumed our ride, managing not to laugh until he was out of earshot.

We were north of Wimborne St Giles, on a hitherto unexplored narrow lane which became ever narrower, until gradually the ground beneath our wheels disappeared under about three inches of water. We cycled along slowly and cautiously for some time, before realising that the tandem was feeling a bit wobbly.

"I think we've punctured now," Allan said. "Damn! That back tyre's not got much tread left in it. We need a new one."

Fortunately, we managed to reach a small patch of dryish ground outside a pretty cottage called Cloud Nine. Now it was poor Bob being turned ignominiously upside-down, while Allan fitted a new inner tube. As he finished, the rain began to pour down in torrents. We put on our capes, I tied my rain-mate under my chin and we soggily climbed back on to the tandem. After we'd carefully negotiated several inches of flowing flood water for the best part of a mile, my husband suddenly asked a rather crucial question.

"Do you remember me putting that packet of spare patches back in the saddlebag?" he said.

Definitely not, was my reluctant and unwelcome reply. Allan groaned, brought the bike to a halt and checked the saddlebag. No patches.

"We'll have to go back," he said. "It would be sod's law for us to puncture again."

There are moments in life when the law of sod really sinks its teeth in and this was one such moment. We found our way back all right but only to discover the small piece of dry ground was now also submerged under at least an inch of water and no little packet could be found.

"We'll have to set off for home," Allan said. "And hope for the best."

We weren't even back on the tandem before Allan realised our back tyre was flat once again.

"We're stuffed," he moaned. "What on earth are we going to do?"

We did the only thing possible, which was to knock on the door of Cloud Nine and ask to use the telephone. Allan spent ages trying to give my dad directions to the remote spot where we were stranded, after which we had plenty of time to get acquainted with Dot and Ivy, two elderly sisters who had moved to Dorset from Birmingham. They made tea and passed round the chocolate digestives.

"I always wanted to be near the sea," Dot explained.

"We're not though," Ivy countered. "It takes nearly an hour to reach the coast from here."

"And I liked the idea of living in a village," Dot continued.

"But it's still just an idea, isn't it?" Ivy persisted. "Our nearest neighbours live half-a-mile away."

"I wanted to be part of a close-knit community," Dot carried on, doggedly.

"We never meet anyone," Ivy complained. "There's no shop, no village hall, no post office and no pub. I haven't been to a single bingo session since we came down south."

"Did you call this cottage Cloud Nine?" Allan asked.

"Yes." They both nodded grimly. "Living here is a dream come true."

When my dad eventually arrived, he didn't look too happy. He was possessive of his beloved little VW campervan and hated subjecting it to the filthy, flooded lanes. Gwen, on the other hand, was pleased to get away from the wrestling on TV.

"It brings out the worst in your father," she explained. "I'm afraid he'll have a heart attack, cheering Giant Haystacks as he bounces up and down on the Dynamite Kid's face."

"Apparently Maggie Thatcher is Haystacks' biggest fan," I said. "I expect he taught her a thing or two about finishing off Edward Heath."

Before setting off for home, we swathed poor, filthy Bob in the spotless dust sheets which Dad had brought with him, taking care not to allow the smallest muddy drip to speckle the campervan's pale blue carpet.

"Driving in this weather is a lot more stressful than watching wrestling," Dad muttered, turning the wipers up full. "It's getting dark now, too."

"I'll drive, if you like." I could see Allan was keen to wrench the wheel away from his father-in-law.

"He won't let you." Gwen sighed. "I've already offered, several times."

She was an intrepid driver and loved a challenge but had unfortunately scraped the campervan once, when reversing it out of the drive, and now Dad kept finding new hiding places for the keys. At long last we arrived back in Zelston and they helped us offload the tandem. My rain-mate fell out of the saddlebag and I saw my elegant, perfectly groomed stepmother give it an appalled glance.

"Thanks so much," I said. "Sorry for wrecking your afternoon."

Dad said nothing and Gwen patted his arm.

"Never mind, darling," she said. "At least you didn't miss Big Daddy. He's on next week."

By way of contrast, our second serious breakdown that year occurred during a pleasantly mild spell of good weather, warm enough to plan on taking a picnic lunch.

Churchyards make excellent picnic spots, being peaceful and generally blessed with a bench. One of our favourites surrounds the beautiful little church at Chalbury, near Wimborne, and we decided to cycle there on a Saturday just before Christmas. Set on a hilltop, with wide views all around, there can be few more idyllic spots. We lifted our faces to the pale, wintry sunshine, our thoughts with Allan's mother, who we had recently lost.

After reading a local history book, I'd become intrigued by the life of a 19th century woman whose father was rector at Chalbury for more than 40 years. Born in 1862, Mary Frances Billington was one of Dorset's most remarkable women. A pioneering female journalist, she worked for 28 years as The Daily Telegraph's first woman reporter. During the First World War she travelled to France and interviewed Quaker nurses in the military hospitals. She once wrote that for a woman to succeed in the male-dominated world of British journalism they needed true grit, a quality Mary's photograph suggests she possessed in abundance.

The Billington family grave is hard to find. It was Allan who eventually discovered the memorial stone, enveloped in green moss and hidden away in a quiet corner of the churchyard, its lettering faded and practically illegible. It's poignant to reflect that this neglected spot is the final resting place of an extraordinary and almost forgotten woman, whose ambition and energy could never be curtailed by ordinary life in a little village. But despite my respect for Mary's achievements, I suspect that rather like that other feisty female journalist – Janet Street-Porter – she is perhaps most comfortably admired at a safe distance.

Disaster struck while cycling away from Chalbury, when Allan's seat pin broke and we very nearly came toppling off the bike. He was lucky to escape serious injury. Fortunately, there was a phone box close by and we rang Richard and Annabelle, who promptly drove to our rescue.

"Come round for some home-brewed apple cider," they suggested, and we were happy to agree. One glass turned into several more, after which Richard staggered into Blandford to buy fish and chips. Shortly after midnight, they found a couple of ancient sleeping bags and we settled down in front of their log-burning stove. Apple cider tends to give me indigestion and I spent a troubled night, dreaming that Janet Street-Porter was wrestling Mary Billington in a muddy corner of Chalbury churchyard and being cheered on to victory by my dad.

TOP TANDEM TIP

Occasionally, the stoker will need to ease off the saddle to briefly alleviate bum pain, or take their hands off the handlebars to adjust their woolly hat, blow their nose or unwrap a barley sugar. A familiar, straight stretch of level road should be chosen for this manoeuvre, which must be accomplished as speedily as possible, without any interruption to smooth pedalling. Jerky movements will almost certainly lead to querulous enquiries from the front rider, along the lines of "What the hell is going on back there?" If it's the last barley sugar, you could be in serious trouble.

CHAPTER NINE

Lovelorn legends, throwing black pudding and Stumble Holme

THEO and Jess, now Dr and Mrs Wood, returned from America in the spring of 1986 with the news that a baby was on the way. Naturally, Theo's immediate thought was how this would affect cycling and the first stage was to equip their tandem with a baby seat. When Jess told me she had now learned to ride a bike, I couldn't help feeling I was being left behind in more ways than one.

In late spring, my dad and Gwen came up with an interesting proposition. They had just retired and were ready to spoil themselves with a series of cracking good holidays.

"We've decided on the Lake District first," Gwen said. "Do you fancy coming with us?"

"That's a great idea," Allan said. "Are you taking the campervan? I should think it's just about big enough to sleep all four of us – and we could fit the tandem in, too."

I saw Gwen shudder. So did Dad, who immediately galloped to her rescue.

"That's not quite what we had in mind," he told us. "The campervan's getting a bit too elderly for long trips. No, we'll go in the Triumph Herald."

"Then we can share the driving," Gwen added and Dad frowned.

"You're not really used to driving the Triumph Herald, darling," he pointed out.

"Then more practice is just what I need," Gwen said sweetly. "Isn't that right? Darling?"

She smiled and I knew Dad would – as always – be putty in her well-manicured hands.

"Right," Allan said. "So no camping then?"

From her bag, Gwen produced a brochure entitled *Top Hotels In The Lake District.*

"We've found one we fancy," she said. "The White Moss House Hotel at Grasmere. It looks wonderful, doesn't it Jim?"

"You sure that place isn't a bit too posh for us?" Dad sounded nervous. "Apparently they serve drinks in the drawing room. What is a drawing room, anyway?"

"You know perfectly well it's just a posh ... I mean another word for lounge. The food is sensational, there are fantastic views of Rydal Water and the hospitality is warm. So long as you can afford to pay," Gwen said. "Which we can."

"But we can't," I reminded them.

"Perhaps we could stretch to B&B," Allan suggested. "And we can take the tandem up there on the train."

Dad and Gwen glanced at each other and my stepmother suddenly proposed what was – to us – a ludicrous suggestion.

"Do you have to take the bike? We'd have so much more fun if you weren't cycling."

"That's right." Now Dad was joining in. "We could go for walks, the four of us. Longish walks. I'm not quite over the hill yet."

"Well, perhaps not too long, darling," Gwen demurred. "Obviously we'll stop for a pub lunch. And afternoon tea, of course. I can't wait to try Grasmere gingerbread."

It took all evening, a lot of honesty and masses of negotiation and compromise, but eventually we worked out a holiday itinerary which suited the four of us. We'd go to the Lake District for about a week. Dad and Gwen would wallow in their classy hotel, saturated with gourmet food, while we would stay B&B.

They'd enjoy steamer trips on the lakes, visit museums, stately homes, gardens, craft centres and castles. They would take gentle strolls around the lakes, while we sweated along the steepest roads we could find. We'd avoid all rip-off tourist attractions, choosing instead to push the tandem up each and every notorious and dramatic mountain pass, which Dad – or more likely Gwen – would drive up in the Triumph Herald.

"We've got to spend some time with you kids," Gwen said. "There's no point otherwise."

"You can treat us to a few dinners at your fancy hotel," I suggested, and Dad's face paled.

"Tea shops are definitely something we have in common," I added. "I want to sample that gingerbread too and a pudding I've read about, called Cumberland Rum Nicky."

"We must stock up on Kendal Mint Cake," Allan said. "That's great for beating the bonk."

Dad looked puzzled and uncomfortable. Gwen looked puzzled and intrigued.

"What's that about bonking?" she asked, and I laughed.

"It's a cycling term," I explained. "For utter exhaustion when blood sugar levels get too low. Don't they do chocolate-covered Kendal Mint Cake now?"

"No," Allan said – but I knew he was lying.

So in September 1986 we left the cats in Richard's care, loaded Bob up with panniers, saddlebag and front bag and caught the London train to Waterloo. As we didn't have camping stuff to carry, I'd insisted on taking two books – *The Secret Diary Of Adrian Mole aged 13¾* and *Lovelorn Legends Of The Lakes.* And 10 pairs of scruffy knickers. I'd been hoarding my threadbare knickers all year so I could chuck worn ones away, rather than bring them home, thus gradually lightening the load. Allan said Real Cyclists didn't wear pants at all. He was welcome to his opinion and also to dealing with the subsequent unsavoury problems it presented at the end of the day, when there was no way of getting his one and only pair of shorts washed and dried.

We were so worried about getting lost while cycling from Waterloo to Euston, to catch the Windermere train, that Theo had offered to meet us at the station on his bike and guide us through London. He and Jess were again living in Cambridge, so he didn't have very far to come, but nevertheless it was an extraordinarily generous gesture.

It was almost five years since we'd met up and I felt quite emotional, seeing Theo again. I wished more than anything that we were all going to the Lake District together, and judging by the way Theo was wistfully eyeing up our fully-laden tandem, he was feeling much the same.

"Next year perhaps," he said. "There's bound to be life after babies."

But I feared it was certain to be a different sort of life altogether.

Cycling through London was terrifying but it didn't take long, which made us even more appreciative of Theo's kindness in coming to nanny us on our way. I was practically in tears as I hugged him goodbye, especially when he handed over a packet of Jess's cheese and chutney sandwiches, which she'd made especially "for old times sake".

The journey to Oxenholme took 3½ hours and then we transferred to a Windermere train. Here we had an altercation with a stroppy guard, who first made it clear that our tandem took up too much room and wasn't welcome, then tried to manhandle it into the van himself. We weren't putting up with that and I remonstrated with the guard, while Allan found a safe corner for Bob to complete the final stage of his journey up north.

It was raining when we reached Windermere, at the end of a very long day travelling. The distant outline of vast mountains could be seen over the mist-enshrouded waters of the lake. We hadn't booked any accommodation ahead of our holiday so set about finding a B&B straight away. The first place we tried had a double room but no shed or garage for the tandem. The landlady couldn't understand why we weren't bothered about inspecting the bedroom but were making a big fuss about Bob's accommodation.

We had to make do with leaving the tandem in the back garden, in a sort of lean-to with barely adequate cover from the by now torrential rain. Allan locked Bob and draped some plastic sheeting over him, before covering the saddles with shower caps. He'd accumulated quite a store of these, during his hotel stays on working trips around the country.

We squelched our way into Windermere looking for dinner, which we found in the Elleray Hotel. The Cumbrian Tatie Pot was excellent, although I was horrified to find out afterwards that there were slivers of black pudding among the tender chunks of lamb.

"I won't be eating that again," I told Allan.

"Why not? It was delicious."

"The main ingredient of black pudding is pig's blood." I shuddered "Thank goodness Theo and Jess aren't here."

"It's very popular in Lancashire." My Yorkshire husband frowned. "That's the only thing wrong with it, as far as I'm concerned."

"There's an annual black pudding throwing competition in Lancashire," I said. "It's supposed to have started during the Wars of the Roses, when the soldiers ran out of ammunition and started chucking food at each other instead."

"What happens these days?"

"Competitors hurl black puddings at a pile of Yorkshire puddings. Whoever knocks down the most is the winner. Something like that."

"Waste of good food."

He was right, I suppose, but I thought I'd rather throw a black pudding than eat one, any day. Over coffee in the lounge, Allan spent half-an-hour or so perusing the map, while I read up on a few Lovelorn Legends, before giggling over the tribulations of Adrian Mole.

The following morning dawned warm and sunny. We were going to look for a B&B in Grasmere later but Allan had a long day's cycling planned first, even with a fully-laden tandem. Before we left, I asked the landlady if she would fill our flask with hot water and was stunned to be charged an extra 20p for this act of kindness!

"We'll make for Ambleside," Allan said, bending and folding the OS map until it fitted into its plastic holder on the front bag. After constant manhandling and frequent exposure to rain, our maps were lucky to survive a holiday. "Then we'll do the Kirkstone Pass, which means taking a narrow road called The Struggle."

I'd been watching people boarding a steamer boat but those few words certainly caught my attention.

"The Struggle?" I said, suspiciously. "Why's it called that?"

"Dunno," Allan shrugged. "The roads around here are bound to be hilly. We're fit enough."

Fit we may have been but stamina alone is not enough to help anyone survive The Struggle. All cyclists attempting this particular challenge need – in the words of my Chalbury heroine Mary Billington – True Grit. Bucketsful of the stuff.

Surely the most aptly-named road in the Lakes, this three-mile ascent starts with a one-in-four climb out of Ambleside. Naturally, we were off the bike straight away and pushing Bob very slowly up the hill. Even though I was putting every ounce of strength I had into helping, I could feel that Allan was having trouble just keeping the tandem from slipping backwards. Panting and bent almost double, the muscles in my legs screaming with pain, I tried to push even harder. Motorists weren't having an easy time of it, either. Every now and then cars would creep past us, leaving behind them the burning smell of hot engines and clutch linings.

The road stretched in front of us, with miles of barren hillside on either side and at its summit – far, far ahead – was a miniature white dot which had to be either a mirage or the Kirkstone Inn. I longed to stop pushing, just for a few seconds, but I knew that wouldn't be fair on Allan, who must surely be feeling even worse than me. There was a brief spell of downhill, when we stopped for a drink and some Kendal Mint Cake, but this was swiftly followed by a steeply climbing section of zig-zagging path which continued relentlessly, until we eventually crawled up on to the main road and the longed-for Kirkstone Inn.

Thankfully, we bought pints of orange juice and lemonade, which we drank while gazing out over the view and marvelling aloud at our achievement. We'd made an early start from Windermere and it wasn't even midday, so Allan decided we would stick to his original plan. Any change would mean going over the Kirkstone Pass again in the opposite direction – and neither of us had nearly enough True Grit to face that twice in one day.

We put on jerseys for the descent, as a chilly little wind had sprung up and we were cooling off rather too quickly. Freewheeling downhill was terrific and hurtling towards Patterdale we must have hit 40mph, glimpsing only the briefest flicker of blue as we raced past Brothers Water.

We bought lunch and ate our picnic overlooking Ullswater, the second largest lake and 7½ miles long. Towering mountains loomed over the water, which sparkled in late summer sunshine. Sheep with thin, black-and-white speckled faces grazed quietly on the lower slopes, while a flock of swallows soared towards the banks of scree. Allan spotted a buzzard soaring high, a baby rabbit dangling from its beak.

After lunch, we saw a sign for a walk beside the shores of the lake and because the footpath looked rideable, we decided to take it. The views were fabulous and it was well worthwhile, even though the path turned into a narrow track and we had to walk much of the way. The kissing gates were a particular problem because we needed to remove the panniers before Allan could lift the tandem over them. At the end of the walk, we arrived at Pooley Bridge and enjoyed tea and Cumbrian lemon cake at a little cafe. Allan was studying the map and looking worried.

"Unless we go back over Kirkstone Pass, it's going to be a long ride into Grasmere," he said.

"How long?" I helped myself to the last sliver of my husband's cake.

"More than 20 miles," Allan admitted, and I practically choked on the illicit, lemony crumbs. "Quite a lot more, probably," he added. "But the scenery is fantastic and it's a beautiful afternoon."

Half-an-hour later the rain began pelting down in torrents. We sheltered for a while but really there was no choice but to cape up and get on with it. The wonderful views retreated behind banks of dismal cloud and even the sheep seemed to disappear somewhere drier. None of the roads around here stayed flat for long and it was hard work.

About 10 miles from Grasmere we stopped for a brew and to eat soggy Kendal Mint Cake. The skies darkened and there was a crack of thunder, before hailstones began hurtling down, bouncing into our flask cup and spattering tea on our hands. Allan rummaged in the side pocket of a pannier and dug out one of the shower caps we used to protect our saddles. Despite my misery, I couldn't help laughing when he pulled it on to his soaking wet head. I'd have to treat him to a natty rain bonnet like mine.

As we cycled into Grasmere, the rain stopped and the sun burst into life. But we didn't care. All we wanted was to find a bolthole, where we could peel off our sodden clothes and sink our exhausted, aching, chilly bodies into the depths of a lovely hot bath. I knocked at the door of the first B&B we found and at the sight of me oozing on to her doorstep, the stylish young woman took a horrified step back into her hallway.

"Do you have a double room?" I asked, watching her expression alternate between shock, dismay and embarrassment, before finally settling into steely resolve, when she spotted Allan lurking beside the tandem, his shower cap dripping dismally. To make matters worse, he'd taken off his shoes and socks and was in the process of wringing his socks out on to her petunias.

"I'm sorry," she said, with a thin little smile. "But I've got good carpets. I'm sure you'd be much happier at the youth hostel up the road."

I squelched my way back to Allan, imparting the humiliating news that we were about as welcome as a skunk at a garden party.

"You'd think they'd be used to wet people around here," he moaned. "It is the Lake District, after all. What happened to a warm Cumbrian welcome?"

Thankfully, this was exactly what we found at the next place we tried, a small guesthouse rather intriguingly called Stumble Holme. When the door opened, I took a deep breath and attempted a charming smile. A smell of baking drifted from the kitchen and the middle-aged man in front of me was holding an oven glove. He gave me the once-over but his expression was amused rather than hostile and his quick eyes caught sight of Allan dripping beside the gate.

"I've a large double room," he said. "Ensuite, with the tiniest peep of a lake view, weather permitting, which it occasionally does, although not often. It'll be £17 a night and I'm Ian."

"That sounds wonderful, Ian." I said and then remembered the most important thing. "Is there somewhere for our tandem?"

Ten minutes later Bob was cosily settled in the garage and all our wet things were either strewn around the bedroom or draped over two hot radiators. We flopped on the bed, making short work of Ian's tea and scones, while the bath filled with water. Bliss.

Unfortunately, we had to be quick because Dad and Gwen would be waiting to hear from us. Looking – I hoped – more like a normal person, I went downstairs carrying the tea tray and our saturated cycling shoes. Ian was sitting at the kitchen table reading the paper. He looked up and spotted our shoes straight away.

"I'll put those beside the Aga," he said. "Bring the rest of your wet stuff down, too. There's nothing an Aga does better than dry clothes and bake scones."

"The scones were delicious," I said. "Thank you so much. Could I use your telephone? We're going for a meal with my father and stepmother this evening. They're staying in Grasmere too, at the White Moss House Hotel."

"Very nice." Ian smiled. "Of course you can use the phone. I'll give you a door key and don't forget to bring those wet clothes down on your way out. I can recommend the food at The Drunken Duck, not far from Hawkshead."

So this was where we suggested going and Dad and Gwen were happy enough to agree, especially when Allan offered to drive, meaning they could both have a drink. They'd enjoyed their day, most of which seemed to have been spent sitting on a steam train travelling from Haverthwaite to Ambleside and back again.

"I'm starving," Gwen said, picking up a menu. "We didn't bother with lunch, did we Jim?"

"Too much breakfast." Dad patted his tummy, carefully. "We had the Full English. Beautiful sausages, beautiful. Nothing like real Cumbrian sausage."

"We can't eat like that every morning, darling," Gwen rebuked him. "You don't want that nasty indigestion again, do you?"

"I might give the black pudding a miss tomorrow," Dad conceded. "And perhaps just the one fried egg. But nothing you can say will stop me going back for more of that sausage."

"What have you kids been up to?" Gwen asked. "Did you go for a little bike ride?"

While waiting for our steak with Cumberland sauce, we tried to explain what our little bike ride had entailed, but it was clear that from the comfort of their railway carriage they hadn't grasped the challenges presented by the Lake District countryside.

"The scenery is so pretty," Gwen enthused. "There was a lovely gift shop at Newby Bridge. I bought a scarf and some of that Kendall Mint Cake. We haven't eaten it yet, though."

"Can we have it?" I asked eagerly. "Ours disintegrated in the rain."

"Did it rain?" Gwen asked and we stared at her in bewilderment.

"It came down in stair rods all afternoon," Allan said. "Where were you?"

"We arrived back at the hotel in time for afternoon tea," Dad said. "Perhaps it rained and we didn't notice."

"We were having such a good time chatting to that charming couple from Somerset," Gwen said. "Pippa and Frank. They recommended those Windermere spice biscuits."

"I thought you hadn't eaten since breakfast." I helped myself generously to chips, not worrying too much about sticking to my fair share.

"We didn't have lunch," Dad corrected me. "Afternoon tea is included in the hotel price. But I only had two Windermere biscuits. And a slice of Grasmere gingerbread."

"So whatever you're doing, you have to plan on being back at the White Moss by the middle of the afternoon?" Allan sounded shocked.

"Decadent, isn't it?" Gwen agreed. "So much healthier to be out in the fresh air on a tandem, getting drenched. My steak is delicious, by the way. This is a very nice pub."

"There's a story in Lovelorn Legends about how it got its name," I said. "But it's a bit far-fetched. A 19th century landlady is supposed to have found all her ducks sparked out in the cellar and thought they were dead. So she plucked them and was just about to pop them in the oven when one of them opened its eyes and started quacking. Apparently a beer barrel had a sprung a leak and the ducks got sozzled before passing out cold."

"Is that why it's called the Dopey Duck?" Dad looked puzzled.

"Drunken Duck, darling." Gwen laughed. "Though I rather like Dopey Duck myself."

"The landlady put them in knitted waistcoats until their feathers grew back," I said, with a giggle. "Perhaps it should have been called the Dressed-Up Duck."

"Or the Death-Defying Duck," Dad suggested, getting the hang of it.

Only my stone cold sober husband failed to find any of this witty repartee amusing. He just wanted to know what was *Lovelorn* about that legend but no-one knew or cared.

Allan and I had brandy mincemeat tart with rum butter and clotted cream but I was hardly surprised when the other two gave pudding a miss. Over coffee we discussed plans for the following day.

"How about a walk?" Allan suggested. "We should do Helvellyn. Via Striding Edge."

"I don't think my boots are up to that," Gwen said. "The heels might be a bit too high."

"We've only got cycling shoes," I reminded Allan. "With leather soles. They won't give much grip, going up mountains."

By the look on my husband's face, I could see he thought I was going over to the enemy.

"I've got a book called Lake District Walks For Motorists," Dad said, helpfully. "Some of those look pretty good."

"Any in particular?" Allan sounded suspicious.

"There's a 3½-mile walk round Rydal Water," Dad said. "But I think you could quite easily shorten it by a couple of miles."

"That sounds lovely, darling," Gwen enthused.

Allan and I exchanged furtive glances.

"Maybe we should stick to bike rides," I said. "That's what we're best at. I just hope we don't have any more rain."

"I'm sure it won't rain." Gwen dismissed such negative thinking. "Let's meet up for dinner again tomorrow. Pippa and Frank recommend The Mortal Man at Troutbeck. It's not far away but, of course, someone will have to drive."

With a hopeful little cough, Dad picked up the bill and produced his wallet. My husband gave in without a struggle.

"Shall I drive tomorrow evening?" he said.

Back at Stumble Holme, Allan spread the still rather damp map out on the carpet and began planning the following day's ride, while I tried to tidy up our room a bit.

"I think we'll make for Wastwater," he said. "Via Wrynose and Hardknott. Let's stay here for the rest of the holiday. It's so much easier, cycling without all the gear."

"Yes, I like it here," I agreed but I wasn't really listening. I was looking at the photograph on the chest of drawers. It was of a much younger Ian, smiling down at the woman by his side. They were standing outside Stumble Holme.

"This must be his wife." I showed Allan the photograph. "Where is she, do you think? We've not seen her."

"No idea." Allan barely glanced up. "She's probably around somewhere."

"I wonder." I frowned at the photo. "He's obviously besotted with her but she's not even looking at him. And she's wearing a lot of red lipstick. I think she looks hard and selfish. I bet she's left him."

"Don't jump to conclusions," Allan advised. "She'll probably be serving breakfast tomorrow."

TOP TANDEM TRIVIA

The Tandem Club produces a booklet, Twicer's Much Fun, with cartoons drawn by Johnny Helms, Cycling Weekly's longest-serving contributor. His cartoons delighted readers for 63 years, by personifying the essence of the British club cyclist. Helms died in November 2009, aged 85. One of the cartoons in Twicer's Much Fun depicts a man leaving home on his solo bike, telling his disgruntled-looking wife: "We've got a perfect marriage – why risk spoiling it by buying a tandem?" In another, a chap is opening a seasonal card which bears the message: "Happy Christmas from our tandem to your tandem."

CHAPTER TEN

The charming Somerset couple and a kindly postman

S HE wasn't though. The dining room was just off the kitchen, where we caught an occasional glimpse of Ian scurrying between Aga, toaster and kettle. The waitress was a cheerful young woman, who presumably lived in Grasmere. She and Ian worked well together and the kitchen was lively with the sound of their laughter.

"I reckon there's something going on there," I whispered to Allan. "I don't blame him. He deserves someone nice."

"He's probably already got someone nice," he whispered back. "Such as a really nice wife."

There were two other guests, a very young couple who gazed into each other's eyes with besotted devotion. Both had ordered beans on toast with fried eggs for breakfast. It sounded as if these two were walking the Grasmere Ale Trail and were being frequently and thoroughly drenched.

"Are me socks dry?" The lad looked up from his beans and I could see he was even younger than I'd first thought. Probably still in his teens.

"I don't know." The girl stopped eating. "Where did you leave them?"

"In me boots. Under the bed."

She stared at him and I could well imagine what she would have said, if only he hadn't been her Galahad and the man of her dreams. Pithy comments such as: "Well, they're still soaking wet then aren't they, you pillock?" or "What did your last slave die of?" or even "Do I look like your mother?"

Ian was full of admiration when Allan told him where we were bound.

114

"Hardknott and Wrynose twice in one day," he marvelled. "You must be fit."

"Twice?" I looked at Allan, accusingly.

"There's no other way back," Ian said. "Let's hope it doesn't rain."

"Have you heard a forecast?" I asked him. "It's beautifully sunny at the moment."

"You could be lucky," he conceded. "There's rain coming in later but it might not arrive until teatime. Take plenty of Kendal Mint Cake with you."

It was only 9.30 when we set off and I winced with pain the second my bum hit the saddle. Fortunately, this excruciating pain doesn't last long and it's just a question of repeating the mantra "This Too Will Pass" with enough conviction, before it actually does. After just a few miles, we approached Little Langdale and the start of Wrynose Pass. Apparently, members of staff at the information centre are often asked the way to Rhino Pass or even Buffalo Pass.

Although we did manage to cycle part of the way up, in places the gradient climbs to one-in-three and, at its narrowest, it is impossible for cars to pass each other. Once again, when vehicles crawled by, we could invariably smell overheated engines. The Three Shires Stone lies at the top of the pass at 1,281 ft and marks the point where the three historic counties of Lancashire, Westmoreland and Cumberland used to meet. We descended into the Duddon Valley via a relentless sequence of steep hairpin bends. The views were tremendous, with Coniston Old Man looming from the southern hills and the Langdale Pikes rearing upwards in the north.

Negotiating Wrynose had been thrilling but not frightening and I was almost wondering what all the fuss was about. But that was before encountering the notoriously scary Hardknott Pass. Here the road seemed to stand on end practically from the start and we couldn't even begin to cycle up it.

The most exciting/terrifying stretch of tarmac in the Lake District, Hardknott is arguably England's steepest road, with one-in-three sections which seem to last forever. The twisting hairpin bends are vicious and we could see alarming skiddy tyre tracks where motorists had struggled to keep control of their vehicles, while shuffling around, trying to pass each other.

Fortunately there weren't many cars that morning, so at least we didn't have much traffic to contend with. After laboriously pushing the tandem more than a mile uphill, we finally puffed our way to the top and were looking forward to a blissful whizz down the other side. But hang on a minute ... what was the warning message on that stern road sign looming up in front of us, trying to spoil our fun?

CYCLISTS ARE ADVISED TO DISMOUNT AND WALK THE DESCENT

"Cobblers to that!" Allan declared indignantly. "We've worked hard for this freewheel and we're jolly well going to enjoy it!"

But in fact, we were forced to take the steep and winding descent very carefully and even stopped twice to allow Bob's wheel rims to cool down. Because a tandem weighs much more than a solo bike, on long downhill stretches the brake has to be applied harder and for longer. Inevitably the wheel rims become very hot, increasing the risk of a blowout.

We cycled through the tiny village of Boot and stopped for a few minutes at Eskdale Green to watch the little trains go by on the Ravenglass and Eskdale Railway. Then it was on into Wasdale, where we cycled along a fantastic road bordering the lake. The famous Wastwater screes, almost 2,000ft high, towered over the opposite shore. Stopping for a moment to exclaim at the view, we heard the distant rattle of stones and boulders plunging into the water. Wastwater is the loneliest and most dramatically beautiful of the lakes, spectacular in its bleak, forbidding grandeur.

We locked the tandem, before having lunch at The Wasdale Head Inn and a look around. The deepest lake in England lies at the foot of the highest English mountain and modestly tucked away in a quiet field can be found the smallest church. The roof beams of St Olaf's are believed to have come from Viking ships and churchwardens' staves have a Herdwick ram's head on one side and a ewe's head on the other. Exploring the little graveyard is a sobering experience, with several poignant memorials to climbers who lost their lives on the slopes of adjacent mountains.

It was still only early afternoon when Allan spotted a sign leading towards the water, bearing the simple and unthreatening words LAKE WALK.

"That must go all the way around Wastwater," he said. "Shall we try it?"

"Have we got time?" I asked. "Remember we've Hardknott and Wrynose to do again."

"The lake's only three miles long," he said. "So we've plenty of time and we might as well make the most of this wonderful sunshine."

The path started off innocently enough and it was fairly easy going for a while. But I began to worry when we encountered the first sections of scree because I knew cycling shoes with smooth leather soles weren't the ideal footwear for those conditions.

"I don't like this much," I admitted, expecting Allan to be reassuring. But to my alarm he didn't reply and his expression was tense.

The route rapidly became more challenging, with increasingly long areas of slippery scree. The path was climbing steadily now and the shining stretch of water seemed to glitter ever more menacingly beneath us. Fear bubbled up inside my tummy.

"Do you think there's much more of this?" I asked.

"I'm afraid so," Allan said. "And it looks as if it's going to get tricky."

After a few minutes, we saw the main boulder field ahead of us. The path more or less disappeared and there was no alternative but to pick the best route possible across the steep, rock-strewn slopes of scree. No matter how carefully I trod, rocks wobbled and slipped beneath my feet. Shaking and sweating with terror, I hung on to Allan's hand. He made the mistake of telling me not to look down and of course I immediately did just that and was confronted by the sight of a sheer drop into the 258ft of water beneath us.

I wished I hadn't recently read about Margaret Hogg, the woman killed by her husband in 1976 who spent eight years at the bottom of this very lake before her body was discovered by divers. Peter Hogg, an airline pilot, had strangled his wife after finding out about her three-year affair with a banker. He wrapped her body in a carpet and tied it to a block of concrete before dumping it in the lake. Due to lack of oxygen, Margaret's corpse did not decompose and was easily identified. If Peter Hogg had rowed just a few yards further before dumping his wife's body, he may never have been brought to justice, because at its deepest Wastwater is beyond normal diving depth.

It was easy going after we regained the path but that three-mile walk had taken us well over two hours and by the time we were back on the tandem it was late afternoon. I felt utterly drained and in the distance the sky was turning ominously black.

The storm managed to hold off while we wearily pushed our way up Hardknott and made a careful descent, but as we approached Wrynose the first heavy drops began to fall and the rain started pelting down. Soon every view was submerged by the deluge and all we could see was a couple of feet of shining tarmac immediately in front of us.

The temperature dropped several degrees, followed by a loud crack of thunder directly overhead, after which sheet lightning momentarily lit up the soaking wet black crags surrounding us. We turned on the dynamo lights and felt thankful there were hardly any motorists around on that grim and dismal afternoon. One of the few we saw was driving an MGB and he stopped his car specifically to photograph a pair of lunatic cyclists, freewheeling down Wrynose in torrential rain.

By the time we reached Grasmere, we were once again as wet as it is possible for two cyclists to be and every weary bone ached. My icy fingers fumbled to turn the key in the locked door of Stumble Holme, expecting to see Ian hurrying to greet us. But the house was quiet and no-one was about. We struggled to undo the laces of our sodden, heavy shoes and draped our cycling capes on hooks inside the porch, where they dripped into the log basket.

"Thank goodness it didn't rain like that while we were walking on the mountain," I said, as we dragged the bike bags upstairs. "I expect we'd both have ended up at the bottom of the lake, although probably no wetter than we are now."

"I wonder how long it would have taken your dad to report us missing?" Allan pondered, not attempting to ridicule this grisly scenario.

"We're supposed to be meeting them in half-an-hour," I groaned.

"I'm sure Ian won't mind if we use the phone," Allan said. "I'll ring and explain what's happened."

He returned a few minutes later, while I was luxuriating in a blissfully hot bath, my wet clothes once again strewn around on radiators.

"Your dad said not to worry, they'd have dinner with the charming Somerset couple instead."

"Nice to know we're so expendable," I grumbled.

"He sounded concerned when I told him we nearly plunged into the icy waters of the deepest lake in England," Allan consoled me. "And he sends you his love."

"What did they do today?" I felt only slightly mollified. "Did they attempt that strenuous trek around Rydal Water?"

"No, they visited Holker Hall house and gardens. It hardly rained at all and they were back at the hotel in time for afternoon tea. But your dad was upset because there wasn't any Grasmere gingerbread."

"Tragic." I sloshed around a bit. "We mustn't forget to give Ian some money for the phone call, when he comes back."

"I've done that." Allan grinned. "He was picking his wife up from the station."

"Oh." I tried hard not to feel meanly disappointed that my theory had just been shredded.

"Pauline's been visiting their daughter, who's just had a baby," Allan said. "A pink one. You might have to dodge hundreds of photos."

The rain had stopped and we were feeling much better and very hungry, so we decided to walk into Grasmere and eat at a little restaurant we'd noticed called The Rowan Tree. On the way out we handed our wet clothes to Ian, who had again offered to dry them over the Aga. Pauline was busy cooking and when she smiled at me, I felt embarrassed and uncomfortable.

Dinner was delicious and over coffee I wrote postcards, which mainly featured pictures of wet sheep in sodden fields and captions saying they Wished Ewe Were Here.

The following morning dawned sunny and beautiful, all our clothes were dry and even our cycling shoes were just about wearable. Pauline served breakfast and was so friendly that I felt guiltier than ever. She told us the forecast was pretty good. No rain until afternoon, lots of sunshine and quite warm.

"Very similar to yesterday's forecast," I reminded Allan, as we cycled out of Grasmere. "And look what happened then."

"It'll be different today." My husband was used to his role as the optimistic half in our relationship. "And if it rains in Keswick we can shelter in the shops."

Our route took us along the shores of Thirlmere Lake, once two small lakes but now a picturesque 3½-mile long reservoir, created to provide water for Manchester. The small villages of Wythburn and Armboth were submerged during the building of the reservoir.

"Armboth House was haunted," I told Allan when we stopped to admire the view.

"This is bound to be about somebody drowning," he said.

"Yup. A bride back in the 18th century, on the eve of her wedding day. It was Halloween, so she was asking for trouble. Someone saw her being pushed into the water but the murderer was never caught."

"Probably the bridegroom had second thoughts and done her in."

"He was certainly the chief suspect. Every following year on the anniversary, peals of ghostly church bells were heard and a ghostly dog could be seen swimming towards a ghostly table laid for the wedding breakfast."

"Perhaps he mistook the wedding breakfast for a dog's breakfast," Allan suggested. "We'd better get a move on. We won't be able to spend very long in Keswick."

It was a shame because I rather liked Keswick and would have enjoyed exploring the tempting little shops. But I settled for buying delicious-looking but expensive smoked duck and brie sandwiches and juicy slices of damson plate cake, which Allan told me I didn't deserve to eat until we'd climbed Whinlatter Pass. Fortunately, of all the passes in the Lake District, this is the least strenuous. The road winds its way up through Thornthwaite Forest before dropping down into the pretty village of Lorton, which we were cycling through when I remembered our postcards, lying forgotten in the front bag. I'd just deposited them safely in the pillar box, when I was struck by an unwelcome thought.

"I didn't put stamps on them," I told Allan.

"Are you sure?" he said.

"Positive. I meant to stick them on after breakfast and I never did. They're still in my purse."

We stared at the pillar box helplessly.

"When's the next collection?" Allan asked.

This turned out to be 9.30 the following morning, so hopeful visions of a kind and friendly postie just 10 minutes away faded into the ether. Then I had something of a brainwave.

"I know. I'll put the stamps in the pillar box, with a note explaining what we've done and asking the postie to stick them on for us."

"That's probably against the postal workers union rules," Allan said. "Or health and safety, or something."

"Can you think of a better idea?" I asked.

"No, it's worth a try. Have we got a pen?"

We had a pen but no paper, so I removed my slice of damson plate cake from its brown paper bag and scribbled a polite and pleading message on the bag, before putting the requisite number of stamps inside it and depositing both in the post box.

"With any luck he won't be put off by the sticky red fruit stains," I said. "I do hope he's a nice, kind postman with a sense of humour and not too squeamish."

He must have been all those things because on our arrival home we found that everyone had received their cards. It would have been good to thank him properly but I made do with writing a letter to Royal Mail, singing his praises. I considered sending it on its way minus a stamp, just for fun, but Allan said they might not see the joke.

We ate our lunch in the sunshine beside Crummock Water, watching a rowing boat move slowly towards the distant shore, tiny against the rocky mountain backdrop. This is possibly the least accessible of the major lakes and therefore comparatively peaceful, despite the lure of its wild, rugged beauty. Buttermere and Crummock Water were probably once one lake and are now separated by only a narrow, half-mile strip of land. I thought Buttermere was the prettiest of the lakes we'd visited so far and would have liked to do the walk around it, but we didn't really have enough time.

"I'm surprised you're so keen," Allan said. "After yesterday."

"Apparently this is a low-level, easy, family walk with fantastic views," I replied. "So there's no comparison."

"Not like the Buttermere Round, then."

"What's that?"

"A one-day walking challenge. It's a circuit of the seven mountains surrounding Buttermere. Competitors walk about 12½ miles and climb to 5,780 feet. I quite fancy doing it."

"Content yourself with surviving Wastwater," I advised. "I've read about a different sort of Round altogether. This one was a coach trip."

"A coach trip!" Allan sounded horrified. "What could possibly be interesting about one of those? Or is it another of your legends?"

"No, this is on record. It was a 19th century coach trip, costing five shillings, which was a lot of money in those days. It started in Keswick, went up Borrowdale and over Honister Pass, then returned to Keswick over Whinlatter."

"We're going back over Honister. The gradient is one-in-four at times. I'm surprised coaches were up to it in those days."

"They weren't. Passengers had to get off and walk up the steep bits."

"We'll be doing that, too," Allan said. "We'd better get a move on."

Honister Pass was tough going but we had a tail wind on the uphill, so it could have been worse. The freewheel down into Seatoller was scary and one of the few times I've been grateful for a head wind because at least it slowed us down a bit. As we hurtled along towards Borrowdale, the sky turned that familiar inky black we'd come to dread and seconds later torrents of rain fell down. Knotting my rain mate under my chin, I brooded on the cruel contours of the Lake District.

"If we were crows," I said, "Grasmere would only be about six miles away. But for us on a tandem, it's nearer 20."

"At least there's no choice," Allan said. "So we can't argue about it. Remember Polperro?"

He'd never let me forget it. We were in Cornwall and this memorable incident occurred at the end of a very long day in the saddle. We'd stopped beside a signpost directing us along the main road to Polperro, 11 miles away. Our map wasn't much help, being on too small a scale.

"They're trying to make us take the long way round." Allan pointed to a twisty lane off to the left, a bit further down the road. "I'm sure Polperro is only a few miles down there."

"That lane's not signposted," I said.

I had visions of cycling miles down a little track, which would get narrower and nastier until it ended up in a ramshackle farmyard, where a pack of vicious dogs would surround us, snarling and growling. If we were lucky enough to survive that onslaught, we'd have to ride all the way back up the lane and, at the end of it, there would still be 11 miles to cycle into Polperro.

"I'd rather go the way we know definitely takes us there," I insisted.

"That's potty! It means cycling miles further than we need to."

But I got my own way and a very long, hilly and winding way it was too, with far too many big, impatient lorries. Despite the lateness of the hour, we found a lovely B&B in Polperro, where the equally lovely landlady confirmed that Allan was right and there was indeed a quiet lane, which tourists were not encouraged to use.

"Nice for cyclists," she said. "So much quicker and it avoids that nasty, busy main road."

The road leading into Keswick hugs Derwent Water and is no doubt very scenic on days when the rain isn't tipping down and it's possible to see more than a yard in front. Cold and miserable, we stopped outside rather a posh-looking tea shop just outside Keswick. Allan locked the tandem, complaining bitterly about his sodden shoes and freezing feet.

"I'll just go and suss the place out," I said. "See if we're likely to be turned away on account of them having good carpets."

It did look quite classy but there was a group of walkers in there, who appeared not to have been ordered to leave their boots outside the door, so I thought we could risk it.

We sat at a table near the log-burning stove, which was wonderful, as was the strawberry cheesecake, smothered with clotted cream. The bill came to £4, more than we'd ever paid for afternoon tea before but it was well worth it.

Climbing back on to the bike again was horrid because we were damp and squelchy and the saddles were soaking wet but at least it had stopped raining. Nevertheless, it was hard to summon up much enthusiasm for the ride back to Grasmere and we weren't in the best of spirits when a young cyclist on a snazzy bike came tearing past us, without even a cursory nod or the briefest of greetings.

"So rude," I fumed. "Doesn't he know Real Cyclists always exchange a few words?"

I had several stock phrases for these occasions. My favourite, if the encounter seemed destined to be brief, was "Nice Day For It", said enthusiastically or with irony, depending on the clemency of the weather.

"I reckon he's on a training run, heading for Thirlmere Lake," Allan said. "If we put a bit of effort into it we'll catch him up, the young whippersnapper."

The lad had clearly been showing off because half-a-mile further on there he was in front of us, taking it easy. Well, he'd seriously underestimated the stamina of this intrepid tandem duo. Noses stuck in the air, and looking to neither right nor left, we whizzed past him, cycling hell for leather. Two minutes later I glanced around and there he was once more, gaining on us with every second.

"He's behind us!" I shrieked – but it was too late. Grinning, the youngster streaked past.

But we were determined not to give in and grim resolve pumped strength into our aching legs and filled our cheesecake-stuffed bellies with steely fire. Heads down, we raced along behind, slowly gaining ground until, approaching the lake, we overtook him once more.

Pedals flying, we began racing along the road bordering Thirlmere Lake, expecting any second to have the youngster on our back wheel once again. But after a few minutes, to our bewilderment, we spotted him approaching the lake from another direction. How had he managed that? Where had he come from? What was his plan? We'd no idea but were certain he had us in his sights and we tore around Thirlmere as if the lad was the devil himself, out to stab us with his scalding pitchfork. Only gradually did it dawn on us that we'd lost him and the excitement was over. We hadn't had so much fun for years.

TOP TANDEM TIP

The stoker's pedalling efforts <u>must never be questioned</u>. The front rider should remember that a harmonious relationship is worth far more than the temporary alleviation of probably ill-founded suspicions. If there is ever the opportunity to ride with someone different on the back of the tandem, then comparisons will probably be made. But unless these are in favour of the regular stoker, the front rider would do well to keep his observations to himself or, if questioned, lie with conviction.

CHAPTER ELEVEN
Rubbish directions, rescuing sheep and gruesome gurning

THAT evening we met my dad and stepmother at their hotel and Allan drove us to The Mortal Man at Troutbeck. It was soon obvious that something was wrong. Gwen wasn't her usual bubbly self and Dad seemed sunk in gloom. They neither exclaimed in admiration as I told the tale of the race around Thirlmere, nor chuckled over Allan's amusing description of our unstamped postcards.

"So what have you been doing today?" I finally asked.

"Muncaster Castle," Dad said, tersely.

"I've been reading about that in Lovelorn Legends. There was a 16th century jester who used to get his kicks by lurking outside the castle and sending lost travellers in the wrong direction."

"That book is marketed under false pretences!" Allan protested. "There's nothing *Lovelorn* about half these legends." But everyone ignored him.

"The jester was called Tom Fool," Dad said. "He haunts the place."

"Were you back at the hotel in time for afternoon tea?" Gamely, I ploughed on.

"We were practically back in time for lunch, never mind tea." This was Gwen's first contribution, crisply delivered.

"Well, Pippa and Frank had to get packed," Dad muttered.

"Oh, you went to the castle with them?" Whatever could have gone wrong, during an outing with the Charming Somerset Couple?

"Unfortunately." Gwen sounded even crisper.

"Weren't they good company?" Allan picked up the baton.

"Let's just say we're not sorry they're leaving tomorrow." Gwen studied the menu. "Has everyone decided?"

The atmosphere began to thaw during the consumption of avocado and prawns, improved over game pie with Cumberland sauce and was noticeably better with the arrival of lemon curd galette slice, helped along nicely by two bottles of Le Piat d'Or. But I was curious – and somewhat concerned – about this unusual discord between the two lovebirds, and when Gwen went to the ladies, I followed.

"It's just your father being over-protective," she said, in response to my carefully-worded enquiry. "He thinks Frank made a pass at me."

"Wow!" I was agog. "And did he?"

"No. Well ... I'm not sure really." She applied lipstick carefully and I thought what an attractive woman she was, besides being 11 years younger than my dad.

"I think he just accidentally bumped into me. But his hands were ... very slightly where they shouldn't have been. Obnoxious little man. And your father noticed."

"What did he say?"

"Nothing. Just went quiet, like he does. But later he said I should have given Frank a good slap. I told him he was being ridiculous and he accused me of enjoying the attention!"

"Where was Pippa when all this was going on?"

"In the gift shop, buying tea towels. It was a good gift shop," Gwen added, slightly more her usual, animated self. "I bought a very pretty vase. Fancy bothering about tea towels on holiday. I'm trying to persuade Jim to buy a dishwasher but it's an uphill struggle."

"I know all about struggling up hills," I reminded her. "But never mind that. Everything will be all right between you two, won't it?" I guessed I probably sounded like an insecure 10-year-old.

"Of course it will." Gwen gave me a hug. "Don't worry, you won't have a twice-divorced father on your hands."

Back in the dining room, she patted Dad's hand before sitting down, and the look of relief on his face was quite touching. Over coffee we talked about plans for the following day. They were thinking of driving to Silloth and going for a pleasant stroll along the Esplanade. Not too arduous, nothing requiring a lot of puff or clumpy walking boots.

"I'd like to drive there, darling," Gwen said, sweetly.

"Of course, darling." Dad didn't even hesitate.

"And back again." Even more sweetly.

"Good idea. I'll enjoy taking in the scenery."

"You know that *Ideal Home* magazine I've been looking at, darling?"

"Um... yes."

"There's an excellent article about dishwashers. I'll show you when we're back at the hotel."

"I'll look forward to that, darling." My father knew when he was beaten. "Avant-garde, that's us. We'll be leading the way in The Close."

"Now, let's talk about Saturday." Gwen glanced meaningfully at Dad, whereupon he made quite a performance of picking up the bill, frowning at it and reaching for his wallet. My stepmother then gave Allan and me the full benefit of her persuasive smile.

"We want to go to the Egremont Crab Fair," she said. "And we'd really like you kids to come as well. Do say yes. We'll have such fun."

"I've read about that," I said. "It's famous for the World Gurning Championships."

"That's right." Gwen agreed. "We can't possibly go home without seeing those."

"What's it all about?" Allan was looking puzzled and less than enthusiastic.

"It's a competition to see who can pull the most revolting expression," I said "The winner is whoever manages to look the most hideous."

"You're making a good start with that sour look on your face, Allan." Gwen could be a tad acerbic occasionally.

"That's the last day of our holiday and we'd be spending it off the bike," my husband mumbled, reinforcing his despondent expression with a tinge of rebellion.

But it would take more than a half-hearted display of mutiny to throw Gwen off-course. She glanced at Dad again and, putting his glasses on, he examined the bill carefully.

"They certainly know how to charge in this place," he said, frowning.

I kicked Allan under the table and tried to give him a *don't be so selfish, we might even enjoy ourselves and, apart from that, we can't afford to pay for this meal* look.

"What else happens besides gurning?" my husband asked.

"Oh, it's all very exciting. People throw lots of apples at each other."

Allan looked unimpressed.

"There's a greasy pole to climb," Gwen continued.

Allan fiddled with the salt and pepper pots.

"And a pipe-smoking contest!"

Allan looked up in disbelief.

"I know what this is really about." I'd suddenly remembered something else about the Egremont Crab Fair. "Dad's heard about the wrestling."

Allan's face now asked whether this could get any worse.

"I would love to see a bout of Cumberland and Westmorland wrestling," Dad admitted. "I've heard a lot about it. Apparently it's a marvellous spectacle. All the contestants wear embroidered bathing trunks."

Allan's expression acknowledged that things had, indeed, become a whole load worse.

"So that's settled then." Gwen smiled. "We're all going to Egremont on Saturday."

Back at Stumble Holme, Allan had a bit of a moan and I tried to console him by pointing out that the weather forecast for the following day was looking surprisingly good.

"We'd better make the most of it then," he said, burying himself in the OS map. "Stop messing about and go for a Really Long Ride."

Over breakfast, Allan told Ian and Pauline the route he'd planned for us and they looked suitably impressed and nonplussed. It turned out even they hadn't ventured into the wilderness we were headed for.

"Better stock up with food," Pauline advised. "There won't be a shop for miles around on those fells."

Feeling like intrepid explorers, we followed her advice and bought lunch in Ambleside. It was a beautiful sunny day and we were already down to T-shirts, for the first time on this holiday. We cycled along a horribly busy road into Windermere, where Allan checked the map and a disorientated lady asked me: "Is the sea down there?"

We turned off at Stavely and headed north, cycling for several miles along a peaceful and very pretty road, with a swollen river racing by its side. We reached the beautiful valley of Longsleddale, where the mountains reared darkly in the distance. But we were safely surrounded by neat green fields bordered by stumpy stone walls, in which the rather waterlogged Herdwick sheep quietly nibbled grass.

We cycled over ancient stone bridges and past a scattering of pretty cottages. Intriguing little tracks meandered off into the hills and we saw an occasional walker high above us. This was a remote and lonely place, which in winter would surely feel isolated. But on a warm morning in late summer, it seemed the whole of Cumbria could offer nothing more perfect.

We stopped beside a church, where there were picnic tables and public toilets. It was far too early for lunch but we had a cup of tea and some Kendal Mint Cake, lifting our faces to the sunshine and enjoying a silence broken only by the occasional bleat or chirrup.

I investigated the ladies and could hardly believe what I found. This was unlike any public toilet I'd ever seen. Fragrant and sparkling clean, it was a pleasure to linger there. There were fresh flowers in a pretty vase above the wash basin and a choice of rose or lavender-scented soap. From the rota pinned to the wall, I learned that W.I. ladies took it in turns to keep the place clean. Appreciative visitors had written messages of thanks, underneath the list of names. I had to practically force myself to leave this little oasis.

"There's a legend associated with this valley," I told Allan, while I was applying suncream. "About a Doctor Lickbarrow, who lived here in the 17th century and was suspected of dabbling in black magic. Apparently, when he was very ill, someone told him about a pair of pigeons who were having a fight close by ... "

"As you would," Allan agreed. "If you were trying to take someone's mind off his troubles."

"When the black pigeon won, the doctor said that was a bad omen for him and, sure enough, he died soon afterwards."

"Another *Legend* with no lovelorn content," Allan said. "Unless it was two male pigeons scrapping over a good-looking bird."

We hadn't cycled much further before the road narrowed and soon petered out into a track, leading off into the fells. According to the map, after a couple of miles we'd meet up with a road which would take us around Haweswater reservoir. What we didn't know was how rideable this track would turn out to be. However, coming towards us, walking his border terrier, was a friendly-looking chap, who we hoped might know the answer. Sure enough, he confidently promised us that we were in for a treat.

"Marvellous scenery and a very reasonable track," he said. "I should think you'll be able to cycle most of it quite easily."

"So we shouldn't have any problem finding Haweswater?" Allan asked.

"You'll soon get your first glimpse of it in the distance," said the pleasant fellow. "Enjoy yourselves."

With hindsight, this short and misleading encounter could have several explanations:

- The man had a mistaken idea of terrain which could be described as rideable.
- He was an ancestor of the jester, Tom Fool.
- He was a compulsive liar.
- He was a sadistic nutcase.

The terrain was beautiful, certainly. It was also extremely hilly and the track rapidly disintegrated into a stony and muddy trail, barely negotiable. Allan resorted to carrying the tandem across long and boggy stretches of moorland. It was slow going and we were forced to slosh our way through many a marshy swamp. Consequently, our shoes were soon soaked and filthy, and only Bob was escaping unscathed.

"It can't be much further," Allan panted. "We should be able to see Haweswater soon. Maybe round this next corner."

But once around the corner, all we could see ahead was a cyclist wearing a lime green peaked cap, making even slower progress than us and also carrying his bike. Hoping for an encouraging exchange of words, we got a move on and caught him up. Like us, he was covered in mud and, also like us, he'd chatted to the amiable owner of a border terrier.

"He told me that cyclists ride along this track all the time," green cap grumbled.

"It's barely a track," Allan complained. "Let alone rideable. I've carried our bike for miles."

"Same here. Mind you ..." with a less than envious glance at our tandem cradled in Allan's arms, "that thing looks heavy."

How dare he call Bob a thing! From being a fellow cyclist having a difficult day, green cap had turned into an ignoramus, who thoroughly deserved to be given rubbish directions. Rather stiffly, we said cheerio and left him chewing on chocolate-covered Kendall Mint Cake, while we continued the long plod uphill. I was suddenly reminded of some character-building advice Robert Baden-Powell is credited with having once given his young scouts, and thought I'd share the great man's wisdom with my husband.

"The road to success in whatever you do is the power to endure and to keep on keeping on," I told him. Allan, weighed down by a sturdy tandem, gave me a frosty glare but didn't have enough puff to retaliate and I sensibly shut up.

At long last we caught a glimpse of Haweswater reservoir in the distance. Relieved to know that we were at least headed in the right direction, we ate our lunch perched on a scratchy stubble of grass, with endless miles of purple, violet and bronze moorland stretching in every direction. Only the occasional screech of a predatory hawk broke the silence. We carefully picked our way down the steep and stony descent until the track widened, before reaching a very minor road and eventually a small car park. Thankfully, we subsided on to a bench at a solitary picnic table, while Allan scrutinised the map.

A middle-aged woman, wearing wellies and a head scarf decorated with prancing horses, wandered up for a chat.

"Where have you come from?" she asked.

"We set off from Grasmere this morning." I told her. "We've been tramping across the fells ever since the road disappeared at the end of Longsleddale."

She stared at us in amazement.

"And with that bike too! But it must have been so exhilarating up on those hills."

"Exhilarating ... yes."

"Did you see the golden eagle? It's occasionally spotted up there."

"I'm afraid not."

"How about an osprey?" she suggested, giving me the benefit of a second chance.

"No. We saw a pair of buzzards."

"Oh, yes. They're everywhere. You're sure they weren't Peregrine falcons?"

She looked at me hopefully and I would have loved to be able to pull something really exciting – a pair of copulating red squirrels maybe – out of the hat, for her delight and gratification.

"My husband found a 50 pence piece in a puddle," was the best I could come up with, and was rewarded by a disappointed little smile. I felt as if we'd wantonly squandered a rare opportunity to get one up on Bill Oddie.

Back on wonderful smooth tarmac again, we soon reached a signpost which informed us we were five miles from Pooley Bridge, on the northern tip of Ullswater. By the time we arrived there, we were in urgent need of a bottomless pot of tea and large plate of cakes. Tea shops abounded in this pretty lakeside village and we bestowed our custom on one whose garden boasted a panoramic view of Ullswater.

"It's a pity we're going home soon and won't have time to visit Aira Force waterfall," I said. "That's supposed to be very impressive and there's a tragic legend attached to it."

"I suppose some silly girl gets dunked in the lake," Allan murmured and I frowned. He could be very annoying at times.

"This legend is genuinely *Lovelorn*," I rebuked him. "The gallant knight Sir Eglamore was betrothed to a beautiful woman called Emma. She spent hours beside Aira Force, watching for her lover to return from war, and one day she fell into the water and drowned."

"Thought so."

"Sir Eglamore never recovered from the death of his beloved and legend has it that he spent the rest of his days living as a hermit, close to the falls."

"Silly chump. These days he'd have had counselling or gone on *Kilroy* to find closure."

I had to giggle. I enjoyed *Kilroy* but was sometimes astounded by the explicit details people were prepared to reveal about their personal lives. I also rather fancied the presenter, Robert Kilroy-Silk, though I liked to think Allan didn't know that.

We enjoyed cycling along the road which hugged Ullswater but it was tough going after that, culminating in a slow crawl up the Kirkstone Pass before descending into Ambleside, then back to Grasmere and Stumble Holme.

It was early evening but fortunately we were in no rush to get showered and changed because Dad and Gwen were spending the evening at their hotel, enjoying a romantic meal in the candlelit restaurant. We were too shattered to think beyond fish and chips and an early night or a Chinese takeaway and an early night. But we weren't sure how Ian and Pauline would feel about us polluting our bedroom with the reek of fried food.

They were in the kitchen when we went downstairs and hailed us companionably. Both were suitably impressed when we told them where we'd been, or at least where we thought we'd been.

"And for once, it didn't rain until you were safely back," Pauline said, which was when I realised that it was steadily tipping down. I wondered which was closest, the chippy or the Chinese. I don't know quite whose idea it was but Ian ended up going to the pub on the corner to buy four of their award-winning takeaway meat and potato pies, while Allan laid the kitchen table and put plates to warm in the bottom oven of the Aga, and Pauline and I scraped carrots. The meal was delicious, especially washed down with a few glasses of Cumberland Ale, and it wasn't long before it seemed as if we'd known each other forever.

My spirits sank slightly when Grandma Pauline produced a dozen packets of photos starring the infant Lily but it really wasn't that difficult to coo and cluck, especially as she had the sweetest little face, underneath a spike of black hair. I also supposed it was valuable practice, with Theo and Jess about to have a baby. I managed to fend off Grandma's tentative suggestion that it would perhaps be my turn next, by assuming the sad and regretful expression I'd pretty much perfected over the years, in response to such enquiries. Tougher measures were needed with nosey people but fortunately Pauline was a sensitive soul and backed off immediately.

On hearing we were bound for Egremont Crab Fair the next day, they looked stunned but that turned out to be because they'd assumed we were going there on the tandem.

"We'd like an early breakfast," I said. "We're meeting my dad and Gwen at nine o'clock, to give us plenty of time to drive to Egremont."

"You'll be very late back if you're planning to stay on for the Gurning Championships," Ian warned. "Better make sure you take your key."

We arrived at the White Moss House Hotel promptly at 9am the following morning, after getting most of our stuff packed in the panniers, ready for the journey back home the next day. Dad and Gwen were waiting for us on a seat in the hotel garden, holding hands. It looked as if the sun was shining again in their particular paradise, as well as in Grasmere on that lovely September morning. There was a map open beside them and this appeared to be the cause of a slight – very slight – dispute.

"I'd really like to go over Wrynose and Hardknott, darling," Gwen wheedled.

"I know darling but it would take longer that way," Dad said and I noticed a slight film of sweat beading his forehead.

"That's what you said when we went to Muncaster Castle," Gwen pointed out. "Whereas, actually, the mountain route is more direct. What do you think, Allan?"

Allan, put unfairly on the spot, looked doubtfully at his in-laws. But a true Yorkshire man cannot tell a lie and, anyway, he was still feeling aggrieved about having to spend the final day of our holiday off the bike.

"Wrynose and Hardknott," he said. "Shall I drive?"

"Yes," Dad said swiftly and with scant regard for the consequences of such betrayal.

"Jim!" Gwen's expression was indignant. Dad capitulated at once.

"Sorry, Allan," he said. "What I meant was … maybe you can drive back. If that's all right of course, darling?"

"We'll see." Gwen was making no promises and she'd withdrawn her hand from his.

We made our way to the pampered Triumph Herald, its gleaming dark blue bodywork a shining testament to my father's devotion. Gwen settled herself behind the steering wheel, with Dad hunched beside her and Allan and I squashed together in the back. She pulled on smart leather driving gloves and glamorous sunglasses, revved the engine, executed a showy three-point turn out of the car park and we were off.

As it was still relatively early, there wasn't much traffic in Ambleside and we soon began climbing steeply through Little Langdale, which took us on to the Wrynose Pass, with its formidable stretches of one-in-three. Fortunately, there were still very few other cars around and we encountered none on the sharp hairpin bends. It seemed that Gwen was well able to cope with this motoring challenge and was certainly enjoying herself.

"I thought this was supposed to be tricky," she said, taking one hand off the steering wheel to pat Dad's quivering leg.

"There's still Hardknott," Allan warned. "That's longer and tougher. More one-in-threes and even hairier hairpin bends."

At the foot of this pass is a cluster of warning signs, seemingly designed specifically to terrify the timid driver, but of course Gwen was not of their number. Putting her foot on the accelerator she made a dash for it. The poor Triumph Herald emitted screeching noises which must have wrung my father's heart strings and a smell of burning rubber leapt in through the open windows. I just hoped we wouldn't meet any cars coming in the opposite direction and, as luck would have it, we didn't.

What we did encounter was possibly worse. Half-a-dozen cyclists were crawling along the road ahead of us and there was no way we could over take them. Flustered for the first time, Gwen stalled. Cursing, she selected first gear and had another go. Barely inching along, we followed the little group of valiant cyclists. They had all my admiration and, right now, I wished I was one of them.

"Bloody cyclists!" Gwen swore. "Just our luck to meet a few idiots out on bikes."

At last she managed to overtake them but it was a risky manoeuvre and one which I felt she was lucky to get away with. This view was shared by the cyclists, judging by the number of two-fingered salutes they were chucking in our direction.

"Well done, darling." Dad half opened his eyes and risked breathing again. "Reckless people like that make this a dangerous road for the cautious motorist."

Allan twitched and I gave him a warning look. Gwen sat up straighter and smiled at her husband.

"Best keep your eyes on the road, darling," Dad suggested, somehow managing to stop his voice from rising more than a couple of octaves.

Just when I thought we were over the worst, we came upon that time-honoured Lake District hoof hazard – a couple of sheep blocking the road ahead of us. Gwen slammed the brakes on again and this time vented her vitriol on the unheeding woolly duo, who ambled gently along. Then suddenly Allan spotted something beside the hedge.

"Stop!" he said, rather unnecessarily, I thought. "There's a sheep stuck in the ditch."

Now Dad and Gwen are both fond of animals. They're thinking about getting a nice little dog, although obviously nothing with big, muddy feet, and they have an annual subscription to *Wildlife* magazine, not to mention buying all their Christmas cards from the RSPCA. So I did think they were showing themselves in rather a poor light, when Dad said something along the lines of "sod the silly bugger, let it sort itself out" – a sentiment with which Gwen agreed, albeit in much more colourful language.

But Allan took no notice and, opening the car door, he was out and across the road. Sure enough, a waterlogged Herdwick sheep had got itself tangled up in a ditch full of brambles and was struggling ineffectually to escape. Allan wrestled with the terrified animal for a few seconds but it was far too exhausted to resist for long and he dragged it out of the ditch, tugging the spiky, trailing brambles from its woolly coat before releasing it.

This bit of excitement seemed to motivate the other two sheep because with a few bleats and after just one false start, they all scooted through a gap in the hedge and out of sight. Splattered with mud and possibly more bedraggled than the animal he had saved, Allan got back in the car, well pleased with himself.

The Triumph Herald juddered its way to the peak of Hardnose and the worst was definitely over. Over that is, except for the descent, when the cyclists we'd previously encountered came tearing past us, some of them shouting and gesturing when they recognised the car. Gwen ignored them, while Allan and I hunkered down out of sight.

"I thought that went pretty well," my stepmother said, looking to Dad for support.

"You did brilliantly, darling. And don't worry about the car, it was due for a service."

Gwen seemed to decide to let him get away with that. Possibly because she had just noticed the pong emanating from her son-in-law's clothing.

"Get them to valet it as well, Jim. Allan stinks of wet sheep and he's dropping clods of mud and probably worse all over the back seat."

We arrived in Egremont with time to spare for a much-needed cup of coffee, before the apple cart was due to arrive and the throwing commenced. Gwen was particular about where we settled ourselves to watch the spectacle. She wanted to have a good view but without running any risk of being wacked in the face by an apple.

"Don't you worry, pet." An elderly woman close by was amused by Gwen's dithering. This hardly seemed like the same fearless woman who'd just taken Hardknott Pass by storm.

"The apple throwing might look random," the woman continued. "But sometimes people are specifically targeted. See that chap over there ..."

She pointed to a man wearing a flat cap. "He'd better watch out. His wife's on the apple cart and she's got a good aim, has Dot. Will should never have got drunk at his work's Christmas bash and made a fool of himself with the Saturday girl."

"When did this Crab Fair begin?" Dad asked her.

"It goes back to 1287, pet. The Lord of the Manor started the custom of distributing crab apples and that's how the event got its name. But these days they use ordinary eating apples."

"What's the greasy pole in the high street all about?" Allan asked.

"That's 20 feet high and thoroughly greased with lard. There's always a prize at the top for the first person who manages to climb all the way up. They used to win a side of mutton in the olden days. Recently it was a pound note, until a couple of years ago, when they introduced that silly little coin."

"Here comes the apple cart!" Gwen said and we all turned to watch.

The crowd surged forward, shouting for apples, which were generally thrown without venom, although Will seemed to have vanished, so maybe he wasn't taking any chances.

We wandered around for a while, looking at the stalls and watching street entertainers. Then we had a pub lunch before making our way to the main arena, where the wrestling was about to start.

Cumberland and Westmorland wrestling probably dates back to the Norsemen and was once well established throughout the country, but is now almost exclusively Cumbrian. I was very impressed by the costumes worn by many of the competitors. These consisted of white vests and coloured velvet trunks, white long johns and socks which matched the colour of the trunks. All this finery was somewhat spoilt when the skies darkened in that familiar way and the rain began teeming down, accompanied by a strengthening wind.

But this change in the weather suited Dad. Accustomed to the theatrical showmanship of his TV heroes, Giant Haystacks and Big Daddy, Cumberland wrestling wasn't quite gutsy enough for him. There was little in the way of loud grunting, sobbing, moaning or cursing. But when the competitors began getting soaking wet and slithered around in the mud, he brightened up and started to enjoy himself. The atmosphere grew even more darkly dramatic, when thunder and lightning were added to the mix and for him, at least, it was all over far too soon.

"Let's go and find a cup of tea and get warm," Gwen said.

"What a shame it rained so hard," Dad fibbed. "Are you all right, darling?"

I realised then that besides being damp and bedraggled, Gwen looked rather pale.

"I do have a slight headache," she admitted.

"You've been getting these headaches a lot recently." Dad frowned. "I wanted you to see the doctor before we came away."

"Don't fuss, Jim." Gwen patted his hand. "I'm sure some tea will see it off."

We ended up drying out in a little hall, where a local history group was providing refreshments and also playing a video showing highlights of the Egremont Crab Fair over the past 20 years. Cumberland wrestling featured strongly and Dad was able to learn a lot more about it. After shaking hands, the two men 'tak hod', which means locking arms behind each other's back, with the aim of toppling their opponent to the ground and breaking their hold. If both men fall, the one on top is deemed the winner. Bouts seldom last very long and, to the uninformed spectator, the technical subtleties are not immediately obvious, which explained why Dad had been ever so slightly disappointed.

Egremont's pipe-smoking contest is probably unique and the competitors are each given a pipe stuffed with baccy and the winner is the man (this challenge seems only to attract men) who is the first to smoke his pipeful. The average age of the contestants on the video looked to be around 97 but this was probably due to deeply carved wrinkles set in the sallow faces of serious chain-smokers. An illusory reek of stale fags seemed to seep into the stuffy little hall and several people began coughing.

But it is the World Gurning Championships for which the fair is really famous. Entrants put their heads through a horse collar and grin or 'gurn', each attempting to pull the most hideous expression possible, while being cheered, jeered and heckled by a wildly enthusiastic audience. The bald, the toothless and those boasting squints or giant hairy warts do tend to have an advantage, which is seldom the case in most popularity competitions. The title of World Champion is keenly contested, although the story goes that the competition was once won by an uninhibited onlooker, who just happened to be watching.

Singing traditional hunting songs is another unique feature of the Egremont Crab Fair and when the video finished a couple of local singers rounded off the session with some live entertainment. Allan knew most of the songs and joined in the choruses. We'd enjoyed ourselves but when the curtains were drawn and the room flooded with daylight once again, we realised that Gwen was looking very white and Dad was worried about her.

"I think we should be setting back," he told us. "I'm sorry to cut your day short but my poor girl really needs to get to bed as soon as possible."

"I'll be all right," Gwen protested. "I don't want to spoil things for Jackie and Allan."

We assured her that we didn't mind and in fact I soon realised it suited Allan rather well.

"I expect you'd like me to drive back," he offered solicitously and Gwen sighed but gave in without protest, which proved how ill she was feeling.

Dad had a go at persuading Allan to use the main road but that wasn't what my husband had in mind at all.

"Let him enjoy himself, darling," Gwen said. "Remember we're all going home tomorrow, so this will be his last chance to tackle Hardknott and Wrynose."

Allan is a competent and experienced driver, with none of my stepmother's exuberance or panache and the journey back was almost boringly uneventful. We were all very quiet, for different reasons, but I felt the holiday had passed far too quickly and there were so many roads we hadn't explored. Maybe we'd bring the tandem back to the Lake District one day, with Theo and Jess when we were all old and withered, and try our luck in the gurning competition. I could wear my rain mate – that should put me streets ahead, besides being useful because, of course, it would certainly still be raining.

TOP TANDEM TRIVIA

Boris Johnson gave Prince William and Kate Middleton a £500 tandem as a wedding present. On a visit to Fortnum & Mason with The Queen and The Duchess of Cornwall, Kate was overheard telling Boris how she and her husband often rode the bike around their garden but hadn't yet been brave enough to take to the streets.

CHAPTER TWELVE

An elderly primigravida
and in love with The Lizard

THE following year was difficult and very sad. Gwen was diagnosed with a tumour a few weeks after our holiday and surgery was unsuccessful. She was only 57 when she died and my dad was devastated. We missed Gwen too. Her zest for life was endearing and infectious and it had been heart-warming to see how much my father loved her.

Reclusive by nature and without a sociable wife to lead the way, Dad became very solitary, scurrying to the local shops only when absolutely necessary and fending off sympathetic and friendly overtures from neighbours. He looked after himself well enough and Allan and I found ourselves politely discouraged from visiting too often, or attempting to prise him away from the sanctuary of his bungalow.

I was hurtling towards my 40th birthday when we decided that the time had come to have a baby. It wasn't the right time, of course, because it had finally dawned on me that this would never arrive. We'd just have to be like everybody else and take a chance. Theo and Jess now had two children and on the rare occasions we saw them, future cycling holidays together were seldom mentioned.

Despite being classed as an 'elderly primigravida', I became pregnant with startling ease. In the words of Allan's cousin's wife Betty, I'd been "puddinged". Allan and I were immediately consumed with the sort of excitement we'd seen overwhelm so many of our friends and we felt absurdly clever and hugely pleased with ourselves.

Mum was elated and wanted to tell everyone immediately. I'd decided to wait three months before grabbing the headlines, in case of miscarriage, which is more likely if you are an elderly primigravida. So I only gave Mum permission to tell my auntie, who was on the phone straight away, saying how thrilled I must be and naturally I'd be staying well away from that dangerous tandem.

Sharing the news with my dad was difficult. He was pleased but said what a shame it was we'd waited so long because Gwen would have loved being a step-grandmother. Talk about piling on the guilt. Dad also said that at least having a baby would get me off the tandem. In fact, everyone seemed united in agreeing that pregnant women should not go cycling.

"You mustn't take any chances, Jackie." Joy was thrilled and rather clucky. "I know everything will be fine and you're going to have a beautiful, healthy little baby and be the happiest family in the whole world ... " Nobody could ever accuse Joy of half-heartedness, only warm-heartedness. "But you will stay off the bike, won't you?"

Whether cycling was a risky activity during pregnancy was one of the first questions I asked my female GP, who didn't hesitate before telling me to pack it in. It was the fact that she didn't hesitate which prejudiced me against slavishly following her advice. She hadn't asked how much cycling I did or suggested I see how I felt about it as the pregnancy advanced. And surely it was important for pregnant women to stay fit?

It was early spring too, with hopefully lots of lovely warm summer weather on the way. Allan said he'd pedal twice as hard, so I could take it easy on the back, and he promised not to complain about walking up even the shortest of hills. Eventually I decided that the woman best qualified to provide a sensible answer to the dilemma was Ruth Merchant. She and Jack had been cyclists all their lives, so her opinion should be worth hearing.

I think Ruth felt the weight of responsibility because first of all she asked what my mother thought. It was then that I realised Mum was just about the only person not to have expressed a view. True to form, she probably didn't want to put me under any pressure. And in her own quiet way she was a bit of Real Cyclist herself, usually choosing the bike over the bus when going into Winton for her shopping.

"Ideas about pregnancy and babies change all the time," Ruth mused. "Theories go in and out of fashion. I tended to follow my own instincts."

"So what did your instincts tell you to do about cycling?" I persisted.

"I didn't stop altogether until it became too uncomfortable," Ruth said. "I managed to cycle a short distance to the shops until well on in pregnancy."

"There was a piece on the radio about a woman who cycled to the hospital when her contractions began. She had a 20-minute labour before giving birth to twins."

"That's ludicrous," Ruth said firmly. "And what's more, I don't believe a word of it."

I rather fancied arriving at the hospital on the back of the tandem, with my nightie in the saddlebag. I already had the perfect T-shirt. Kate had given me a customised one emblazoned with the words PREGNANT – PLEASE PASS. She'd wanted to add ELDERLY PRIMIGRAVIDA but there wasn't room.

But for a variety of reasons, I didn't continue cycling after the fifth month. For one thing, despite having a small frame and never weighing more than 7½ stone, I ballooned in size. I also developed a variety of aches and pains and suffered from severe and persistent heartburn. Although I didn't know it, being forced to abandon my plans and admit defeat was all good preparation for the days ahead when Baby would be Boss.

I had a short and easy labour and on 27th November 1988, Jolyon David was born in Odstock Hospital, near Salisbury. In those far-off days, new mums and babies stayed in hospital for about a week, which I didn't mind at all. I'd never even held a baby before, if you discount that day at the library shortly before I went on maternity leave, when a former member of staff brought her eight-week-old daughter in to be admired.

"Give her to Jackie to hold, she needs the practice," suggested a woman from Lending. Everyone thought it was hilarious when I demonstrated my incompetence by barely knowing which way was up. They all agreed that I had spent too much time riding a tandem and not enough nurturing my maternal instincts. Luckily for me, most of the blame for this was unfairly dumped on Allan.

Soon Jolyon was home and the joyful but exhausting journey into parenthood embarked upon. Life was dominated by feeds, changing nappies and wistfully harkening back to a time when seven hours' sleep a night was the norm.

I did no housework for weeks and one day, passing through the sitting room after having a shower and noticing a thick layer of dust on the coffee table, I swiped the worst of it off with some knickers which were en route to the washing machine. Allan managed to get out on his bike for the occasional hour at weekends but the tandem gathered even more dust than the coffee table and Jolyon's baby seat remained pristine in its packaging.

This was a turbulent time for me, with moments of great happiness, which were all too often overshadowed by worry and fear. Towards the end of my pregnancy, my mother had been diagnosed with cancer of the tongue. This was a cruel blow, just when she was looking forward to becoming a grandma. She had surgery at the Royal Marsden in London, followed by radiotherapy at Poole Hospital, and at first the prognosis looked hopeful. But soon the disease tightened its grip and Mum died before our son was a year old, so he never knew either of his grandmothers.

Due to a cold winter and my mum's illness, we made no attempt to start cycling as a family until the Easter after Jolyon was born. But with the arrival of spring sunshine, we decided it was time to introduce the little chap to his baby seat at the back of the tandem. Although the most intelligent and good-looking child on the planet, our son did not possess a placid temperament and we approached this significant event with caution.

We tucked him up cosily, wrapped in plenty of layers, all the while chatting cheerfully about the great adventure ahead and how he was going to enjoy himself very much. He was all smiles and chirrups as we wheeled the tandem down the garden path – far, far more carefully than it had ever been wheeled before. I hoped he wouldn't begin to howl until we were at least out of the village, as I doubted if many neighbours would share our belief that a bike ride was a good afternoon out for a four-month-old child.

Feeling very self-conscious and thankful there was no-one around, we cycled out of the village and onto the A31, a hazardous road and one which we left as quickly as possible. There was still no sound from behind me and I reckoned Jolyon was trying to decide whether to play the part of contented participant or enraged prisoner. After a few minutes I called out: "OK, back there?" Silence. Looking around, I realised our son was well able to take momentous initiations in his stride. Fast asleep, he was probably dreaming about his first Ferrari.

As the summer progressed, the three of us ventured out on the tandem more often and friends' opinions about our behaviour varied. Some agreed with my dad, who thought we were foolish and reckless. The wisest people, I was to realise later, encouraged us to enjoy the moment because once our son was old enough to speak his mind, there would ensue a tussle of wills we were unlikely to win.

But while he was little, Jolyon was generally happy to go out cycling and he certainly enjoyed the attention he received. Seldom did we go unnoticed and enchanted onlookers cooed in horrified delight. "Oh, look at that gorgeous baby! Bless his dear little heart. But what on earth are his selfish parents thinking about, risking their child's life on these dangerous roads?"

Jolyon soon learned to play to the gallery. Occasionally, he'd attempt world-weary nonchalance but generally he waved at admirers and liberally distributed angelic smiles.

Cycling with a baby on the back drastically reduced our mileage and we always seemed to be stopping for some reason. Usually to pick grass. For months Jolyon had an obsession with carrying bunches of grass. And he was only content with a specific type. Our eyes were constantly peeled for the long sturdy stuff, topped with brown tufty bits, which he favoured. Even now, more than 20 years later, we'll be cycling along a country road and one of us will sigh nostalgically and say "Oh, look. Some of that grass Jolyon used to love."

The issue of sleeping often dominated our rides. Sometimes we wanted him to sleep. More often, we would prefer to delay his nap, hoping to have some peace later on at home when we were shattered. By way of encouragement, Allan and I could often be heard belting out *The Grand Old Duke of York* or, more soothingly, *Twinkle, Twinkle, Little Star*.

A tandem plus baby seat is a long machine, so there was quite a distance between our son and his sharp-eyed father. Consequently, it was my job to relay observations from parent to child, by which time it was often irrelevant. The deer had disappeared into the hillside, the blackbird flown from the cow's head and the cuckoo stopped singing, long before Jolyon received the information.

My dad's physical and mental health was deteriorating and his behaviour was quite bizarre at times. When Jolyon started crawling and then learning to walk, Dad was terrified he would damage something in the bungalow and he started putting more and more stuff out of sight and covering up the furniture. Anything Gwen regarded as precious had been carefully wrapped up and squirreled away shortly after her death.

When Jolyon and I went to see his grandad, we would find his front room practically bare of any sort of ornament, everything hidden away specifically because of our visit. A few photographs were put on high shelves and the sofa and chairs swathed in old sheets "in case of accidents". It must have meant hours of work, both before we'd arrived and after we'd left.

When Jolyon was almost two-years-old, we borrowed my brother-in-law's caravan and went to the Cotswolds for a week. The tandem came too, of course. Michael's caravan was five-star luxury after a tent and the only drawback was the dreadful lights, which were so weak that I couldn't read my book. This was misery for me, especially as I was in the middle of *500 Mile Walkies* by Mark Wallington, definitely the funniest book I've ever read. Thankfully, after a couple of days Allan located a hook-up point and plugged us into mains electricity, which meant I could read and giggle comfortably, while he cooked the tea safely.

Jolyon loved the camp site and lost no time in making friends with the nice lady in the next caravan. Unfortunately, he would sometimes prefer her company to ours and began to object noisily when his irritating parents insisted on plonking him on the back of the tandem.

"He likes it really," I'd say, trying to fasten a struggling, furious toddler into his seat. "Once we're off, he's all smiles."

Judging by her doubtful expression, I'm sure the nice lady didn't believe a word of it.

We enjoyed ourselves, and I loved the Cotswold villages, but this was a very different sort of cycling holiday. A healthy two-year-old tends to be quite weighty and at the first hint of a hill we ground to a halt. I would then get off and walk, while Allan pushed the tandem with Jolyon on it. Twenty miles of this wore us out more effectively than the 70 or 80 of pre-baby days. By the time we returned to Dorset we were beginning to realise that life really had changed, if not forever, certainly for a very long time.

The rot didn't really set in until Jolyon started school. Up until then he probably thought every little lad spent Sundays on the back of a tandem. We'd bought a trailer bike, which enabled him to pedal if he wanted to but not if he didn't. We chose to believe that he would want to, at least some of the time. Our son had other ideas. He might deign to put a bit of effort in, if the gradient of a hill reduced us to begging or bribery, but generally it was staggeringly hard work for his parents. Good for the fitness though, I suppose.

The final straw came because of influence wielded by a boy called Freddie, on the day Jolyon went to this little chap's fifth birthday party. Naturally, we took advantage of an afternoon's freedom by going for a bike ride, which we managed to combine with collecting our son from the party. I must admit to feeling a tad uneasy about this, recollecting the refined elegance of Freddie's mother, who was never to be seen at the school gate without eyeliner and high heels.

Sure enough, despite having spent an unenviable afternoon trying to referee a dozen over-excited five-year-old boys and helped only by a bewildered-looking chap dressed as a clown, Natasha still looked ravishingly beautiful. Designer jeans hugged her slim hips and that pale pink jumper had to be softest cashmere. Even the smear of strawberry sauce on her exquisitely made-up face somehow looked enticing, rather than messy. By way of contrast, I was unflatteringly clad in Lycra leggings and a hi-vis waterproof jacket, the weather having taken a turn for the worse. I did have enough self-respect to whip off my rain mate before she opened the door but all this meant was that my hair clung soggily to my red, sweaty face.

Natasha couldn't have been more welcoming, though that was probably because we had come to remove a small boy who was waving a cocktail sausage around and trying to lure an indignant Persian cat from its refuge on top of the kitchen cupboards.

"You must be so fit," Natasha marvelled, pushing silvery fingernails through expensively highlighted hair. "I only seem to find time for Pilates once a week. I'm dreadfully out of condition."

I'm pretty sure Allan disagreed with this modest but inaccurate self-assessment of a woman who was at least 10 years younger than me and doubtless higher maintenance than he could possibly imagine.

But it was difficult to dislike Natasha. Kind as well as beautiful, she'd put a little packet of silver-wrapped chocolate bicycles in Jolyon's party bag. Not that it earned her any thanks. "Why do people think I like cycling?" he grumbled, as we pedalled home in the rain. "And why do you have to turn up looking so different from the other mummies and daddies? Freddie says you're weird. I like Freddie and I don't like this stupid bike."

So thanks to the forthright Freddie, from then on we pretty much stopped cycling as a family. Jolyon had tennis lessons and became a good junior player over the following years. Our evenings and weekends were taken up by driving him all over the south of England for tennis tournaments, plus the ordinary school activities and socialising. Allan found the occasional hour to get out on his solo bike but the tandem was leading a lazy life.

My dad was finally admitted into a care home, where he died after only a short time. I felt sad that my son would have no clear memories of either of my parents, even though they had loved him so very much.

When Jolyon was 10-years-old, he went on a school trip to Dartmoor for five days. I knew I would miss him dreadfully and fret about whether or not he was homesick, even though he was a very independent boy and had never been clingy.

So to take my mind off our son's first foray away from home, we decided to have a short cycling holiday in south-west Cornwall. We were renting a cottage – a new experience for us. Allan was pretty fit but we only managed the occasional ride on the tandem these days and I felt quite apprehensive about how well I would cope with cycling every day.

I still suffered from skin problems but acne had been supplanted by rosacea, a recurrent condition characterised by facial flushing, itchy red spots and painful burning skin. There are specific triggers which make these symptoms worse, such as exposure to sunlight, exercise and alcohol.

A couple of days before we left for Cornwall, my face exploded into a scarlet furnace and I kept gazing into mirrors, in appalled fascination. After congratulating me on presenting with the worst case of rosacea he'd ever encountered, my GP prescribed antibiotics and advised me to avoid sunshine and cold winds. When I explained that we were about to go on a cycling holiday, he smiled, shrugged and told me to at least keep off the booze. He said some women were plagued by rosacea all their lives. Perhaps unfairly, I felt the implication was that I'd done well to stave off its arrival until the menopause caught up with me.

I bought a hideous sun visor with a huge peak and some factor-50 sun block, which smeared my scarlet face in a greasy white film. Recognising that the trauma was making me thin-skinned as well as fair-skinned, Allan wisely refrained from commenting on my appearance.

By removing the front wheel, we'd managed to fit the tandem into the car and even found room for Allan's guitar. We'd like to have taken the cat but it seemed more sensible to leave Thing at home, where Richard had offered to feed him, make a fuss of him and clear up dead mice and pools of vomit. Woe betide us if we failed to come home without plenty of Cornish fudge and biscuits.

Our cottage was at Mawgan, a small village in a valley at the head of the Helford River on the Lizard Peninsular. The owners, Leonard and Madge, lived next door and were friendly and helpful, giving us plenty of information about the area and in particular recommending the food at the local pub. I wasn't keen on this idea because I preferred to keep my face almost literally under wraps for the time being, so we heated up a meal in the microwave.

Poor Allan made a valiant attempt to enjoy the complimentary bottle of wine, watched by his resentful wife, who was sipping orange juice and lemonade. After we'd eaten, I cheered myself up by making a start on my holiday reading – *Dog Days* by Mavis Cheek. I'd recently discovered this writer, who very much tickled my funny bone.

Over breakfast the following day, we saw that our hosts had already taken the tandem out of their shed and Bob was flexing his handlebars, ready for the off. It had been a long time since his last holiday. On the first steep little hill, it soon became obvious that we would not be eating up the miles around here and Allan was horrified to be overtaken by a leisurely postman on his sturdy old bike. After all, we were supposed to be the Real Cyclists.

We cycled to Helford first, a pretty village on the river estuary, and enjoyed tea and scones in a cafe garden, where a robin ate crumbs from Allan's hand. On returning the tray, we noticed a sign asking people not to feed the robins *inside* the cafe!

Dropping down into Coverack, we were caught by a heavy shower and I had a go at wearing my rain mate over my sun visor. Anything, rather than risk the rain washing off my thick layer of factor-50. Coverack was revealed in all its beauty when the sun emerged warily through thinning cloud and we shielded our eyes against the light bouncing off giant waves, crashing against the green serpentine rock of the harbour walls. Not one day of that holiday passed when we weren't at some point transfixed by the sight of waves hurling themselves against a Cornish sea wall.

Roskilly ice-cream was another unforgettable experience. While I licked my way through a double helping of fudge-filled Hokey Pokey Crunch at Coverack, Allan and I agreed that Cornwall was fantastic, the Lizard wonderful and Coverack the shiniest jewel in its crown. Even a puncture on the way back didn't diminish our enthusiasm because it happened at such a pretty place beside the river.

We bought Cornish new potatoes and strawberries for supper from a roadside stall. The Spar at Mawgan provided lamb chops, local mushrooms and tomatoes. I had a bath while Allan cooked dinner and the hot steamy water attacked my face with relish, turning the skin a throbbing, fiery scarlet. So once again it was antibiotics washed down with orange juice for me that evening.

The following days found us reconsidering Coverack's title of number one shiniest jewel in the Lizard's crown. How about Cadgewith? A warm sun lit up that exquisite village, while we ate our sandwiches on the cliff top, overlooking yet more crashing waves. Nothing could be more beautiful than this, we agreed.

But that was before we discovered Lizard Point, so peaceful in comparison with the commercialised Land's End, but every bit as dramatically glorious. And surely nothing could surpass the beauty of Kynance Cove, where the waves not only crashed even more magnificently but were practically turquoise in colour.

On Tuesday evening, I wasn't allowed to skulk behind closed doors because Allan had noticed that there was a folk club at the Cadgewith Cove Inn. I applied a thick layer of slap, hoped for dim lighting, and off we went. Unlike some pub landlords, this one clearly liked folkies and everyone was very welcoming. There was a blend of locals and visitors and Tuesday evenings were evidently something of a tourist attraction. But the compere protected his singers from a surfeit of unwelcome attention, albeit very good humouredly. "No photos, please. They're an ugly lot." Allan's performance received a favourable response and his beloved Patrick Eggle guitar was admired, which always pleased him.

The following day, after cycling to Mullion Cove, we found the small village of Gunwalloe and its church, which is set among the sand dunes, in which legend suggests several chests of treasure lie buried, looted by the notorious buccaneer Captain John Avery. A 13th century bell tower is built into the solid rock of the headland and regular Sunday afternoon services are held here, when sleepy sunbathers run the risk of being woken by the sound of bells ringing out across the beach.

With only a couple of days holiday left, we decided it was time to turn our backs on crashing waves and explore the area around the Helford River. It was hard-going and we did quite a bit of walking and tandem-pushing but Port Navas made all the effort worthwhile. This village is at the head of a wooded tidal creek on the northern side of the river, very pretty and peaceful.

On to Helford Passage, where over more Roskilly ice-cream (clotted cream vanilla) we eyed up the smallish passenger ferry and wondered if there would be enough room for the tandem. No trouble at all, declared the young and handsome ferryman, and he was right. I've got the photos to prove it but, sadly, none of him. The sun shone and it was pretty much perfect. Yes, Helford had to be a contender for the title of Number One shiniest jewel.

What to do on our last day was tricky. We wanted to go back to all our favourite places and eat Roskilly ice-cream at each one, but to begin with it looked as if we were going nowhere. Not by bike, anyway. The shed in which Bob took his rest was locked every night and opened by Leonard or Madge at the crack of dawn, long before we were up and about.

But on this, the final morning, to our dismay we found the shed doors firmly locked and no reply to our increasingly urgent ringing on next door's bell. All was ominously quiet and there were no cars in their driveway. Warm sunshine and cloudless skies presaged a beautiful day and there we were, two cyclists without their tandem, watching precious time disappear. Allan did the sensible thing, which was to panic and hammer on the front door, shouting through the letterbox.

Meanwhile, I went back inside and rummaged through my bag, looking for the introductory letter we'd been sent. Sure enough, both landline and mobile numbers were listed. Fortunately, Leonard was working only a couple of miles away and drove back immediately, to release Bob into our eager hands. In the end, we lost less than an hour but it took Allan a little more than that to regain his equilibrium. The experience had propelled him into what I call one of his Yorkshire Moods and he glowered at poor Leonard, who was astute enough to keep heartfelt apologies to a bare minimum, before beating a wise retreat.

But after that inauspicious beginning, it turned into a lovely day. We cycled to Porthleven and sat on the harbour wall, lingering over expensive but totally delicious crab sandwiches. Crashing waves were naturally an accompaniment to this gourmet feast.

Delightful as Porthleven is, I shall always remember it as being the place where we met a fluffy brown cat, who didn't need rescuing. She was curled up beside the wall, perilously close to passing traffic. When I went to stroke her, I saw a notice in the nearby chippy saying her name was Poppy, she lived locally and was well-loved, so please don't anybody take her away. Well, even if we'd managed to squash her into the saddlebag, she might not have received much of a welcome from his spoilt Lordship back home.

We cycled on along the coast road for a while, stopping to drink tea from our flask on the cliffs near Rinsey, overlooking a tin mine where an episode of *Poldark* had been filmed. Then back into Porthleven, where we bought sea bass from a wonderful fishmonger and Allan roasted it for tea with rosemary and lemon. We shared a bottle of wine and my face only flushed a healthy shade of palest pink. Hurrah! The antibiotics were working at last, just in time for us to go home.

Allan raised his glass to Cadegworth, proclaiming it to be the Lizard's most shining jewel. But I thought he was overly biased by kind comments at the folk club and my vote went to Kynance Cove. Eventually, we compromised by awarding the accolade to Roskilly's ice-cream and we were in complete agreement about making a return visit very soon, to sample the remaining 42 flavours.

TOP TANDEM TRIVIA

'Charlotte's Tandems' are based in Gloucestershire. They lend tandems (free of charge) only to children and adults with disabilities or special needs, who are unable to ride a bike safely on their own. Tandems are available for hire for a couple of months at a time. The charity owns about 100 tandems all over the UK, which are looked after by Volunteer Helpers. St James's Palace has reported that "their Royal Highnesses ...The Duke and Duchess of Cambridge ...were most interested to hear about Charlotte's Tandems and the support you lend to people with special needs..." **www.charlottestandems.co.uk**

CHAPTER THIRTEEN
Falling off the bike, illness and stripping the willow

IN May 2001, Allan was made redundant. His job with a swimming pool company had been stressful but well-paid and except for my role as parish clerk for the previous 10 years, I hadn't worked since Jolyon's birth. But we had to face up to the fact that at the age of 52, Allan might not find another job easily. So I was reluctantly forced into salvaging the family finances and seeking employment, which I found almost straight away at Dorchester library. It was a part-time post in the Home Library Service, providing support to Nicki, the young woman who drove the van to care homes and sheltered housing.

It was hard physical work and at first I was foxed by the unfamiliar computer system. Mess and confusion soon surrounded me in the form of trolleys piled high with books I hadn't time to shelve and notes from staff with mystifying requests and instructions. Several weeks later, I crawled out from underneath this mountain of chaos to meet the somewhat sceptical gaze of Nicki, the colleague with whom I was neglecting to form any sort of companionable relationship.

We probably salvaged the situation just in time. Nicki was almost certainly on the point of categorising me as insufferably serious, with barely a word to say for myself. She herself was cheeky, gregarious, quick-witted, generous and incredibly hard-working. It took a while because in some ways we were complete opposites, but I grew very fond of Nicki and we became good friends. In the difficult days which lay ahead, there were many times when I was grateful for her warm-hearted kindness and the sensitivity she chose to keep well hidden, under a tough exterior.

Allan was out of work for just over a year. Frequent, long and solitary bike rides meant that he was super-fit but when, after so many months of unemployment, he was offered a job with a chemical distribution company, he welcomed the opportunity to become a wage slave once more. Jolyon and I were certainly relieved and pleased to see him suited and booted again –and with a couple of inches lopped off his hair.

Now 13 years old, Jolyon was doing well at school and I was happy at work, so life seemed to be back on an even keel. I still enjoyed going out on the tandem but I wasn't so keen on very long rides now (50 miles was enough) and preferred to stay at home and read a book if it was raining, or indeed if rain was even forecast.

I wasn't too keen on extremes of temperature either, not with my sensitive skin and predisposition to the dreaded rosacea, which was always waiting to pounce. Allan frowned on such self-indulgence and pronounced me in danger of turning into a fair weather cyclist rather than a Real one. I thought he should consider himself lucky that I hadn't chucked out my cycling shorts years ago and even luckier that they still fitted me. Spiritedly, I pointed out the scarcity of women cyclists on Dorset roads and almost total absence of any post-menopausal ones.

Allan might consider cycling 50 miles to be unremarkable but most people thought differently. I even managed to impress Nicki occasionally, until one unguarded moment when I let slip the fact that I couldn't ride a bike, which lowered my credibility by several notches. One day I happened to mention that I needed a new rain-mate and they were hard to come by these days. I could see from her gleeful expression that she was calculating the maximum amount of enjoyment it would be possible to derive from this opportunity. Sure enough, a few days later Nicki solemnly presented me with a small, prettily-wrapped package. Inside were two rain bonnets, one spotted pink and the other blue.

"I didn't want to leave Allan out," she explained. "We don't want his barnet getting wet and soggy."

An interested group of staff were gathering round my desk and Nicki looked at me, hopefully. She was far too nice to embarrass the staid old girl publicly but I knew very well what she was hoping would happen next. The years receded and I recalled an almost identical situation with Joy and Kate, 20 years earlier, back in Poole library.

I knew what I must do and I also knew exactly what Nicki would do and what she had hidden behind her back. Obediently, I shook out the pink spotted rain-mate and put it on, turning to stick out my tongue in the direction of Nicki's mobile phone, as she photographed the moment, while everybody clapped. I wanted to continue the fun later on, by taking a photo on my phone of Allan wearing his own rain-mate but he meanly refused to co-operate.

We've only fallen off the tandem three times in over 30 years. Once was on black ice and then there was the day when my husband lost concentration and steered us into a ditch full of nettles.

On the third occasion we hadn't even found our way into Zelston, let alone on to the A31. A short track leads from our garden into the village and it was here that the tandem skidded on some loose gravel, tipping us both off. Allan was unhurt, due in his blinkered view to rigorous training received during his time as a member of Wimborne St Giles' football team almost 40 years earlier. I, on the other hand, fell as awkwardly as possible and lay winded on the ground for several seconds. I vaguely heard Allan discussing with a dog-walking neighbour whether he should call an ambulance.

"Give me a minute," I gasped, so they helped me to my feet instead and I tottered back indoors and found my way to the sofa. There I lay moaning for some time, before managing to rally enough to get stuck into *The Other Boleyn Girl* by Philippa Gregory. It was great, having access to all the new books again.

The next day I was covered in spectacular bruises and it hurt to move. Allan suggested I take the day off work but stoically I did my duty, feeling noble and heroic, as well as about 90 years old.

"Good weekend?" Nicki asked but without waiting for an answer. "Could you hunt down six cosy murders for Mrs M? It won't be easy, she's read most of them."

"I thought Mrs M was brown bread," I said, getting up carefully.

"False alarm. The really awkward ones go on forever. Have you got a touch of the old lumbago?"

"I fell off the tandem yesterday."

154

I watched as the flicker of sympathy on her mischievous little face was immediately submerged by a tidal wave of hilarity.

"You fell off the tandem?" she squeaked. "Oh no, how dreadful. Did you hurt yourself?"

I beckoned Nicki into the ladies toilet and showed her my technicolour bruises. She hung on to the edge of a washbasin and howled with laughter.

"I'm sorry," she gasped. "I've got this image in my head of you falling off the bike and it's so funny, it really is. Please tell me you were wearing that hideous rain-mate."

Somehow, she soon had me giggling over my own misfortune, even though it hurt to laugh. Then the customer services manager opened the door and I pulled my skirt down quickly. Goodness knows what she thought, as Nicki and I both exited the toilet in a great rush, cackling uncontrollably. When I arrived for work the next day, I found a big packet of cashew nuts and a bar of chocolate on my desk –get-well presents from my contrite but still grinning friend.

When Jolyon was 18 and studying for A-levels, he told us he wanted to take a gap year. We'd been expecting that but what we weren't prepared for was his intention to have 12 whole months in Guyana, as a volunteer with Project Trust, an organisation which specialised in student gap years. But the prospect of waving goodbye to my son was by no means the worst experience which lay ahead for me in 2007.

I'd suspected for a while that something was wrong with me but because the symptoms were embarrassing, I'd put off going to my GP and kept telling myself it couldn't be anything serious. I was fit and healthy – always had been. Allan had just had a few days' holiday and we'd been for a couple of long rides on the tandem. Surely I wouldn't be able to do that if I was ill? Then I watched an episode of *Street Doctor* on TV and suddenly I felt a tremor of real fear. Someone with symptoms identical to mine was warned not to ignore them.

So at last I visited my GP and was reassured when he told me he didn't think the bleeding was anything to worry about but he would refer me to Dorchester Hospital. When my appointment arrived, it wasn't very convenient, so I asked for it to be rescheduled. I did the same with the next one because Allan would be away and I needed someone to drive me home. When the third appointment came through, and it turned out Allan was going to be away then too, Joy offered to take me.

"Don't worry," I told her blithely. "It can wait. There's nothing wrong."

"I'm sure there isn't," Joy agreed. "But you're going and I'm taking you and no arguments."

"This colonoscopy sounds horrible," I muttered.

"Best to get it over and done with," Joy advised. "And I'll be there to hold your hand."

This was exactly what she ended up doing. I got into such a state during the procedure, when it become frighteningly obvious that something was very wrong indeed, that a nurse called Joy into the examination room to try to calm me down.

Somehow, she not only managed to do that but also remained cool-headed enough to ask the questions I was too traumatised to put into words. How blessed I was to have my best friend there. From that day on, Allan was never far from my side, but it was poor Joy who'd had to cope with the initial shock and terror.

The hospital machinery clicked smoothly into gear and letters with the NHS logo began arriving, with alarming efficiency. A CT scan was swiftly followed by an appointment with a consultant, when it was confirmed that I had bowel cancer and would need an immediate operation. The jovial surgeon seemed to positively relish the prospect of sticking a scalpel into me. I was his dream patient: young (in terms of bowel cancer, anyway), thin (no mounds of flesh to hinder said scalpel) and, best of all, I was a remarkably fit 56-year-old. Due to all those years of cycling, he assured me I had every chance of making a speedy recovery.

A few days before my operation, we had to face up to the fact that our dear cat Thing was no longer enjoying his life. He was 24-years-old and we could scarcely imagine being without him. He could hardly move at all now and spent hours just lying on the garden path, trying to summon up enough strength to inch a little further towards the door. I phoned the vet, who was kindness itself and talked me through what needed to be done. Afterwards, we missed him dreadfully and added to my grief was a painful feeling that we'd let him suffer too long because we couldn't bear to let him go.

The prospects of recovery from cancer are improving all the time and yet it is still often viewed as a death sentence, and people's reactions to my nasty news were as varied as they were bewildering. One friend behaved as if I had nothing worse than a bad case of flu, whereas another didn't come near me for several weeks. It's always difficult to hear that someone close is seriously ill but the value of simple human kindness cannot be over-estimated.

I developed a wound infection after surgery, which was treated with intravenous antibiotics, and I spent 11 days in hospital, which included our 33rd wedding anniversary. Nicki brought me a selection of the newest library books but for the first time in my life I couldn't concentrate on reading and found no solace there.

Considering I had ignored the symptoms for so long, I was a lot luckier than I deserved to be. The operation was successful and I didn't need chemotherapy because every lymph node harvested during surgery was free from disease. I returned to work four months later in September, five weeks after Jolyon left for Guyana.

In early October, Allan and I went cycling for the first time since my operation. We decided on Pamphill, near Wimborne, a round trip of about 20 miles. It seemed very strange being back on the tandem again after five months and I felt vulnerable, in a new and disconcerting way. I wasn't in pain any more but there was still minor discomfort. The wound infection had set me back several weeks and destroyed the consultant's prognosis of a swift recovery.

I was used to feeling confident on the tandem, certain that I could cope with the mileage, whatever it turned out to be. Now I was afraid of running out of energy and having no reserves of strength to call upon. But it was lovely to be out once more, and on the homeward stretch I began to believe I really would get back to being my old self again.

There was a coolness in the late afternoon air and a hint of impending autumn. Sadly, I reflected that a whole summer had passed me by, in a blur of painkillers and daytime TV. I'd never take cycling for granted again, I thought. Never turn my nose up at a bike ride, simply because rain threatened. It was so good to be the three of us again – Allan, me and dear old Bob. It would take a while – far longer than I'd expected – but I vowed that when I was fit again, I'd relish cycling more than ever.

Although we never lost touch with Theo and Jess and visited each other occasionally, our plans to spend cycling holidays together never materialised after Yorkshire in 1976. But they had been in regular contact since my diagnosis and came to Dorset to spend a few days with us over the New Year. Having friends to stay was good for Allan and me and shook us out of our rather sombre mood. For a few days, we didn't dwell quite so much on Jolyon's absence and for the first time in a long while we enjoyed ourselves and had fun.

We spent New Year's Eve at Sherborne, where The Yetties were holding their annual ceilidh. A highly successful folk band, The Yetties originated from the Dorset village of Yetminster. The majority of people at the ceilidh were entitled to a bus pass and maybe even a free TV licence, but they showed an energy and stamina which probably put many a youthful party-goer to shame. Certainly no concessions were made to advancing age, dodgy knees, escalating blood pressure or hip replacements.

I wasn't given the chance to stay in my seat, even if I'd wanted to, and I was up for circle dances, six hand reels, longways sets and square dances. I raced up the sides and down the middle, I galloped across and back, I did umpteen baskets and I swung numerous different partners – often a sweaty fellow, sometimes a woman and once a littl'un about 3ft tall. I clapped, hopped and kicked, I Dosey Doed, I formed right hand stars and left hand stars, I waltzed and I Stripped The Willow. Shortly before midnight Jess and I went to the ladies.

"It probably sounds very sad but this is the best New Year I've ever had," I shouted to her in the neighbouring cubicle.

"I was just thinking the same," Jess shouted back. "Hurry up. They're forming sets for the Cumberland Square Eight. That's my favourite."

It was mine too. It sounds sexist but this dance is best performed by big strong men partnered by small, thin women. If sufficient speed is built up and the men aren't intimidated by shrieks of protest, their ladies' feet should leave the floor as they are whirled around. This is the moment many a girl will regret the decision she made to wear a short, swirly skirt. Fortunately, Jess and I were old hands at ceilidh dancing and were both wearing jeans. We shrieked though, long and loud, and were delighted when our men folk carried on regardless.

In the early hours of 2008, we arrived back at Zelston, exhausted but still full of adrenalin. Allan cracked open a bottle of Champagne and we all went a bit misty-eyed as we toasted our respective offspring.

"You wouldn't be without the young ankle-biters." Jess was soaking her sore feet in a bowl of hot water. "But where are they now, when you need a New Year hug and to be told you're the best mummy in the whole wide world?"

"With their respective other halves." Theo poured more fizz. "Well, that's where ours are."

"Jolyon hasn't even got an excuse like that," I complained. "And we didn't have so much as a Christmas card from him."

"But he's in Guyana," Allan protested. "His village is 40 miles away from the nearest shop. The poor lad explained that."

"He could have taken a card with him to post," I said. "Or left one behind for us to find."

"Let's face it," Jess said, pouring another kettleful of hot water into the bowl and closing her eyes in blissful appreciation. "Kids go off and leave you. That's what they're programmed to do. Friends, now ... " she wriggled her toes. "Well, you can rely on friends. Look at us."

"You didn't let me down in my hour of need," I agreed, sleepily maudlin. "A get-well card, flowers, lots of phone calls, a big bag of liquorice allsorts ... "

"Liquorice allsorts?" Jess frowned.

"Oh no, that was Nicki," I remembered. "And she didn't give me them until I was back at work and she could pinch the yellow coconut ones."

"Holidays together," Jess splashed around a bit. "That's when you discover what people are really made of. We've spent cycling holidays together and we're still friends."

"Well, only one holiday, to be fair," Theo pointed out.

"And that was 32 years ago," Allan added. "Goodness knows if we could survive close proximity for a whole fortnight these days."

"Of course we could!" Jess and I were indignant.

"Let's put it to the test." Theo stifled a yawn. "Next summer – where shall we go?"

During the following few days we talked of little else and many holiday destinations were mooted, but it proved impossible to resist the opportunity of recreating our carefree youth, pedalling around the Yorkshire Dales.

"So we're digging out the tents, are we?" Allan looked excited but anxious. "Ours is in the shed and I'm afraid the mice might have got at it."

"We should buy new tents," Theo decided. "There are some brilliant ones on the market these days. Roomy, light and quick to set up."

159

Jess and I glanced at each other. She gave me a stern look which I interpreted as meaning, *'Not a chance. Play the sick card, it's a powerful weapon'.*

"I don't think I'm up to camping," I faltered, in my frailest little voice. "I haven't recovered my strength yet and cycling every day for a fortnight will be quite challenging enough."

Theo looked concerned but Allan was having none of it. When it suited him, he could be a firm believer in tough love.

"You're perfectly well now," he said. "Remember the ceilidh – there was no stopping you."

"You can't compare one evening of dancing to being under canvas for two weeks," I objected, adjusting from frail to stroppy with consummate ease. "We're all 30 years older and I don't fancy sleeping on hard ground these days with only a jumper for a pillow."

"You always had such a sense of adventure," Allan pleaded. "What happened to the girl I married?"

"She turned into a mature woman, who prefers to have a nice clean loo only a few feet away from the comfy bed she's sleeping in," I said, firmly. "The days of taking a chance and crouching in a moonlit field are long gone."

"So what sort of holiday do you have in mind?" he asked, and Jess and I were only too happy to supply the answers.

"We want a self-catering cottage," I said. "With two toilets."

"Two bathrooms," Jess corrected. "And a bidet would be nice, too."

"A dishwasher is essential," I added.

"And at least one TV," decided the woman who used to deride couples who spent their evenings in front of the gogglebox. Once children came on the scene, she'd sensibly ditched her principles without a second's hesitation. Brainy old Theo was a university professor now but still felt ashamed of his family's dishonourable capitulation to media enslavement and refused to watch any TV programme which he categorised as rubbish. This prohibited all the soaps and anything which came anywhere near featuring a celebrity.

"Any other stipulations regarding this holiday cottage?" Allan enquired, with heavy sarcasm.

"A quiet location," I said. "We don't want to be woken up early by traffic noise."

"If we were camping, we could stay in farmers' fields," Allan said. "With nothing but the occasional moo to disturb us."

"A garden," Jess mused. "It would be nice to eat outside."

"We'd be doing that all the time if we were camping," Theo pointed out.

"A log-burning stove," I said. "In case it's cold and wet."

They all scoffed at such a daft idea. This was going to be 1976 all over again, wasn't it? So we were bound to come home with brown knees and noses.

TOP TANDEM TIP

If you are new to tandeming, try to ignore any scornful comments about riding at the back, rather than at the front. Be thick-skinned when dealing with remarks which suggest you are betraying the Sisterhood. Remember the many advantages of being a stoker – i.e no responsibility for steering, braking or changing gear. And furthermore, as the one on the back, you are protected from the worst of the elements because the rear rider gets the full force of lashing rain, freezing north-east winds and hordes of nasty black flies.

CHAPTER FOURTEEN
Tandem number three, Ecky Thump and cursing in rhyme

AFTER 30 years, Bob Jackson was beginning to show definite signs of ageing and although we felt guilty about it, we'd started to hanker after a more modern tandem. In February 2008 we found just the thing at St John's Cycles in Bridgewater, where we'd gone to buy some new panniers and a saddlebag.

Allan spotted the Thorn Vitesse straight away. Mainly black, with gold lettering and touches of red, it was similar to Bob in colour. But this one was second-hand and had apparently been involved in an accident, which rather put me off, but there was no sign of any damage. In fact, it looked spanking new and was the perfect size for us. It could almost have been made-to-measure.

"It's got a drag brake," Allan said. "That's brilliant!"

"Is it?" I'd put my specs on, peering closely for dents or scratches. "Why?"

"It would slow us down on steep downhill stretches, without using the usual brakes," Allan explained. "So the rims won't heat up, meaning no more blow-outs."

"And no more having to stop halfway down a hill, waiting until the rims cool off?" I said.

"Exactly. I've been thinking about getting a drag brake for years. This bike is begging to come home with us."

We took it out for a short ride and loved it – but not enough to seal the deal there and then. £2,000 was a bargain for a Thorn Vitesse with all the trimmings but still a lot of money for us to find. Nevertheless, the minute we were home, Allan rushed to the phone and committed us to buying our third tandem. I left him to it. Unhappily, I sidled into the shed and confronted Bob with the awful news that he was being replaced by a sassy, upmarket youngster.

"We'll never part with you," I promised. "And you'll always be our favourite bike, because of all those adventures we've had together." I whispered that last bit, half an eye on Claud, tucked away in his dusty corner. "Maybe one day, Jolyon will find a nice young lady and you can take them out for a ride," I added, encouragingly.

It must have been my imagination but Bob seemed to flinch, before cowering back against the wall. Perhaps he was remembering the young Jolyon's scornful rejection of cycling and tandems, uttered all those years ago. Or maybe he was just looking forward to a well-earned rest. I patted his handlebars and went back indoors to share in Allan's excitement.

Five months later, we'd got used to riding Thorny and were preparing for our first holiday with him, which was quite exciting. After much deliberation with Theo and Jess, we'd decided to spend a week near Kettlewell in the Dales and then move on to Melrose for a week in the Scottish Borders. Jess had been driving for several years and they had a Volvo Estate, quite big enough to carry their tandem. Allan's company car was a huge Mondeo, so we had no transportation problems either.

We arrived at Frosty Cottage in the late afternoon of Saturday, 5th July, 2008, to find our friends already settling in. Theo and Allan began clucking over the tandems, while I joined Jess in the kitchen, where she was unpacking boxes of provisions. I was pleased to see she'd brought a jar of her homemade gooseberry jam and some brownies.

"I'll put the kettle on," she said. "What do you fancy? There's Lapsang Souchang, redbush or lemon and ginger."

"We've brought camomile, Lady Grey and green tea," I told her and giggled. "Thirty years ago, it was Tetley's, take it or leave it."

"There's half-a-box of Asda's own blend, if you'd prefer a more humble tea bag."

"No thanks, I'll try Lapsang Souchang. And Allan always has Lady Grey."

"Theo and I are keen on redbush at the moment." Jess opened a cupboard, searching for mugs. There was quite a selection of pottery ones, each with its own cheery little message.

"Would you prefer your Lapsang Souchang in *Finders Keepers Losers Weepers* or *Let Not Poor Nellie Starve?*" she enquired. "It's going to give the brain cells quite a work-out remembering everyone's favourite blend of tea."

"It seems nice here." I looked around the kitchen, pleased to see big work surfaces and the vitally important dishwasher. "Funny sort of name, though. Frosty Cottage."

"Surprisingly appropriate," Jess said. "There's a long list of bossy instructions. The switch for the water heater is quite high up and there's a note underneath saying 'No Standing On Chairs' to reach it. I was going to call Theo, then I thought 'sod it' and stood on a chair anyway."

"What else aren't we allowed to do?"

"We mustn't move any of the furniture and we're not to try to wind up the kitchen clock."

"Sounds as if the owner wants to wind us up," I said. "It's not exactly welcoming. Speaking of which, is there a welcome present for us?"

"Yes, that was the half-box of Asda tea bags. Oh, and a packet of custard creams – past their sell-by date."

"I'd rather have one of your brownies," I said.

"Well, don't spill any crumbs," Jess advised. "Apparently we're to leave the cottage spotless and exactly as we found it."

"It does make you feel mutinous, doesn't it? I've a good mind to go round the whole place climbing on chairs and leaving a trail of crumbs."

"I can see you're getting in the holiday mood," Jess said. "The birds can have the custard creams. We're expected to keep their feeders topped up. And water the hanging basket, while we're at it."

"No need for that today."

We looked out of the window and watched the rain teeming down.

Theo and Allan came in, soaking wet. We lit the log-burning stove and huddled around it, enjoying our tea. Allan drank his Lady Grey from a mug warning him that *Fine Words Butter No Parsnips*. Despite the miserable weather, we all felt excited to be back in the Dales and were looking forward to revisiting the fantastic scenery. But for the moment we were happy enough settling into our temporary home.

"I don't like this picture," Allan said. He'd gone into our bedroom and was frowning at a still life of half-a-dozen over-ripe bananas, spilling out of a brown paper bag.

"No worries," I said. "We'll swap it for another one. How about that painting in the hall of a rainbow over the moors?"

Allan duly changed the pictures and when Jess saw what he was up to, she instructed Theo to get rid of the portrait of Queen Victoria in their bathroom.

"I don't want to watch her disapproving of the way I floss my teeth," she said. "There's a nice watercolour above the table. Let's have that instead."

We ate Jess's lentil loaf for supper, accompanied by our own home-grown potatoes and broad beans. Afterwards, Theo produced his fiddle and Allan his guitar and the men serenaded their beautiful wives, who gazed at them adoringly. Well, to be honest, Jess was concentrating hard on her knitting, because she was negotiating a tricky bit of cardigan sleeve, and I made a start on *A Thousand Shining Suns* by Khalid Hosseini.

"I wonder what's on telly?" Jess raised her voice to be heard over a mournful ballad about some silly young girl who'd gone to sea dressed as a sailor lad, searching for her lost love. "I think there are some DVDs in that drawer."

We needed the TV on quite loudly to watch *Inspector Morse* but, after all, the musicians could have taken their instruments elsewhere. True, this cottage had only one living room but there was a big garden and it had nearly stopped raining. So there was no need for Theo and Allan to plonk themselves down on the sofa quite so sulkily. But they soon cheered up when we opened another bottle of Merlot and tried to guess who'd murdered the opera singer. I already knew because I'd been a Morse fan for years and had read all the books but I refused to supply any clues.

"If she'd been a folk singer, you could have sympathised with the killer," Jess said but fortunately Theo and Allan chose to assume she was joking.

The following morning dawned wet and windy. It was cold too. Feeling rather subdued, we ate our breakfast of luxury muesli with mixed berries and organic milk, followed by huge shiny croissants laden with Jess's gooseberry jam. I drank my green tea from a mug reminding me that *If Anything Can Go Wrong It Will*.

"Remember '76?" I said. "When what we called muesli was really 90% oats and 10% sultanas?"

"Washed down with 100% water." Jess laughed. "Goodness knows how we kept going on such meagre rations."

"At least we didn't have rain to contend with in '76." Theo stared out of the window. "Shall we set off now or wait for it to stop?"

Allan was all for not wasting a moment of our holiday but Jess and I were less gung-ho.

"How about you boys have a good look at the maps and sort out some rides, while the weather makes up its mind?" she suggested.

Once they were busy, Jess breathed a sigh of relief and got back to her knitting, and I began reading a book I'd brought called *Ecky Thump*, which was about traditions and customs in the Yorkshire Dales. Our husbands frowned to see us with our slippered feet up on the sofa.

"It's nearly stopped raining," Allan lied. "We've got a ride all planned and we mustn't fritter the day away."

"Jackie's not wasting time, she's doing valuable research," Jess said, to my considerable surprise. "We should know something about the area before we start cycling around it."

"Why should we?" Allan asked. "We never have before."

"Come on, Jackie." Jess ignored him. "Enlighten our ignorance."

"Um, right, yes ... " I dithered but found I was up to the challenge, especially when I heard a clap of thunder not far away and the clatter of hailstones. "I've been reading about Kettlewell's annual scarecrow festival."

"A scarecrow festival?" Jess looked enthralled. "That sounds fascinating."

Exchanging defeated glances, Allan and Theo sat down and endeavoured to look suitably fascinated.

"It began in 1994 as a fund-raising event for the school," I said. "The idea really caught people's imaginations and over 100 scarecrows appeared in gardens, windows and even on rooftops."

"Straw figures do have a long history," Theo observed. "Centuries ago they were often placed in fields at harvest time to appease the fickle gods. In Orkney, the tradition was to make a straw dog."

"These days the scarecrows are more likely to resemble Shrek or Gordon Brown," I said. "It's on for nine days. There's a scarecrow trail to follow and the village ladies serve cream teas."

"Cream teas!" Jess looked genuinely interested now. "Is the festival on at the moment?"

"I'm afraid not," I admitted. "Not until August."

"No point getting excited about it then." Allan got to his feet. "Time to go."

It wasn't just raining as we set off in the direction of Hawes, it was freezing cold too. I wore a vest, thick T-shirt, two cycling jumpers, my waterproof jacket, a woolly hat underneath my rain-mate and Jess's spare overshoes, which I'd borrowed in exchange for my spare rain-mate, which she wore over her cycle helmet. The rain pelted down as we toiled over Fleet Moss, where Allan had told me he wanted his ashes scattered. It was slightly alarming to reflect that we were now 32 years closer to that event. On a more level bit of road, we cycled side by side and began to chat.

"I like the new tandem," Theo said. "That's really good quality tubing."

"It makes for a much stiffer frame than the Bob Jackson," Allan agreed. "Safer, really."

"Are you pleased, Jackie?" Jess asked. "The colours are pretty. I like those red flashes."

"I love my new suspension seat post," I said. "When we hit an unexpected bump in the road, it's not nearly so painful now. I think my bum must be bonier these days."

"You've probably missed your chance of winning the Rear of the Year contest," Jess agreed.

At Hawes we stopped for lunch at a cafe and ordered soup, hoping its heat would be both comforting and warming.

"We camped here in '76," Allan reflected. "Do you remember eating dinner with our cycling capes draped over our heads because there were so many mosquitoes?"

I remembered because it was my blood the little blighters had feasted on, but Theo and Jess had both forgotten.

"I thought we camped at Askrigg," Jess said. "I know we went there."

"That was the village where someone shouted *Can You Ride Tandem?* at us for the first time," Allan said. "At least that won't happen again."

"Don't be so sure." Theo supped his lentil and butternut squash soup. "PG Tips have resurrected the advert. I saw it on TV the other day."

"It's often shown during breaks on *Big Brother*," Jess teased, but Theo wasn't in the mood.

"I'm absolutely frozen," he complained. "There's a shop over the road which sells outdoor clothing. I'm going to buy some thermal vests and socks."

Jess and I went into the little shop next door, where she bought half-a-pound of juicy jellies and I couldn't resist a postcard featuring a miserable sheep sheltering under a tree. The caption read *The weather in Yorkshire isn't always this baaaaaad.* I thought I'd send it to Nicki.

Because it was so cold and wet, we cycled straight back to Frosty Cottage, lit the log burner and hung our saturated clothes on the rails over the fire.

"I've changed my mind about that rainbow picture," I told Allan. "It reminds me how wet it is. Let's have the haymaking one on the stairs. It looks warm and sunny in that."

"I'd like the rainbow picture," Jess said. "It can go in our bedroom, where the mirror was. That mirror is like those in hairdressing salons – makes you look like a wrinkly octogenarian. I've hidden it at the back of the wardrobe."

Until Allan switched on the TV, we'd all forgotten it was men's final day at Wimbledon. The match was late starting because of rain, so we hadn't missed much.

"Looks like it's going to be a walkover for Nadal," Allan said, seeing that the Spaniard was leading by two sets. We all settled down to watch and it felt cosy hearing rain hammering against the windows, while we were dry and snug in front of the fire.

Federer began fighting back and was leading in the third set, when Wimbledon was subjected to yet another downpour, postponing the match for over an hour. I made tea, trying to remember everyone's favourite brew but failing dismally.

"I quite like this Lady Grey," Theo decided, after a few mouthfuls from his *Misery Loves Company* mug.

"It's camomile, actually," I said.

"Oh, yuck." He pushed it away. "I can't stand camomile."

"Have a juicy jelly." Jess offered them around and I reached out for a plump yellow one.

"Remember your teeth," Allan warned and, reluctantly, I withdrew my hand. Most of my teeth were in the last chance saloon and I'd recently spent a fortune at the dentist.

Then the tennis players were back on court and we watched Federer win the next two exciting sets, both of which went to tie-breaks. When rain yet again stopped play, Allan hurried into the kitchen and made a start on

168

supper. This time it was my home-made gruyere, leek and mushroom quiche, with more of our spuds and beans. While he was gone, Theo quietly proffered the bag of sweets.

"Quick," he urged. "Before Allan comes back and tells you to remember your teeth."

We ate supper from trays on our laps, watching the match being fought out against falling darkness and threats of further rain. Nadal won the final set 9-7 after a total of four hours and 48 minutes on court. Including delays for rain, the match had taken almost seven hours.

"Bjorn Borg won the men's final in '76," Allan said. "He beat Nastase in straight sets."

"I liked Nastase," Jess said, giving her husband's knee a little pat. "I always thought he looked rather like Theo."

"Same quick temper, anyway," Theo said, with a grin.

We turned off the TV, after a cheerful weather lady told us that it was going to bucket down over the next couple of days, with northern areas being particularly badly-affected. Localised flooding was probable.

"I don't think young girls should be telling us about the weather," Jess said. "I get distracted by their hair and what they're wearing and then I don't listen properly."

"They never wear clothes suitable for the weather they're forecasting," I complained. "Mostly, you'd think it was going to be 80 degrees in the shade."

"They're teenagers, playing at being mummies and daddies." Theo was joining in now. "It enrages me to be told to wrap up warmly and not forget my umbrella."

"I get annoyed by their concerned expressions, when they urge me to drive carefully or use a high-protection suncream," I agreed.

"Snow is barely on the horizon, before we're advised to leave home only if our journey is really necessary." Theo was well into his stride now. "Whatever *really necessary* means. And in winter, any motorist who dares venture out without a boot full of blankets, shovels and emergency rations is just asking for trouble."

"What grumpy old fogeys we have become." Allan stretched and yawned. "I rather like Andrea McLean. She's pretty and looks shy and rather sweet."

"She doesn't do the weather now," I informed him. "She's gone over to *Loose Women*."

"Oh, I enjoy that show," Jess said and Theo promptly rose to his feet, no doubt fearing the onslaught of celebrity gossip.

"Time for bed," he said. "They're probably wrong and it'll be sunny tomorrow."

It wasn't, though. We ate a rather silent breakfast watching the rain hammering down from a slate-grey sky. I anticipated Allan gearing up for optimistic encouragement and so, it seemed, did Jess. Delaying tactics were called for.

"Come on, Jackie," she said. "Share something from *Ecky Thump*."

I was well-prepared this time and had an interesting little custom at my fingertips.

"You remember we were talking about Askrigg yesterday?" I said. "Well, every August Bank Holiday Sunday, the vicar of Askrigg holds a service from a boat on Semerwater Lake. He was inspired by Jesus preaching from a fishing boat on Lake Galilee. The first service was in 1956 and it's been an annual event ever since. Musicians from Hawes Silver Band accompany the hymn-singing."

"Semerwater is Yorkshire's only natural lake," contributed Theo. "And isn't there some sort of legend attached to it, about a town being submerged in its waters?"

"That's right," I butted in quickly because I'd rehearsed this bit. "The story goes that a whole village, except for one cottage, was cursed by a weary traveller, who was refused shelter from a raging storm. His curse went as follows ... Semerwater rise, Semerwater sink, and swallow all the town, save this little house, where they gave me meat and drink."

"Fancy managing to curse in rhyme," Jess marvelled, but Allan's patience was wearing thin and soon, wearing winter clothes and waterproofs, we once again set off to the brave the elements.

I love Dorset and never want to move, but too many other people seem to feel the same way about my pretty little county and there appears to be more traffic every year. Yorkshire, on the other hand, despite being every bit as beautiful, has miles of quiet roads with few cars, which makes cycling so much more enjoyable. On the lanes leading towards Wensley, we were able to cycle side-by-side and chat. Theo and Jess thought rural roads near them were also peaceful, compared with those in Dorset.

"I never used to be nervous when I was cycling," I admitted. "I only thought of traffic as a nuisance. It didn't terrify me the way it does now. I think it's to do with getting older."

Allan, who was in denial about the relentless march of time, stayed quiet, but Jess agreed.

"When you're young you think you're immortal," she mused. "But by the time you're our age, you've known people who've died, and death feels frighteningly real."

"The less we have of something, the more precious it becomes," Theo said. "Which is probably why we're inclined to take fewer risks with the time we have left."

A watery sun emerged at this point, adding to our enjoyment of the scenic road we were cycling along, which led us eventually to the small town of Wensley. After a pub lunch, we followed a very pretty little road to Bolton Castle, where we stopped, trying to spot a couple of curlews we could hear calling from the protection of the sturdy ramparts.

"We cycled here in '76," Allan said. "The temperature was hurtling towards 90 degrees."

"We didn't come to this castle," Theo said. "I've never been here before."

"Yes you have!" Allan was adamant. "We found a patch of shade here and heated up some soup on one of the primus stoves because the girls had the bonk."

Jess and I bristled at this, denying any memory of the bonk or Bolton Castle, and Allan found himself in a minority of one. This was most unfair, as the photographs at home proved, when he eventually found them long after the holiday was over.

The sun continued to shine as we cycled on into Aysgarth, where we looked at the falls, which were magnificent after the recent torrential rain. Then we shared a pot of tea in the cafe, accompanied by slices of chocolate and black sheep ale cake, smothered in blackcurrant jam and cream. We were all united in agreeing that we certainly hadn't eaten this cake 32 years before, because such a gastronomic experience could never be forgotten.

We bought eggs, mushrooms and tomatoes at a farm shop on the way back, after which it pelted down with rain, and we arrived at Frosty Cottage soaking wet and cold as usual. Allan cooked omelettes for supper, then after coffee and Yorkshire curd tart, we opened the bottle of Bailey's

Irish Cream that Theo and Jess had brought and spent an enjoyable couple of hours playing Consequences. This got ruder and sillier as the bottle emptied and Jess patriotically kicked the picture of Queen Victoria under the sofa, in a loyal attempt to preserve the monarch's dignity. The game reached its hilarious finale with the intriguing line *"And the consequence was she farted and his wig flew off"*.

The following day we woke up to blue sky, with only a few fluffy white smudges marring its perfection. We ate breakfast, exclaiming at the view of surrounding hills, which every other morning had been doused in dollops of thick cloud. It looked as if it was going to be a gorgeous day.

"We'd better follow instructions and water the hanging basket," Jess said, peering out of the window. "Where is it?"

"To the side of the front door," Allan told her. "It's a really nice one. Full of begonias, lobelias and fuchsias. All colour co-ordinated and doing really well."

"Not any more," Jess said. "It's gone."

We all went out into the garden and began a fruitless and ridiculous search because, as Theo said, hanging baskets do not generally play hide-and-seek, neither are they known for a tendency to sprout legs and scarper.

"It's been nicked," he said. "Any passing motorist would have had a good sighting of it from the road. Some opportunist saw his chance and grabbed it. It's probably on its way to a car boot sale this very minute."

"I suppose you're right." Allan gave up prodding the depths of the tiny, murky pond. "But this is such a quiet road and you wouldn't expect rural Yorkshire to have a problem with garden theft."

"Maybe Frosty Cottage was specifically targeted," Jess suggested. "The owners sound a bit peculiar, if that long list of dos and don'ts is anything to go by."

"It's a shame but not our fault," Allan said. "And the sooner we get out on the bikes, the better. No need for *Ecky Thump* today."

It was windy and still a bit chilly, but after Kettlewell we enjoyed cycling the lovely road from Kilnsey Crag to Arncliffe. Then there was a steep hill to climb, laying bare the majestic landscape, bleak and threatening underneath a bank of black cloud which had quickly consumed the bright sunshine. The men were pushing the tandems, while Jess and I chatted. At least, I chatted.

"Isn't this fantastic?" I enthused. "I know the rain's a pest but Yorkshire is so beautiful, despite the rotten weather. I really love it here."

"Me too." But Jess's enthusiasm was luke-warm and she seemed to be walking more and more slowly.

"Allan and I really need this holiday," I confided. "Last year was so grim."

"I bet." She patted my arm. "But you seem fine now."

"I must be tougher than I look," I agreed. "Even climbing this hill isn't really making me puff."

"I'd noticed." Jess stopped for a breather. "Flipping heck, is there much more of this?"

Belatedly, I took the hint and we trudged our way silently to the summit, where our husbands were waiting. A few heavy spots of rain spattered down as we joined them. I was just launching into another eulogy about the splendour of Yorkshire scenery, when Theo interrupted me.

"I've had enough of this," he said. "And the rain's setting in again. I want go back."

"Go back!" Allan stuttered. "We've barely started. Let's have a cup of tea and a flapjack. That'll perk us up."

It did – but not enough to make Theo change his mind. Only Jess could have done that and she didn't seem inclined to try. After some discussion and with our friends' encouragement, Allan and I decided to carry on into Malham. But watching Theo and Jess turn back, I felt forlorn and abandoned.

"The weather is pretty grim," Allan admitted, after we'd cycled along in silence for a few minutes. "Are you sure you're up to this?"

"Quite sure." Straightening my soggy rain-mate, I rallied and pedalled with increased vigour.

Not so long previously, I'd probably have wanted to abandon the bike ride, but recent events had changed my attitude to many things. I still felt I'd narrowly escaped shaking hands with the Grim Reaper and now life had a salty tang, which I relished. I was fit and confident again. More than ever before, I enjoyed being on the tandem and I loved cycling in Yorkshire. It would be great to have warm sunshine instead of rain but I was just happy to be out on Thorny.

When we arrived in Malham, we bought ham sandwiches and Kendal Mint Cake and ate our lunch, facing the looming limestone cliffs. The rain had just about stopped.

"I haven't seen a tandem for years." A cheerful chap, walking a huge black poodle, stopped for a chat. "And now I've seen two in one day."

Two? Bemused, we looked around. Had Theo and Jess changed their minds?

"There's one outside the shop," he explained. "Belongs to Stu and Haley."

"Are they a local couple?" Allan asked.

"I doubt it." Poodle man looked surprised. "The place is full of tourists this time of year. Only about 100 residents."

So how did he know who the tandem belonged to, I wondered?

"We live in a small village in Dorset," Allan was saying. "Our closest neighbour is the village hall. That's more or less in our garden."

"Ah, now I can tell you an interesting story about Malham village hall." The chap suddenly produced one of those little fold-up seats and plonked himself down on it. His dog yawned and lay down resignedly, with its head on its paws. It had half an eye on my sandwich but was well out of luck there.

"It was only discovered a couple of years ago when an electrician came to do an inspection," Poodle man said.

"What was?" This chap seemed to enjoy being mysterious.

"A bugging device," he announced with relish. "Hidden in a 13 amp wall socket."

"Who on earth would want to bug Malham village hall?" Allan was incredulous.

"Good question. There's some who think the W.I. must have been up to no good." Poodle man chuckled. "And the parish council are under suspicion too."

"Well, people can become argumentative at meetings," I said. As parish clerk to Lower Winterborne, I was aware how quickly tempers could flare. "But there's nothing secret about them. In fact it would be good if more people bothered to turn up."

"Personally, I reckon it must have been a jealous husband," Poodle man said. "The place could have been used for illicit romantic trysts."

"Nothing very romantic about a village hall," I objected. "Not if it's anything like ours."

"You're probably right," he agreed. "No reliable heating and not even a carpet on the floor. I suppose we'll never know the truth now."

Giving his comatose dog a prod, the chap rose to his feet.

"Like to be anonymous, do you?" He gave our tandem a final glance, as he went on his way. "Not like Stu and Haley."

"Who the devil are Stu and Haley?" I said, and Allan shrugged.

"Apparently their bike was outside the shop. We'll go past and see if it's still there."

TOP TANDEM TRIVIA

Tandem cycling used to be an Olympic sport but was discontinued after the 1972 Munich Games. The 2,000m Tandem race was a long-time inclusion in the Olympic cycling programme but is largely forgotten now, joining many other discontinued Olympic cycling events, such as the 12-hour race, unsurprisingly held only once in 1896. Tandem cycling was introduced in the 1996 Paralympic Games in Atlanta. Barney Storey MBE, from Wimborne in Dorset, is the world's best sprint tandem pilot. At the London Paralympics in 2012, Barney and his stoker, the partially sighted Neil Fachie, won gold in the kilometre time trial, setting a new world record of one minute 01.351 seconds. Barney has piloted a number of celebrity stokers, such as Channel 4's Jon Snow.

CHAPTER FIFTEEN

Gourmet grub and the spectre
of a toothless daughter-in-law

T HE tandem was locked to a railing beside the shop but there was no sign of its riders. However, their names were engraved on the bike in wavy golden script, against a background of silvery hearts and an angelic cupid firing his fat little arrow in the direction of Haley's padded saddle. More tiny cupids cavorted along the length of her pink velvet handlebar tape.

"Let's go," Allan said, with a shudder. "Before they come back. They must be foreign, American probably."

"Hang on." I was intrigued. "I like Haley's handlebar tape. I wonder if it comes in other colours and designs? I rather fancy a flowery one."

Allan was shocked. "No Real Cyclist would ever desecrate their bike like that. It would completely ruin Thorny's appearance."

We cycled back via Malham Tarn and revisited the pretty little road to Kilnsey Crag. It was quite late when we finally reached Frosty Cottage and Theo already had supper under way. His mood appeared to be a mixture of the subdued and the bolshy, which was because he'd had a go at winding up the kitchen clock and now it had stopped.

"I told him not to." Jess sighed. "But he thought it was losing time and he didn't want to risk over-cooking the salmon."

"Salmon," I said. "Yum."

"We drove into Settle and stocked up with necessities," Theo said. "More Lapsang Souchang, olives, trout and crayfish, as well as salmon, croissants, raspberries, wine and lots of vegetables."

"I'll settle up with you later," I promised. Jess and I were in charge of finances and we were scrupulous about dividing everything down the middle.

"We've broken just about every house rule," Jess said. "It was dustbin day today and we didn't put the rubbish out. There were four exclamation marks next to that on the list of instructions."

"We don't come on holiday to obey petty instructions." Theo banged a saucepan around.

"What's for supper?" My main priority was whether I had time for a bath or would have to make do with a shower.

"Lemon grass and citrus poached salmon," he said. "With mange tout and asparagus. Followed by strawberry oat crumble and clotted cream. It's nearly ready."

Theo was a fantastic cook and I didn't want to risk putting him in a creative paddy by being late to the table for this gourmet feast. A shower it would have to be.

We stroked Theo into a good mood by praising supper to the skies and eating every last mouthful.

"That was rather different from all the fish fingers and rice in '76," Allan said. "And not much like the food Jolyon's eating in Guyana. He's had to learn to fend for himself. Under-cooked noodles and over-cooked onions seem to feature regularly. Oh, and pumpkin curry."

"He's improving." I defended my son's culinary ability. "Last week he made himself a meal of noodles, onions, tuna and fried banana, topped by two fried eggs. Apparently it was delicious."

"When does he come home?" Theo asked.

"August 18th," I said. "Less than six weeks now. We're so excited."

"Has he been able to keep in touch?"

"He usually manages to email every week and he sends excerpts from his diary, which is something of a mixed blessing," I said. "There's far too much lurid detail about narrow escapes from huge snakes, which slither their way into his bungalow."

"Also narrow escapes from death by dangerous driving," Allan added. "The roads in rural Guyana are dreadful and the bus drivers seem permanently drunk."

"I think the chances of him surviving to tell even scarier tales are pretty good now," Jess said. "I wonder if he will have changed much?"

This was something I kept wondering too, but mainly I was just thankful Jolyon was fit and well and maintaining contact so faithfully. His emails were regular, cheerful and affectionate. But Project Trust had experienced tragedy back in early spring, of a sort which must have struck terror into the heart of every parent.

"One of the British volunteers in Guyana was killed," I said. "A girl who Jolyon knew. Pamela was climbing in the mountains with a friend, lost her footing and fell to her death."

Theo and Jess were silent and I understood why. No-one expects to send their 18-year-old off for the experience of a lifetime and never see them again. Terrifyingly, Jolyon had admitted that when he and another lad were on a similar mountain trek, they had taken the wrong path and found themselves clinging to bare, flaking rock above a precipitous drop into the jungle beneath. They'd managed to scramble to safety. Pamela hadn't been so lucky.

"He's enjoying teaching." Allan changed the subject. "The kids call him Sir Jolyon. And there's a crazy woman with hardly any teeth who wants to marry him."

"A toothless daughter-in-law, Jackie," Jess said. "Just the sort of present you were hoping he'd bring home."

I half woke at 7.30 the following morning to hear rain hurling itself against the window, so I turned over and went back to sleep. Damned weather. It hadn't improved by the time we all sat down to breakfast, although warm croissants dipped in cherry and blueberry jam did their best to comfort us. But we were still hungry and the rain was getting heavier, so Allan cooked poached eggs on slices of hot buttery granary toast. Then we lit the log burner and prepared for a long wait, until the weather cheered up a bit.

"Come on, Jackie." Jess nodded in the direction of *Ecky Thump*. "What local tradition have you got lined up for us today?"

"I've run out of local ones," I said. "But if you're sitting comfortably, I'll tell you a tale of murder, remorse and commemorative postage stamps."

"Aha." Theo grinned. "This must be the custom of Tolling the Devil's Knell."

"That's the one," I agreed. "Sir Thomas de Soothill was a 15th century nobleman who lived in Dewsbury, not far from Wakefield. He was prone to nasty fits of temper and – for no good reason – murdered a poor servant man, who'd upset him.

"Not that there is ever a good enough reason for murdering servant men," Allan pointed out.

"According to some accounts, Sir Thomas de Soothill ... " but my gallant attempt to continue the story was once again unhelpfully thwarted.

"Let's call him Sooty," Jess suggested. "I bet everyone called him that."

"I bet they didn't," Allan said. "Not unless they wanted to run the risk of being murdered."

"Order!" I banged a spoon on the coffee table. "OK, Sooty, if you insist ... Sooty chucked the dead servant into a mill pond. Or if another account is to be believed, into the furnace of a blacksmith's forge. Legend has it that he was overcome with remorse and, by way of penance, presented the church with a tenor bell, which became known as Black Tom."

"He should have been thrown into a rat-infested dungeon, then had his head chopped off and stuck on a pike," Jess complained. "Shelling out a few quid for a new church bell is the equivalent of community service. That's disgraceful."

"Sooty called the shots in medieval Dewsbury," I reminded her. "He instructed that the bell should be tolled at funeral pace every Christmas Eve, with one toll for every year since the birth of Christ. It still takes place today."

"That must take ages," Allan said.

"More than two hours," I agreed. "And the last stroke is carefully timed to coincide with midnight on Christmas Eve. Someone keeps a tally so they get it right. The tradition is also known as Tolling the Old Lad's Passing because Sooty left instructions for the bell to be rung at his funeral."

"The devil was supposed to be frightened off by the sound of church bells," Theo said. "The passing bell was rung when someone was on the point of death, in order to scare away the evil spirits, which were thought to be lurking in readiness to pounce on the soul as it passed from the body."

"What was that about postage stamps?" Allan asked.

"I know Tolling the Devil's Knell once featured on a Christmas stamp, sometime in the 1980s," Theo said.

"1986," I said. "The stamp was one of five, all commemorating British Christmas folk customs."

"What were the others?" Jess asked and I consulted *Ecky Thump* but without any luck.

"Dunno," I said, and Theo admitted defeat too.

It was still raining and we decided to go for a walk instead of a bike ride. We drove to Ingleton and did the waterfall walk, which was fantastic and the sun even managed to make an appearance eventually. The 4½-mile trail took us through magnificent woodland, giving glorious views over moorland and with a seemingly endless series of dramatic waterfalls. Allan spotted a little owl sitting on a fence quite close and a green woodpecker flying by. We passed an Indian girl, who was walking with her boyfriend. Jess and I were fascinated that she was tottering on very elegant, high-heeled sandals. On our final sighting of the couple she was limping along barefoot, which must have been equally uncomfortable.

"Theo hates high heels," Jess told me.

"He shouldn't wear them then," I said and giggled.

"He doesn't like *me* wearing them, you twit. I've lived in flatties all my married life. Then last Christmas I decided the time had come to rebel."

"You told him you wanted killer heels for your Christmas present?"

"No, I bought myself a pair of gorgeous black suede shoes with three-inch heels and put them under the tree, wrapped in silver paper and with a tag saying "Lots of love from Theo XXX".

"Well done." I was most impressed. "What did he say?"

"He said he'd protected my feet for 35 years and his reward was going to be a lame wife, crippled with corns and bunions."

"We shouldn't pander to them all the time," I said. "Feminists would be ashamed of us. Did you bring your beautiful shoes with you? I haven't seen them."

"You could have seen them in Cambridge's Oxfam shop, in the New Year," Jess said. "Theo was right all along. Those bloody things were torture."

I couldn't help feeling that three-inch heels after a lifetime of flatties was maybe at least one inch too optimistic but I said nothing. Comfort came first with me too, these days.

For supper, Allan made a crayfish and trout bake with watercress sauce, followed by raspberry orange trifle. He enjoying cooking and had been put on his mettle by Theo's expertise. Jess and I knew when we were well off and were lavish with our praise and appreciation.

"I enjoyed the waterfall walk," Theo said, over coffee and Belgian chocolate truffles. "But did anyone feel there was something missing?"

"Of course." Allan understood immediately. "It felt wrong, leaving the bikes behind. It's riding tandems together that makes our friendship special."

"We'll go on a good long ride tomorrow," Theo decided. "And get really fit."

Jess eyeballed me and I had a quick rummage through *Ecky Thump*, just in case.

Thursday dawned soaking wet and, according to the sympathetic weather lady, there was unlikely to be much immediate improvement, although she was cautiously optimistic about the weekend.

"Go on then." Allan sighed. "What curious custom have you got lined up for us today? But we're not sitting around here for one minute after 11 o'clock. The bikes are beckoning."

"This is all about a traditional Yorkshire delicacy," I told them. "The Denby Dale Pie, to be precise."

"I've heard of that but I don't know a thing about it," Theo said.

"The Denby Dale villagers baked their first pie in 1788, to rejoice over King George III's return to sanity after a mental breakdown."

"I thought he was always known as mad King George?" Jess said.

"Yes, he relapsed but he didn't eat any of the pie, so we can't blame that. Compared to most of the pies which followed at intervals of about 30 years, the first one was a modest affair, containing only two sheep and 20 chickens. A local soldier sliced it up with his sword. The second was the victory pie of 1815, baked to celebrate Napoleon's defeat."

"Was that much bigger?" Theo asked.

"Not a lot," I admitted. "Denby Dale really got its pastry credentials in the pie of 1846. This one commemorated the repeal of the Corn Laws and was eight feet in diameter and stuffed with five sheep, 21 rabbits and 90 chickens."

"Disgusting." Jess the vegetarian shuddered. "Who cut that one up?"

"No-one. The stage collapsed under the weight of the pie and it smashed to pieces on the ground. There was a crowd of 15,000 people looking forward to their lunch and they waded in, grabbed handfuls and gobbled the lot."

"When was the next great bake-off?" Theo asked.

"1887, for Queen Victoria's golden jubilee. That one contained meat so rotten that when the putrid pie was cut into, people retreated from its pong. It had to be buried in quick lime. Denby Dale made a ceremony of the internment and circulated invitation cards."

"The village ladies responsible for cooking the pie must have been in trouble," Jess said.

"No, a top notch London chef was in charge. He did a bunk before the state of the pie was discovered. The women saved the day by baking another one within the week."

"That's more like it." Jess's knitting needles clacked approval.

"How much more of this?" Allan asked. "I'm getting bored and it's nearly stopped raining."

No-one gave me any encouragement to continue, so with dignity I closed *Ecky Thump*. They'd lost their chance to hear the fascinating story of the other seven pies, in particular the interference of Environmental Health during the planning of one baked in 1964. They'd never know about the unpleasant and embarrassing medical tests endured by everybody involved in its preparation and the manner in which the men from the Ministry were finally put firmly in their place, by forthright Yorkshire men. These were just a few of the many intriguing snippets they'd never know and it jolly well served them right.

We decided to cycle to Bolton Abbey and walk to the Strid, a notorious stretch of water where the River Wharfe is forced into a deep and narrow channel. We expected the Strid to look both magnificent and intimidating, after the recent torrential downpours. It had actually stopped raining now but the roads were waterlogged. I was grateful for Jess's over-shoes because without them, my shoes would have been soaked through from all the puddles and spray from passing cars. But it wasn't quite so cold, which made for more pleasant cycling. We reached the village of Appletreewick, where we'd camped in '76.

"Do you remember the non-smoking pub here?" Allan asked.

"Oh yes," Jess said. "It was great. We had a really good evening and didn't come out reeking of cigarette smoke."

Allan stared at her in disbelief. "We didn't even stop for a drink," he said. "It was full of grumpy old people."

"Then we'd feel very much at home there now," Theo said. "But I can't remember going into a non-smoking pub at all."

I remembered it quite clearly but meanly stayed silent because I hadn't forgiven Allan for his ungrateful rejection of *Ecky Thump.*

"Let's see if we can find the pub," Theo suggested. "We could have lunch there."

There are two pubs in Appletreewick, both obviously smoke-free now. Allan was pretty sure it was The New Inn which had been non-smoking in '76 and which we'd abandoned in favour of the more relaxed and welcoming Craven Arms. Three decades later, we decided to give The New Inn a second chance and opted to eat outside, to enjoy every second of the elusive sunshine. We had the place almost to ourselves, until an old chap sat down at the table next to ours and immediately lit up. Allan wrinkled his nose at the first waft of smoke.

"That's the problem now," he observed. "The air outside pubs is polluted. There's really no avoiding the disgusting weed."

Irritably, he kicked at a cigarette butt lurking underneath our table and it rolled directly to the feet of the offending smoker, who promptly kicked it back again.

"You watch who you're calling disgusting," said fag ash Fred, who'd obviously heard my husband's comment. "I suppose you're one of those who'd like to make it illegal for people to smoke anywhere?"

I could see Allan weighing this up, so I interrupted quickly.

"When we came to Appletreewick 30 years ago, The New Inn was non-smoking. Most unusual in those days."

"That's right." The old chap flicked some ash in the general direction of a potted fern. "It were famous for being the country's first non-smoking pub. Right-thinking village folk hung their heads in shame. Mind, people visited from far and wide, just to inhale the fag-free air. But they never came back a second time."

"We didn't stay long ourselves, back in '76," Allan admitted. "About two minutes, actually. The atmosphere wasn't very friendly."

Fag ash Fred grinned. "Aye, livelier folk decamped to The Craven Arms."

Finishing his pint and his smoke, the old chap got up to leave, and spotted our bikes.

"I might have known you'd be cyclists," he said. "I bet you're vegetarians, too. But it takes all sorts. Live and let live, that's what I say."

Looking pleased with himself, he sauntered off.

As the weather was still reasonable, we pedalled on to Bolton Abbey, where we left the tandems locked together in the car park while we followed a footpath through the woods. The track was muddy and stony and our cycling shoes weren't ideal for difficult walking, so we trod carefully and even more carefully when we finally reached the slippery rocks around the Strid.

It is at this spot where the River Wharfe suddenly narrows and the water rushes through with menacing force. The Strid is so-called because it is said to be a stride wide and narrow enough to jump across. A risky escapade, even when dry weather has coerced the river into a deceptively gentle trickle. But that day, after recent flooding, the Wharfe was in turbulent, arrogant mode, subduing us into respectful silence as we listened to the roar of heavy water battering its way past every obstacle.

A stark sign warned visitors to take care. **DANGER.** THE STRID IS DANGEROUS AND HAS CLAIMED LIVES IN THE PAST.

"A honeymoon couple drowned here only last year," Theo said. "It was several weeks before their bodies were found."

"I remember reading about that," Allan agreed. "Apparently the water can rise up to five feet in less than a minute."

I'd moved well back from the river. Ever since that death-defying walk around Wastwater lake, I'd not felt inclined to take any chances.

"How about a nice cup of tea in the cafe before we head home?" I suggested and, to my relief, they didn't need any persuading.

When we eventually turned back, the rain had set in again and the sky was that leaden slate grey we'd all come to dread. We were cycling on a quiet road, side by side, when a Land Rover suddenly skidded up behind us and the driver leaned on his horn, gesturing for us to separate into single file. When we did so, he overtook us much too fast and far too close. I squealed as the vehicle tore past with only inches to spare. Thorny wobbled alarmingly and Allan swore, treating the motorist to a few gestures of his own. Theo and Jess's tandem had stayed steady but we were all shaken and angry.

"It's either ignorance, stupidity or a combination of both," Theo fumed. "Wouldn't you just love to be able to get your own back?"

"He's probably in Lancashire by now," Allan muttered. "Going at that speed."

However, half-a-mile down the road we spotted the Land Rover parked outside a cottage, with no sign of its driver. The men considered banging on the cottage door, in the hope of giving our bad-mannered motorist a punch on the nose, or at least a few choice words. But in the end we pedalled off, our anger somewhat dampened by the rain, which was now falling down in torrents.

But revenge is a dish best served cold and we were certainly getting rather chilly when we suddenly realised that the same Land Rover was once again careering up behind us. We'd been cycling in single file because of the deep puddles narrowing the road, but with barely a word spoken Theo and Jess came alongside us and we cycled steadily on, ignoring the barrage of furious hoots.

We must have managed to force him down to a frustrating 10mph for practically a mile before meeting a lay-by, when he was finally able to overtake. Four grinning faces briefly encountered an irate and purple countenance, hurling obscenities through a lowered window. It's not often cyclists are given the opportunity to wreak vengeance on an arrogant motorist and we revelled in the satisfaction of it.

Theo was so pumped up that he took the lead, cycling straight through puddles with abandon, deaf to Jess's complaints. Allan and I had trouble keeping up with them but we thought they'd have to stop soon, as there was an anonymous junction coming up and we'd need to consult the map.

Allan's eyesight was still pretty good and he could just about read maps without recourse to glasses, but Theo was not so fortunate and his specs were on and off every five minutes and frequently steaming up because of the rain, much to his irritation. Still euphoric with victory, he couldn't be bothered groping in his pocket for the wretched glasses, so at the junction he made a guess, turned right and pedalled off into the wet and misty murk, without a second thought or a backwards glance. If it hadn't been for Allan's warning shout, they'd soon have been well on their way into the wilds of Hebden Moor, from whence few return, or so I've heard tell.

Back at Frosty Cottage, we lit the log burner and draped our sodden clothes yet again on the drying racks. No-one felt like cooking, so we damped down the fire and Allan was elected to drive us to the pub, where we opted for the full works, this being our first restaurant meal of the holiday. Theo and Jess both had garlic mushrooms followed by fish pie, while Allan and I started with Yorkshire puddings and onion gravy.

"My mum used to serve Yorkshires like this," Allan said. "It was supposed to fill us up before the main event, but that never worked."

"It would be a shame if it worked today." Jess eyed my plateful. "One of those Yorkshire puds would go down well with these garlic mushrooms."

I was happy to share my starter but secretly rather relieved that neither of them could dig their forks into my main course, which was home-made meat and potato pie. Dessert was no problem, as we all decided on sticky toffee pudding with ice-cream and hot caramel sauce.

"We're certainly eating well," Jess said. "Generally, on a cycling holiday we might expect to lose some weight – but not this year."

"Our last day in Yorkshire tomorrow," Allan said. "Where shall we go?"

"We've got to clean Frosty Cottage," I reminded him. "So we can't do a long ride."

"It'll have to make do with a lick and a promise," Allan said firmly. "We're not wasting our final day scrubbing floors."

Theo and Jess nodded agreement, so I said no more. I was no keener on housework than anyone else and wasn't about to suggest doing more than my fair share.

TOP TANDEM TRIVIA

The record for the longest tandem ride is held by Phil and Louise Shambrook. It took this British couple three years to cycle around the world, clocking up 23,701 miles. They left Brigg, in Lincolnshire, on 17th December 1994 and completed their ride on 1st October 1997. Another British couple – Kat and Steve Turner – who were married in the Devon village of Bigbury-on-Sea in August 2011, spent a two-year honeymoon riding 20,000 miles around the world on their tandem.

CHAPTER SIXTEEN

Cheese and carrot sarnies,
rough wooing and hot foot

O N Friday we awoke to a delightful absence of rain but cloudy
skies suggested that this could be short-lived. Chivvied along by
Allan, we were on the bikes by 10.30, the time when generally I
was narrating some fascinating tradition from *Ecky Thump*. This was
slightly annoying because I'd been rather looking forward to politely
refusing to oblige, due to the ingratitude certain people had shown on the
previous day, although I might possibly have capitulated after being
suitably cajoled and coaxed.

We were half-way to Grassington when the heavens opened and the
familiar wet stuff bucketed down. Naturally this coincided with us
puncturing, on a barren stretch of road with only a dripping tree for shelter.
Allan fitted a spare inner-tube as quickly as possible, but by the time we
got going again we were all damp and chilled. Fortunately, there was a
good choice of tea shops in Grassington and we were soon steaming nicely
in a lovely warm fug and waiting to be served with egg and chips and big
mugs of hot tea.

"Are you here for long?" asked the waitress, putting a plate of bread and
butter on the table.

"It's our last day," Allan said. "We're off to Scotland tomorrow."

"It knows how to rain there too," she said, with a smile. "But I think the
weather forecast is better for next week. It's hardly fit for cycling today."

Looking out of the window at the relentless rain, it was difficult to
disagree. It's hard to feel completely dejected while eating egg and chips
but we certainly weren't at our cheeriest.

"How about visiting the folk museum?" suggested the waitress. "At least you'd be dry."

"We went there in '76," Theo told her and Allan looked up from his food in surprise.

"Did we? I don't remember it," he said.

"Neither do I," Jess said. "Does anyone want that last slice of bread and butter?"

"I'll halve it with you," I offered. "I remember going to the museum."

"You can't possibly remember because we never went there." Allan scowled.

"I think we wanted to get indoors out of the boiling hot sun, believe it or not," Theo said.

"That's right," I agreed. "We were tired and hot and because the museum contained the word 'folk', you and Allan suggested looking around."

"Were you working here in '76?" Jess asked the waitress, who was piling plates on to a tray.

"No, love," she said. "I was only seven. And your memories must be playing tricks because the museum didn't open until 1979."

Well, that left us very little to argue about. Making a herculean effort, Allan managed not to crow too loudly.

"I wonder what else we're remembering wrongly?" Jess pondered.

"If in doubt, ask Allan," Theo said. "He's the elephant in the room."

After buying food at the Spar for our supper, we cycled back to Frosty Cottage in the rain and after the usual drying process out came all the cleaning stuff and the hoover. It didn't take long before the house had resumed what we chose to believe was an acceptable level of cleanliness. There was nothing we could do about the broken clock or the missing hanging basket and there was a stubborn mark on one of the chairs, which Theo had stood on while wearing muddy cycling shoes. And we'd moved the pictures around so many times that none of us could be sure of their original positions. We spent ages searching for the portrait of Queen Victoria, which eventually turned up, for some inexplicable reason, in the peg bag. Given the job of writing a few lines in the visitors' book, I felt so guilty about our misdemeanours that I was gushy with appreciation and even said thank-you for the stale custard creams.

We ate our supper of baked potatoes and salad in front of the TV and watched two *Prime Suspect* DVDs, which meant we didn't get to bed until nearly 1am. Consequently, we overslept and still had most of our packing to do before the eviction time of 10am. We were 17 minutes late shutting the door of Frosty Cottage behind us, a final transgression which I'm certain was being observed by someone, somewhere, even if they weren't actually visible.

Allan and I stopped at Richmond for an hour or so, while Jess and Theo drove on into Scotland. It was mid-afternoon when we arrived at Melrose and decided to stock up on food before finding our cottage. The small town was very much the sort of place where hungry cyclists could find a tempting selection of tasty, gourmet grub. We bought olives stuffed with sun-dried tomatoes, a goat's cheese and red pepper quiche, soda bread, Border biscuits, a crab and gruyere flan, raspberries and tiny new potatoes, a Selkirk Bannock, homemade lemon curd and a bottle of whisky. It all cost a fortune and I had to divert my eyes from a tempting little dress shop on the other side of the road. Never mind, there would be other opportunities.

The cottage, endearingly and aptly named The Back O' Beyond, was a couple of miles out of town and not easy to find, being attached to an old country house in its own grounds and beyond the Sat Nav's capabilities. Theo and Jess were drinking tea in the kitchen.

"This seems OK," I said. "No long list of rules?"

"It's much more relaxed," Jess said. "And the welcome present is a Border tart, which looks delicious. Well, it is delicious. Ask my husband."

Jess indicated the crumb-strewn plate in front of a guilty-looking Theo. But none of us really minded and there was plenty of food after all. I explored the cottage and spotted the usual pluses and minuses for the finicky, middle-aged grumpies we had become. The rooms were quite big and it was peaceful, so no traffic noise. But stuff cluttered all the surfaces – vases of dried flowers, china figurines, a collection of glass giraffes, and soft cuddly toys lolling on the beds and most of the chairs.

We had the desired dishwasher and an open fireplace with two big baskets full of logs and coal, but the TV was tiny and its screen was partly obscured by the dangling legs of a stuffed clown. There was a separate toilet and cloakroom but only one bathroom, in which houseplants trailed luxuriant leaves and fronds over all the shelves and even along the edge of the bath.

We sat down with a cup of tea and a packet of strawberry cream shortbread cookies.

"We can treat ourselves to a drop of the hard stuff, later on," I said, and Theo looked interested.

"Did you buy some scotch in Melrose?" he asked.

"A bottle of Dalwhinnie, 15-year-old Highland single malt," I told him.

"We must owe you loads of money," Jess said, rather to my relief. "I'll get my purse."

We dined well that evening and sampled the whisky, which Theo's educated palate pronounced excellent. Even after the clown was dumped in a cobwebby corner of the broom cupboard, the TV proved a disappointment. Reception was dreadful and we soon resorted to making our own entertainment, in the usual form of knitting, guitar-playing and book-reading.

I settled down with *A Thousand Splendid Suns*, which I wanted to finish quickly, as I knew Theo had his eye on it. He'd offered to swap it for the latest C. J. Sansom historical crime novel, which he'd brought with him. It was his own copy, which seemed like wanton extravagance to me – the library girl – whose home was always bursting with books but who owned few of them.

"Are you going to treat us to the Scottish equivalent of *Ecky Thump*?" Jess asked me.

"Sorry. I haven't brought another book with me and I think I must have left *Ecky Thump* behind in Frosty Cottage."

"Tragic." Allan faked a sigh. "Never mind, Frosty's next visitors are in for a real treat."

"There are a couple of good guidebooks here," Theo said. "We can take them with us when we're cycling."

"So where shall we go tomorrow?" Allan was spreading the maps out on the floor. "I think we should follow some of the Border Loop's 250 miles of way marked routes, mainly along quiet roads. We can pick it up in Melrose."

"Sounds great." Theo eyed the Dalwhinnie. "Let's drink to a good day's cycling."

"Let's not." Allan said. "I want to be in a fit state to enjoy it."

We woke to sunshine filtering in through the thin, cotton curtains. It was breezy, with puffy clouds scudding across a pale blue sky. We breakfasted in high spirits, then Theo starting making sandwiches to take for a picnic.

"Grated cheese and carrot," he said. "Is that OK?"

"Er ... yes." It was too late now to suggest buying lunch from the scrumptious deli in Melrose. Theo was already parcelling up a stack of doubtless very healthy sarnies. Oh well, holidays were all about new experiences, even potentially inedible ones.

We cycled into Melrose, where I tried to slow down to show Jess the nice little dress shop, but Allan stamped firmly on the pedals and we soon left the town behind us. The Border Loop took us along a quiet, hilly road into the village of Stow, where Jess spotted the Cloud House Cafe and Gallery. Perfect timing for morning coffee. The place seemed popular with locals and we could understand why, when we were served with excellent coffee and generous pieces of buttery shortbread. Paintings by Scottish artists hung on the walls and there were notices about forthcoming events at the cafe.

"Oh, look," Jess said. "There's a session at lunchtime today."

Traditional folk singing in Ireland and Scotland is often referred to as a session and is usually very good indeed. In Ireland we'd found the best ones were impromptu, so the visitor is very lucky to stumble across one of those. I saw now that there were several guitars and a violin in a corner of the room and a small group of people well past the first flush of youth, who looked like hardcore folkies. Theo had already wandered across and was chatting to the fiddle player.

"Shall we stay here for lunch and join in?" Jess suggested.

Being tone deaf and having spent a lifetime miming rather than singing, I wasn't that keen, but I could see Allan was likely to have trouble making a choice between music and cycling. Maybe I should try to influence his decision.

"It's turning into a lovely day," I murmured. "Such a treat to see the sun at last."

"Yes." Allan turned to look out the window. "We really should make the most of it."

"I don't think I'll be able to drag Theo away." Jess nodded towards her husband, who was deep in conversation with his new fiddle-playing friend. I was pretty sure she had no intention of even trying to drag him away and, furthermore, I strongly suspected she had her knitting tucked into a corner of the saddlebag, ready for just such a contingency as this.

"Take the guidebook with you," Jess said. "And we'll have to buy lunch if we stay here, so you might as well have our cheese and carrot sandwiches."

After politely refusing this generous offer, Allan and I set off alone to explore the countryside north of Stow, still following the Border Loop. We cycled along high and lonely roads, the hills unfolding around us in swathes of green and purple, speckled with dusty gold by splashes of sunshine. Skylarks soared and circled and we marvelled at the ability of these small brown birds to sing tirelessly on the wing.

We stopped to eat our picnic near Heriot Water, biting warily into the sandwiches. However, they were surprisingly tasty and the birds didn't do so well from our leftovers as might have been expected. We also ate the rest of the Border biscuits and slices of Selkirk Bannock, spread thickly with butter and lemon curd.

The Border Loop towards Innerleithen took us along scenic, almost traffic-free roads through the Moorfoot Hills, where we were very excited to see a sign warning motorists to look out for otters crossing the road. A couple of strenuous climbs awaited us but we were enjoying the ride and there was a tail wind, which helped make it easier.

Seven miles from Innerleithen and in a lay-by at more or less at the highest point on the road, we saw a grave stone, painted starkly black and white and described simply as The Piper's Grave. We stopped for a proper look and I rummaged around in the front bag for my specs and the guidebook.

"This is the last resting place of an itinerant 18th century piper," I informed Allan. "He used to go round the local pubs, taking wagers that he could play any tune a customer cared to name."

"Not a bad way to earn a living," Allan conceded.

"One evening he started bragging that he could play non-stop all the way between Traquair House and Edinburgh Castle, without repeating a tune. That's about 30 miles, so no-one believed him and everyone in the pub dug deep into their pockets to take him up on his bet, reckoning they could make some easy money."

"Surely they were right," Allan said. "That was a crazy claim to make."

"Sounds as if you would have staked your last sixpence," I said. "The inebriated throng set off into the night, staggering behind a surprisingly sober and sprightly Pied Piper."

"I bet they didn't get very far."

"Most of them gave up and went home," I admitted. "But there's always a hardcore ... "

"Always," he agreed. "Especially among folkies."

"So the piper and his followers eventually reached the treacherous, rain-swamped wilds of the Moorfoot Hills, infamous as the hideout of robbers and rapists, who the local Polis were too terrified to pursue into their lairs."

"Does it actually say that last bit?"

"Not exactly," I confessed. "And there's really no need for me to exaggerate the story because the truth is pretty shocking. The miserable Scottish cheats."

"Keep your voice down. What happened next?"

"The piper was going great guns and the others suddenly realised that it was a long trudge back home, so one of them stuck a knife into the windbag of his pipes. The piper soon ran out of puff but refused to give up, until he had a heart attack and died at this very spot."

"What happened to his pipes?"

"Buried right here with him."

"I bet someone stuck a knife in the piper, not his bagpipes," Allan said. "Probably one of those robbers or rapists."

"The same robbers and rapists who were figments of my imagination?"

"I've never been a fan of the bagpipes," Allan said, as if that excused any amount of appalling behaviour. "It's jolly windy up here and I'm getting cold. Let's press on."

So onwards we pressed and managed to more or less bypass Innerleithen, via a combination of the Border Loop and Route One of the National Cycling Network, a long-distance cycle route that connects Dover and the Shetland Islands and covers 1,736 miles. We passed a sign to Traquair House, starting place for the ill-fated piper's final journey.

Cycling back towards Melrose, we enjoyed frequent sightings of the River Tweed, which forms the border between England and Scotland. At Caddonfoot we stopped to watch a couple of men fly-fishing, thigh-high in the waters of the magnificent river.

"They'll be catching salmon," Allan said. "The Tweed is famous for salmon fishing. It's beautiful here, isn't it?"

"Gorgeous," I agreed. "Much as I love Dorset, I think I could live here quite happily."

"Remember, they have real winters in Scotland," Allan said. "I think you've spent too many years being a soft southerner to adapt now."

Maybe he was right and, anyway, I'd be lonely, hundreds of miles away from Joy and Kate.

At the Back O' Beyond, we were pleased to see Theo wearing a pinny and cooking dinner. Theo's meals were always a culinary treat and this imaginative creation of pasta with prawns in a creamy garlic sauce was very much up to standard, accompanied by walnut bread and followed by raspberries with white chocolate ice-cream.

"I'm sorry about those cheese and carrot sandwiches," Theo apologised. "I expect they were revolting."

"No, I enjoyed them," I assured him, but he still looked doubtful.

"We had a delicious lunch at The Cloud House Cafe." Jess smiled. "Smoked salmon and asparagus omelettes, followed by strawberry bread and butter pudding. We chucked our sarnies into the hedge on the way home. The session was good, too."

"Fergus let me play his fiddle," Theo said. "And I sang a song. Mind you, most people sang two."

"Well, yours did have 18 verses," Jess reminded him.

"19," Theo corrected her. "But I'm sure everyone enjoyed it."

Allan managed to persuade the TV to work by moving it around to underneath the window, which meant we had to reposition the sofas too. Shades of Frosty Cottage. We drank scotch and fell asleep while watching an episode of *Midsomer Murders*, waking up with a jolt when the grandmother clock chimed midnight.

Monday dawned cloudy but dry and the forecast was good. We bought food for a picnic lunch in Melrose and then tried to find Dryburgh Abbey, which proved surprisingly difficult. However, we were determined that today we would not cycle straight past all the historic sites, intent simply on clocking up the miles. But this admirable intention did not include actually paying the entrance fee. We compromised by taking photographs of Dryburgh Abbey, admiring this stretch of the wonderful River Tweed and prowling around on the free side of the magnificent ruins, while I read out chunks from the guidebook.

"The Abbey was established in the 12th century by Premonstratensian priests from Alnwick in Northumberland," I said. "An austere sect who believed in living a hard, penitent life."

"I expect it was destroyed by the English," Theo said, and I nodded.

"Yes, severely damaged in 1544 by a raiding party led by the Earl of Hertford during Henry VIII's Rough Wooing."

"Rough Wooing?" Jess said. "What on earth was that?"

While I was still searching through the index, brainy old Theo supplied the answer.

"Henry VIII wanted to break Scotland's close ties with France, so he tried to establish an English-Scottish alliance, by arranging a marriage between his young son Edward and the two-year-old Queen Mary."

"But the Scots didn't trust Henry." I'd found the right page now. "They hid Mary in one castle after another and refused to sign the marriage settlement. Henry was furious and told his soldiers to put everything to the fire and the sword. The army did its best to destroy every abbey and kill all who resisted."

"Just one of the many reasons the Scots hate the English." Theo looked glum.

"I thought it was something to do with football," Jess said. "Or is it tennis? Andy Murray's not keen on the English, is he?"

"That misunderstanding connects both football and tennis," Allan said. He knew a lot about tennis because Jolyon had played for so many years. "In an interview, Andy Murray was asked who he'd be supporting in the 2006 World Cup and he said anyone but England. But he was only joking."

"Well, maybe," Theo conceded. "The Scots still have one big weapon against the English and that's the wee beastie."

"Midgies?" I frowned. Mosquitoes loved to feast on me but so far this holiday I'd been unbitten.

"They aren't a problem this far south," Allan said. "But in the Highlands and on the west coast, it's a different matter."

This was a blow. I'd fallen in love with Scotland and wanted to explore more of it.

"You can buy a mesh headnet, Jackie," Jess said, with a giggle. "They cover your head and shoulders and are quite a fashion statement, so I've heard. Maybe you could find one that would accessorise with your rain-mate."

"The Scots like to say it's only the wee beasties that stop the English outstaying their welcome," Theo said. "And they only pretend to be joking. Rather like Andy Murray."

From Dryburgh, we cycled the short distance to Scott's View, so called because it was much admired by Sir Walter Scott. We only spent a few minutes enjoying the fantastic scenery across the Eildon Hills and River Tweed because Allan began complaining that the day was fast disappearing and we'd hardly done any cycling. So it was noses down for a bit of serious pedalling, following a circuitous route to Kelso. Allan allowed us a 20-minute breather at Smailholm, where we ate our lunch looking up at the tower, another place favoured by Sir Walter Scott and used as the setting for one of his ballads.

On the outskirts of Kelso, Theo noticed that the tread was practically gone on part of our front tyre. Fortunately, Simon Porteous Cycles was able to sort us out and while Allan and Theo occupied themselves rummaging around among boring bike-related paraphernalia, Jess and I set off in search of more interesting retail outlets.

There were several attractive shops, including an unusual one called Itzy Bitzy, where Jess fell in love with a beautiful golden brown and apricot pashmina and I found it impossible to choose which of the cashmere jumpers I liked the best. Then we spent ages peering into the window of a bridal boutique.

"I made my own wedding dress," Jess said. "I was an old lady of 22 but Theo was only 20."

"Well, it worked out all right," I said.

"Yes, it's been 35 years. I wonder how many miles we've pedalled on the tandem since we tied the knot?"

"Thousands," I said. "Same as us. We must ask the boys what they think."

"We've certainly sampled several hundred tea shops," Jess said. "Talking of which, there's one over the road and I'm gasping for a cup of tea and a scone with cream and jam."

"Good idea," I said. "I'll text Allan and tell him where to find us."

Before we set off back, we bought food for supper and Allan put himself in charge of cooking. Sea bass was on the menu, grilled with oregano and tomatoes, accompanied by Jersey potatoes and followed by treacle tart and clotted cream. As we neared Melrose, it started to rain but it was just drizzle compared with the Yorkshire deluge we'd endured. We ate supper sitting around a spluttery coal fire, discussing the number of miles we'd cycled over the last three-and-a-half decades. We reckoned each couple must have clocked up at least 100,000 miles.

Doing so many sums must have exhausted Allan because he didn't wake up until 9am the following day. So we were late setting off, which didn't really matter as we had planned a relatively short ride to Hawick. The weather was a mixture of sunshine and cloud but the clouds were of the puffy white variety, so we felt fairly optimistic. Heading first in the direction of Selkirk, we followed some beautiful roads over the hills. We stopped at the top of Smasha Hill to admire the view, which was when I spotted a plaque in the shape of an open book. This turned out to be a memorial cairn to the poet Will H Ogilvie and lines from one of his poems were inscribed on the plaque.

The hill road to Roberton
Ale Water at our feet
and grey hills and blue hills
that melt away and meet
with cotton flowers that wave to us
and lone whaups that call
and over all the Border mist
the soft mist over all

Let oil, nor steam,
nor wings of dream
deprive of us our own
the wide world for a kingdom
and the saddle for a throne!

I consulted the guide book, pages flapping wildly in the wind, and discovered that Will Ogilvie was born near Kelso in 1869 and lived in Australia as a young man, writing popular bush ballads about his adventures in the outback. He returned to Scotland in 1901 and made a reputation for himself as a Border poet. After his death in 1963 his ashes were scattered on the hillside.

"I like his poem," I said. "I wonder what a *whaup* is?"

"It's the Scottish name for curlew," Jess told me.

I stared at her, most impressed, and she looked modestly pleased with herself. It was usually Theo who came up with the answers.

We cycled on to Hawick, where we walked through the busy town, looking for somewhere to have lunch. We found a cafe not far from the river and locked the tandems to a lamp-post. where we were able to keep an eye on them from our window table. We ordered toasted sandwiches, which took ages to arrive, and I vaguely noticed Allan's face assuming what I called his Yorkshire expression. He didn't really like to spend long over lunch, viewing it as wasted cycling time. Theo was reading *The Guardian*, oblivious to the minutes ticking past, and Jess and I were chatting, so my husband's temper was simmering up to the boil all by itself. When the toasted sandwiches arrived they were delicious, except for Allan's, which was quite badly burnt.

"You could ask for another one," I suggested. "Mine is really tasty."

"And mine," Jess agreed. "I think you should say something, Allan. That toast is definitely incinerated rather than crunchy."

"We'd only have to wait another 20 minutes while they cooked it," my husband muttered, trying to cut a slice of sandwich and succeeding in catapulting a blackened crust across the floor.

Jess and I needed to visit the ladies and unfortunately there was only one cubicle, which was already occupied, and we had to wait several minutes. I let Jess go first and soon heard the sound of laughter from behind the closed door.

"What's so funny?" I asked.

"You'll find out," she said. "Someone must have been feeling very cross to put a notice like this in here."

I was used to reading humorous poems in the staff toilet at the library. I had to try to remember to wear my specs when I went to the loo, otherwise everything was just a blur. Sometimes the poems were quite rude and it was interesting to ponder on who'd put them there. But in this toilet it was obvious that a furious cafe owner was responsible. The instruction was in angry black print, big enough so I could read it, even without my specs.

Please DO NOT steal the toilet rolls. If you need one that badly, you can ask a member of staff, who will be happy to provide you with one free of charge.

"Hard to believe some women's handbags are stuffed full of pilfered loo roll," Jess said. "But it would be hard to pin this on a man."

Giggling, we went back into the café, where there were no husbands to be seen. Then we spotted Theo beside the tandems, but no sign of Allan.

"He went off in a strop," Theo told me. "What took you so long?"

"We had to queue," I said. "Where is he?"

"No idea. He snarled something about wasting the day sitting around in cafes, breaking his teeth on rock-hard toast and then he stamped off."

I fancied Theo couldn't help rather enjoying this. He was the one with a reputation for having a short fuse, so Allan indulging in a tantrum made a pleasant change.

"Oh, let's push the bikes down the high street," I said. "He can't have gone far."

He hadn't. He was skulking a few yards away, pretending to be fascinated by a display of hay fever remedies in the window of Boots. I glared at him and he glared back for a few seconds, but I could tell his heart wasn't really in it.

"Let's get out of here," Theo said. "I can't wait to get back on to quiet roads."

"There's a good fishmonger just round the corner," Allan said. "I thought maybe I could cook trout and vegetable risotto for supper."

"That's his signature dish," I said, promptly forgiving my husband's display of pique. "But what about the other ingredients? You need asparagus, butternut squash and parmesan."

"Melrose will have all those," Theo decided. "So that's supper sorted. Now let's get on with what we do best."

We cycled back via the Minto Hills, which weren't too much of a hard slog but still rewarded us with spectacular views of the Border countryside, then through Lilliesleaf and Bowden and finally back to our cottage, via Melrose, where we bought lots of extravagant food and hand-made chocolate truffles.

Allan excelled himself and supper was wonderful. We tried to stay awake long enough to watch another episode of *Midsomer Murders* but the programme worked its usual, soporific magic and we were all soon slumbering gently on the sofas, in front of a comfortably crackling fire.

The following day was Allan's birthday, so he was allowed to choose our destination. He opted to head for the hills and we began by retracing our cycle tracks to Lilliesleaf, where we bought deliciously indulgent food for lunch from the Jammy Coo coffee shop. Then we turned off at Ashkirk, crossed the Ale Water and headed for Ettrickbridge. A strong head wind meant tough going on the high and exposed moorland roads, but we were all feeling pretty fit by now and enjoyed the challenge. At Ettrickbridge we stopped beside the river to eat our picnic and Theo pointed in the direction of a commemorative stone on the old bridge.

"That looks like some sort of family crest," he said. "Does the guidebook mention it?"

"Let's see ... " I rummaged through the pages. "Yes, it's the Harden coat of arms. Apparently some 17th century ancestor called Auld Wat was returning from a border raid one dark and rainy night ... "

"That means he'd killed and pillaged some of his Northumberland neighbours," Theo translated.

"He had a baby in his arms," I continued. "An English baby, I suppose. The river was in flood and Auld Wat's horse stumbled crossing the ford and the infant was swept away in the surging waters."

"That poor child's mother," Jess said. "Why did Auld Wat steal the dear little baby?"

"I don't know ... oh, yes. The lad was the heir to the Nevilles of Ravensworth, a powerful Northumbrian family."

"Told you." Theo looked triumphant.

"Auld Wat was filled with remorse about the child's death and built a bridge over the river."

"So that in future he'd have more success stealing English babies from their distraught mothers. I hope he met a sticky end," Jess said, fiercely. She'd obviously taken against Auld Wat in a big way.

I settled back with a second cup of tea, doing my best to ignore Allan purposefully putting stuff back in the saddlebag.

"Apparently Ettrick and Lauderdale are twinned with a town in France called Trois Rivieres," I said.

"There's a village called Dull in Perthshire, which wants to pair up with a town in the USA called Boring," Theo said. "If they succeed, they're going to throw a wild party to show that none of Dull's 84 residents are boring."

"I'd love to cycle through Dull," I said.

"We won't be going anywhere near Perthshire," Allan said. "Let's get a move on. Remember, it's my birthday and what I say goes."

"Don't push your luck," I warned, but rose to my feet and lifted my face to the sun. It was a lovely day, the warmest we'd had since we came north.

The road towards Selkirk was beautiful, in a steep and hilly sort of way. We were soon off the bikes and pushing them, down to T-shirts for the first time on this holiday.

"At this rate, we'll be getting hot foot," Theo said, and I groaned.

"I hadn't even heard of hot foot until recently," I said. "Is it one of those age-related nasties? Like high blood pressure and liver spots."

"I don't know about that but cycling shoes which fit too snugly can be to blame," Theo said. "It's very painful."

I agreed with him whole-heartedly. Hot foot was a fiery, burning sensation on the soles of the feet, exacerbated by pedalling and sometimes almost unbearably agonising.

"Insoles are supposed to help," Theo said. "And thin socks. Some people suffer more than others. It's never been a problem for Jess but then she's always worn sensible shoes, no ghastly stilettos."

Jess glanced at me smugly and, remembering her Christmas high-heeled shoes, I stifled a grin.

"I've never worn stilettos either," Allan said. "But I get hot foot occasionally."

"Back in the boiling summer of '76, none of us had it," I reminded him. "I'm sure it's something to do with advancing years."

"I suppose I must just have young feet," Jess murmured.

We stopped for a cup of tea at the Waterwheel tea room, just outside Selkirk. While we were locking the bikes, an elderly couple came up to admire our tandem.

"We used to have a Thorn Discovery," the chap said. "But it wasn't as good as that bike of yours."

"Do you still ride it?" I asked.

"No," he said, abruptly. "A combination of old age and ill health stopped us cycling. Although we do ride electric bikes now."

I noticed his wife was stroking the Thorn logo, very gently.

"Do you miss it?" I asked, regretting my insensitivity too late.

"We had a good few years on the bike," he said. "And we're grateful for that. Be sure you make the most of your fitness."

While you still have it, were the unspoken words, and I gave a little shiver.

"Did you sell your tandem?" Jess asked, and I looked at her in horror. She was committing a bigger faux pas than me!

"Good heavens, no." The man looked shocked. "It's in our son and daughter-in-law's garage."

"They even ride it occasionally," his wife said. "Mainly to please us, I think, but they'd never part with it."

"They will one day," the chap said, and a silence followed, during which we all interpreted his meaning. The silence continued as we watched them drive away.

"Those two are Real Cyclists all right," Allan said, eventually. "Even if they do ride electric bikes."

"I'll never complain about hot foot again," I vowed. "Or being saddle sore."

"It does make you realise how lucky you are." Theo put his arm around Jess.

"I've been telling you that for years," she said, but there was a slight tremor in her voice.

TOP TANDEM TIP

Options for transporting tandems by car:

a) Inside the car if it's big enough and you don't mind losing seats and luggage space.
b) Vertical or horizontal on top with power-assisted rack, if you can afford it and want to avoid manual lifting.
c) Vertical or horizontal on top with rigid rack, if lifting a tandem to head height isn't a problem and you won't be travelling on any ferries.
d) In a trailer, if you are happy towing one.

CHAPTER SEVENTEEN
A naked cyclist, a dog called Tarry and a 24-carat gold friendship

RATHER soberly we made our way into the Waterwheel and ordered tea with scones and strawberry jam. "A chap could do without all these reminders of the Grim Reaper on his 59th birthday," Allan said plaintively.

"Out for dinner tonight," I consoled him. "Birthdays do have their plus side."

"I'm glad I brought my posh frock," Jess said. "But I think I've got sunburn, which means a silly cyclist's tan on my arms, and that will ruin the sophisticated effect I usually aim for."

"You never look sophisticated," Theo said. "You're too smiley. Jackie, you haven't caught the sun at all."

"She smothers herself in factor 30 every day," Allan told them. "Even last week, when the rain pelted down."

"All those years cycling without effective sun protection did my skin no good at all," I said. "I've had two rodent ulcers removed during the last five years."

"If I ask what a rodent ulcer is," Jess said, "will it put me off my scone?"

"Nothing ever puts you off your grub. The medical term is basal cell carcinoma. Caused by sun damage and unless removed it carries on growing until it takes over your entire face."

"Stop right there," Allan demanded. "We may all have cast-iron stomachs but no-one wants to hear about your experiences under the surgeon's knife."

Another long climb out of Selkirk awaited us but we were pleasantly stoked up with food and the wind was behind us now, which made it a lot easier. Back at the cottage, we showered and donned our glad rags. I encouraged Jess to use some of my concealer on her red nose.

"I don't usually wear make-up," she said.

"It's not make-up," I protested. "It's only a dab of concealer."

"What else have you got?" Jess searched through my meagre jumble of cosmetics. "What's this?"

"Orange nail varnish. I paint my toenails with it. It's interesting how even quite ugly feet suddenly look rather sexy with painted toenails."

"I've got youthful feet, as you know," Jess reminded me. "Can I borrow it?"

"Certainly. Lipstick, mascara?"

"No. I think orange toenails will be quite enough of a shock for Theo."

Jess drove us into Melrose and we soon found Burt's Hotel, where we'd made a reservation. It seemed rather a classy establishment and therefore eminently suited to four ravenous cyclists, suavely disguised as two elegantly-attired, middle-aged couples, who seldom did anything more energetic than walk the labrador.

It was hard to make a selection from the enticing menu but eventually I decided on goat's cheese mousse, followed by venison, while Allan chose roasted sea bass and a starter of scallops with cauliflower puree. Theo and Jess both opted for smoked salmon, followed by aubergine and artichoke cannelloni.

"This is very civilised," Theo said. "We didn't do anything nearly so sophisticated in '76."

"We went to The Black Swan in Helmsley for dinner," Allan reminded him. "That was pretty swish. I had avocado with prawns and coq au vin and chips."

"Those were our chips," Jess said. "You kept pinching them. I wonder how much that meal cost? Under £20, I bet."

"It was £17.50," Theo said, and we all stared at him. He shrugged. "I just remember these things. At least today we don't have to worry about whether our purse can take the strain."

"Not while we're still working," Allan said. "But it'll be different for Jackie and me when we retire. I'd like to go at 60 but there's no chance of that. My pension's not huge."

"We could always downsize," I suggested. "That does have certain attractions, like less housework. Of course, some people worry that retirement will be boring."

"Not me," Allan said. "Plenty of time to go cycling and play my guitar."

"My dad died when he was 60," Theo said. "He only had a few months of retirement."

"Which proves there's no point trying to second-guess the future," Jess advised. "And just enjoy the moment. This cannelloni is delicious."

Over pudding, the conversation moved from retirement issues to speculation about infirmity and care homes, subjects which had never received much of an airing back in '76.

"My legs are really aching," Jess complained. "It must be walking up all those hills."

"I've got some embrocation you can have," I told her. "In fact, I've brought a new one which I've not opened yet. You can review it for me."

"I should think we'll all be going home a few pounds heavier after this holiday," Allan said. "Not like '76, when I lost half-a-stone in a fortnight."

"I've ditched the scales," Jess said, pouring more sauce on her sticky toffee pudding. "Being cuddly isn't a bad thing as you grow older. When you have a fall – have you noticed that elderly people never simply fall down, they always have a fall – you're not so likely to break your bones if they're well padded. And plump grandmas are much nicer than skinny ones."

"Has one of the kids been hiding something from me?" Theo enquired.

"No, but they're bound to reproduce sooner or later," Jess promised him.

"Your knitting will go into overdrive then," I said. "I wish I had a daughter, as well as a son. A boy grows up and leaves home for a woman who he expects his mother to love as much as he does. Although Jolyon did say he'd look after me when I was old."

"How about me?" Allan asked.

"Not you. Of course, he was at that gorgeous age when little boys adore their mums. About four, probably. But I've chalked it up and I'll hold him to it, if my daughter-in-law wants to plonk me in a care home."

"Could we discuss something more cheerful, like funeral plans?" Allan suggested. "Remember it's my birthday and I'm the oldest person round this table."

"And probably the fittest," I assured him. "I saw a fortune teller years ago, who predicted you would live well into your 90s."

"And without setting eyes on me," my husband marvelled. "That has put my mind at rest."

"Let's drink to Allan." Theo raised his glass. "And to all our tandems – past, present and future. May we always have sheds big enough to accommodate them, so they never find themselves at the mercy of our children."

The bill came to £150, so was approximately eight times the price of our long-ago meal in The Black Swan. At the Back O' Beyond, we didn't chat for long before seeking out the comfort of our beds. Jess had her aching legs to massage and the rest of us were ever so slightly inebriated. Another symptom of advancing years seemed to be an inability to stay awake much after 11 o'clock at night, especially after indulgence in rich food and alcohol.

Theo and Jess had decided to visit Edinburgh the following day, but we'd opted for another bike ride. We heard them moving about surprisingly early and by the time Allan and I surfaced, they'd already had breakfast and were ready to leave. They were both looking very perky.

"How are your legs this morning?" I asked Jess.

"Fine," she said. "I feel like a new woman. Ready for anything."

"That's because you're going to spend the day doing lazy tourist stuff," I told her.

"No." She gave me the hint of a wink. "It's got quite a lot to do with your orange nail varnish."

It seemed odd, setting off cycling on our own, and at first I felt a bit sulky. Vetoing Edinburgh had been more Allan's idea than mine. But the sun was shining, it was all set to be a beautiful day and after buying delicious sandwiches in Melrose, I began to cheer up.

We cycled to Galashiels via a network of cycle paths and then started to follow the high and scenic road towards Innerleithen. A cyclist came up fast behind us, but instead of swooping past with a quick greeting, he slowed down for a chat and almost straight away we realised that this was not simply another touring cyclist or a local out on a training run. This was Mike Tomlinson, husband of the late Jane Tomlinson, who had died the previous year from breast cancer. Mike and his daughter Rebecca were cycling from John O'Groats to Land's End, a long-distance ride generally known as the End to End. They were fund-raising for cancer and children's charities in Jane's name.

"My wife was a tremendous cyclist," Mike said. "In 2006 she spent nine weeks riding 3,800 miles across the United States. That raised £250,000."

The enormity of this achievement overwhelmed me. I'd heard quite a lot about Jane and the phenomenal endurance challenges she'd taken on, after her diagnosis of terminal cancer in 2000. I'd also read the book she'd written, called *You Can't Take it With You.*

"Jane and her brother did two long-distance rides on a tandem," Mike told us. "In 2003, they cycled the End to End, even though she had to stop twice for chemotherapy. And the following year they cycled 2,000 miles across Europe. Altogether, Jane raised almost £1.85 million for cancer charities."

He glanced back, obviously looking for Rebecca.

"I'll stop and wait here," he said. "We're aiming to reach Hawick today. Good to meet you. Enjoy the rest of your holiday."

I felt quite emotional as we left Mike behind, realising how very fortunate I was to be fit and healthy, cycling these beautiful Scottish roads and with a future to look forward to.

"How much money have we brought with us?" Allan asked, slowing to a halt.

"Only about a tenner," I said. "What's in the saddlebag?"

We always carried a reserve stash with us, dropping a pound coin in every now and again, and sometimes it accumulated to quite a lot. Allan tipped out the waterproofs and spare jumpers until he reached the coins rattling around in the bottom of the saddlebag. All the silver added up to nearly £15 and, scooping it up, I ran back to Mike, who was still waiting for his daughter. He was very appreciative, even though it was only a fraction of the amount we would have liked to give him.

We ate our lunch beside the River Tweed and then cycled into Innerleithen. It was immediately obvious from the banners and decoration that something special was happening in the town. We stopped for a wander along the main street and I soon spotted a sign advertising the St Ronan's Border Games. I remembered seeing this mentioned in the guidebook, which I'd unfortunately left behind at The Back O' Beyond.

The sun was very hot now and we both fancied a cold drink. Allan wheeled the tandem into a shady bus shelter, where I waited while he went into a nearby shop. A lad of about 12, wearing a T-shirt bearing the slogan *Fat People Are Hard To Kidnap*, sauntered up, kicking a Coke can.

"Nice bike," he said, then frowned. "Are you waiting for a bus?"

"No, no," I assured him, trying not to giggle. "Just keeping out of the sun for a minute."

"Oh, that's OK, then. Because they'd never let you on, you know. Not with that bike."

"Absolutely," I agreed, solemnly.

"Are you here for games week?" asked Kidnap Kid. Unlike most youngsters of his age, he appeared willing to pass the time of day with an old fogey.

"We're just passing through," I told him. "But it looks interesting. Are the games held every year?"

"Yup. We've been learning about it in History." From his expression, I gathered this had not been a wholly enthralling experience. "The first Border Games were in 1827. It was named after Saint Ronan, the patron saint of Innerleithen."

"What was special about him?" I asked.

"He was a bishop and he had one of those staff things that bishops carry around," the boy explained. "Innerleithen was a hotbed of sin and evil in those days," he added, wistfully. "The devil was having a high old time. So one day, Saint Ronan lay in wait for the devil and told him to scarper. Then he bashed him over the head with his bishop's staff."

"And ever since then, Innerleithen has been a model of rectitude?" I suggested.

"I dare say." Kidnap Kid shrugged. "It's dead boring here, anyway. The games are the only interesting thing that happens. And they aren't nearly as exciting as they used to be. Back in the old days, there was something called a handba' match."

"A handbag match?" I was puzzled, and he grinned.

"Handba'. Handball. Teams from Innerleithen and Traquair used to slug it out in a field next to the river. They were all trying to score goals, but the ball spent most of its time in the water."

"Sounds like a hard job for the ref," I said, and the lad gave me a pitying look.

"There was no ref," he scoffed. "Not many rules either and hundreds of players. Lots of them ended up in the water, fighting. Loads were drowned."

"Drowned? Really?"

"Well, maybe not." Kidnap Kid reined in his imagination a few notches. "But it was dangerous and people were hurt. That's why they stopped doing it."

Glumly, he kicked his Coke can against the wall of the bus shelter.

"There must be something good about the games these days?" I hoped so, for his sake.

"The end is the best bit. There's a torchlight procession up Curly Hill to a bonfire, where there's a ceremony and they pretend to burn the devil. It finishes with fireworks."

"That sounds fun," I said, hearing myself sound like a hearty grandma.

"It's OK for kids," he agreed, with a world-weary shrug.

His mobile beeped and he perked up, abandoned the old lady and her tandem and disappeared up the street. *Fat People Are Hard To Kidnap.* I'd save that one up to get a few laughs at an appropriate moment. But I'd be wise to choose my company carefully.

We cycled on to Selkirk, where we stopped for tea and cakes at a deli/cafe, the Waterwheel being sadly closed. On our way back to Melrose, we found several quiet cycle paths, which we mostly had entirely to ourselves – except for one notable encounter. After negotiating a sharp bend along the track, we suddenly saw two cyclists ahead of us – a man and a woman. It was a few seconds before it dawned on me that except for shoes and his shirt, the chap was stark naked. I decided to employ my usual salutation, when stuck for an appropriate greeting.

"Nice day for it," I called out jovially, as we sped past.

Returning back rather late, we found Theo preparing supper. The enticing aroma of linguine, tossed with basil, lemon and cream and accompanied by sourdough bread, reminded me how hungry I was, and I rushed to beat Allan to the shower.

Before retiring for an early night, Allan vacuumed, Jess and I cleaned the bathrooms and Theo put the rubbish out and mopped the kitchen floor. Housework done, on our return from cycling tomorrow, we could relax and enjoy our final evening together.

The following day was Friday and our last day in Scotland. We wanted to make the most of it by doing a fairly strenuous ride to St Mary's Loch, between Selkirk and Moffat. We'd decided to put the tandems in the cars and drive towards Innerleithen, park up and set off cycling.

We awoke to rain. Rather glumly we sat down to breakfast – trying not to spill croissant crumbs on the clean carpet – and listened to the weather forecast. It sounded promising but we'd been in Scotland long enough not to feel too hopeful. Nevertheless, we made an early start and parked on the outskirts of Innerleithen well before 10am.

We followed the B709 as far as The Gordon Arms Hotel before turning right along the A road and heading up the Yarrow Valley. The rain had lessened to an intermittent drizzle but there was no sign of any sunshine yet and we were beginning to feel hungry. Breakfast was a distant memory and had in any case mostly consisted of finishing up the leftovers. Fortunately, we found the wonderful Glen Cafe, situated on the shores of the Loch of the Lowes, by St Mary's Loch. Its appearance – that of a long wooden hut – is misleading because inside it is warm and welcoming with an appetising menu.

Looking out at the thickening drizzle, we decided to comfort ourselves with huge portions of carbohydrates. Jess had double egg and chips, I ordered a bacon roll and a raspberry oat crunchie, Theo decided on baked potato stuffed with tuna and lemon coleslaw, while Allan sank his teeth into a juicy steak and onion baguette.

"Have you seen all those posters?" Theo said. "This cafe is a hub of the local community."

"It hosts regular music suppers." Allan peered in the direction of the noticeboard. "Sounds just the sort of evening we'd enjoy. What's more, it's been recommended by The Guardian as one of the best roadside cafes in the country."

"Oh, well." Jess grinned at Theo. "If The Guardian says so, it must be true. Those chips were definitely among the best I've ever tasted. Don't take my word for it, though. Ask Jackie, she pinched half of them."

"You had most of my raspberry oat crunchie," I protested, looking around the room properly for the first time. "There are lots of locally-made crafts for sale here. I like those bamboo T-shirts."

"Made from organic cotton," Theo said. "Very eco-friendly. This is a great place."

Glen Cafe was certainly relaxed, with customers sitting around on comfy sofas, some enjoying a game of chess while they drank their coffee. Lingering here for hours seemed to be positively encouraged. But our lingering time was regrettably limited and we soon set off to explore St Mary's Loch.

The afternoon proved to be the sort of cycling experience you wistfully bring to mind during the depths of a miserable winter, or when you're trying to convince a sceptical friend that the back of a tandem is the perfect way to enjoy outstanding scenery.

Over three miles long, St Mary's Loch is the largest natural loch in the Scottish Borders. Although easily accessible by road, its aura is one of peaceful remoteness. Surrounded by the steep hills of the Ettrick Forest, its beauty has been praised by numerous poets, including Wordsworth, Walter Scott and James Hogg, a 19th century poet known as the Ettrick Shepherd.

At Cappercleugh, we were faced with a steep climb towards Megget Water, which soon forced us to dismount and start pushing the bikes. The road continued steadily uphill, climbing ever more steeply to eventually reach the Megget Reservoir dam. At this point, the weather took pity on us and our labours were rewarded by pale sunlight, lighting up fantastic scenery stretching all around, including a view of Broad Law, the highest hill in southern Scotland.

We stopped for a breather and I wandered across to the noticeboard. No-one else could be bothered moving, so I imparted snippets of information.

"The Megget Reservoir carries water to Edinburgh," I told them. "It supplies up to one hundred million litres every day."

"That's a lot of cups of tea," Allan said.

"Three hundred million, to be precise," I said. "Or enough water for one million baths."

"It's wonderful here," Jess murmured. "So peaceful."

"It wasn't always. In the 16th century this area was infested with outlaws, some of them quite high up in the world. William Cockburn, a laird in the Megget valley and a notorious bad boy, was found guilty of theft and slaughter and had his head chopped off."

"I expect they did something imaginative with his head," Theo said. "They usually did back then."

"It was stuck on a spike at the Tolbooth of Edinburgh, as a warning to others," I said. "What's a Tolbooth?"

"Me Sir, please Sir, me Sir!" Jess waved a hand in the air, before Theo could reply. "Yesterday's trip around Edinburgh wasn't wasted on me," she said. "The Old Tolbooth was a particularly manky prison, also used as a court and council chamber."

"The place had more than its share of beheadings and hangings," Theo said. "Heads were left to shrivel on spikes for up to a year, sometimes longer."

"And today we don't even have the death penalty," Allan said.

"Watching people suffer has always provided entertainment," Theo continued. "People used to pay a penny to stare at the lunatics in Bedlam. A visit to the madhouse was a good day out. As well as picnic lunches, they brought long sticks with them to poke the inmates."

"Nowadays we have reality TV," Jess observed. "So nothing's changed much."

The sun obligingly elbowed its way through the remaining thin film of cloud, as we climbed back on the bikes and followed the reservoir road for a long stretch of stunning scenery. After Meggethead, we climbed again for over a mile before glimpsing Talla Reservoir ahead, at which point the descent became very steep indeed, even slightly scary.

We cycled alongside the reservoir for a couple of miles, before dropping through the forest to Tweedsmuir and following the A701 towards Broughton and Peebles. There was more traffic here than we'd so far encountered, but still a mere trickle compared with Dorset roads in high season. Just before the B702 turning right to Peebles, we spotted a sign to The Glen Holm Centre, which included the welcome words *Tea Room*.

This was a diversion from the planned route and we were tight for time, so we were a little concerned when the narrow road went on further than we'd expected. But eventually Glen Holm, set on a working hill farm, came into sight and proved well worth the effort.

We were greeted by a soft and shaggy dog, who looked pleased to see us in a quiet, tail-wagging sort of way. The tea room led off into a spacious sitting room.

The waitress took our order of tea, scones with jam and cream and chocolate brownies.

"You're in for a treat," she promised. "Fiona does all the baking and she's a fantastic cook."

"The menu certainly looks good," I said. "I like your interesting children's meals. Little kids are so often offered nothing except flab and chips."

Partly from hunger but mainly from a lifelong inability to resist the proximity of the printed word, it had taken me less than a minute to scan the entire menu.

"Fiona and Neil are very proud of their catering," the waitress said. "We do B&B and evening meals too."

"What's the dog's name?" Allan asked, and she smiled.

"That's Tarry. He knows he's not allowed into the tearoom but it's hard for him because he likes people so much."

At the sound of his name, the dog looked up and resumed the tail-wagging. Between his paws lay a much-chewed ball. The waitress went over, patted his head and rolled the ball down the length of the sitting room. Tarry immediately raced in pursuit, carried his prize back to the demarcation line and resumed the prone position, but this time looking hopefully in our direction. Now we knew how the game worked, his eyes pleaded, surely we would want to join in? No pressure, of course.

Allan succumbed and went over to throw the ball. Once more, Tarry sped after it, returned and flopped down again, head on paws.

I am not a dog lover and I had no problem ignoring Tarry and concentrating on my scone. But both Theo and Jess gave in and obligingly played chuck the ball several times.

"Go on, Jackie," Jess urged. "You know you want to."

"She doesn't." Allan laughed. "Tarry's charms are wasted on my wife. The only four-legged friends she likes are ones that miaow and treat you with lofty disdain."

Jess went to the ladies, the men disappeared outside to the bikes, and I was left to pay the bill. Tarry's tail stopped wagging and his ears drooped. His face was mournful, humble and full of kindness. I completely understand, his expression seemed to say. I know you had a very frightening experience quite recently, involving a springer spaniel with a nasty set of gnashers. So of course you don't trust me at all, which is a shame because a nicer, friendlier dog you are never likely to meet.

"Oh, all right then," I muttered, and for the first time in my life, I picked up a chewed, damp ball and did what was expected of me.

Heading towards Peebles, we needed to get a move on, as it was still at least 20 miles back to Innerleithen. Fortunately we were well fortified by our Glen Holm tea. We cycled past the entrance to Dawyck Botanic Gardens and through Stobo, before turning right on to a minor road leading to Lyne Station.

It was fairly slow going along a couple of footpaths, where we had to get off and walk. Tandems don't negotiate tracks very well, being more difficult to manoeuvre than solo bikes, but it is often worth the effort to avoid heavy traffic on major roads.

Eventually we dropped down into Peebles and after a couple of false starts, we found a cycle lane which took us to the edge of this busy little town. After that, the route was easy to follow and there was only one significant hill. I drew a sigh of relief as we approached Traquair village because I knew we were now only a couple of miles away from Innerleithen, where our ride had begun, almost eight hours previously. We were so tired that we didn't exchange more than a few words while loading the tandems into the cars and returning to The Back O' Beyond.

After several cups of tea and leisurely baths, we finally began to think about supper. No-one felt like cooking.

"We could go out to eat," Allan suggested. "It is our last night, after all."

"Oh no." Jess yawned. "I can't be bothered getting all tarted up again."

"Me neither," I agreed. "But the cupboards are bare, except for a stale croissant and two tins of red kidney beans left behind by the last visitors."

"That's quite a challenge for the culinary imagination," Jess murmured. "Allan, are you up to it?"

"All I'm up to is taking orders for fish and chips," he said. "There's a chippy just down the road in St Boswell's. Will that do?"

We gratefully assured him it would do very nicely and off he went, with instructions not to forget the pea fritters and to bring back plenty of those little sachets of tomato sauce and mayonnaise. It wasn't really chilly but we lit the fire anyway for the cosy effect and made the table look pretty, with red candles and a jug filled with creamy roses from the garden.

When Allan returned, we sat down in front of plates laden with battered haddock, thick crunchy chips and pea fritters, all washed down with a couple of bottles of Rioja. Pleasantly replete, we flopped in front of the fire, faced with the onerous task of finishing off the whisky. Sleepily, we began to reminisce about our holiday.

"Most unforgettable memories," Allan suggested. "Like in '76. Theo, you first."

"Getting soaking wet and freezing cold on the very first day." Theo shuddered. "And eating wonderful chocolate and black sheep beer cake in the cafe at Aysgarth."

"That list of instructions at Frosty Cottage," Jess said. "The fierce notice in that ladies loo about people who pinch toilet rolls. Allan's trout and vegetable risotto. Oh, yes," she giggled, "and Jackie's orange nail varnish."

Allan looked puzzled, but Theo just grinned.

"The Ingleton Waterfall walk," I said. "Those cheese and carrot sandwiches. And Stewart and Hayley's tandem, especially the pink velvet handlebar tape."

"I do wish I'd seen it," Jess complained. "You didn't even take a photograph."

"All the fantastic views along the River Tweed," Allan said. "Glen Holm and playing ball with Tarry. But my very favourite memory is that speeding Land Rover which overtook us ..." Theo interrupted before he could finish.

"How could I have forgotten!" He waved his empty glass around. "We caught up with him when he stopped to fill up with petrol ..."

"It was a narrow lane and we cycled side by side ..." I gave a gleeful, tipsy hiccup.

"Refusing to move over when he came hurtling up behind ..." Jess sniggered, also tipsily.

"Even though he tooted and hooted and gibbered with impotent rage!" Theo finished, triumphantly.

"It's the only time I've had revenge on a motorist," Allan said. "That certainly is a memory to cherish."

"All our memories deserve cherishing," Theo declared. "And so does our friendship."

"There's a song about friendship, or is it a poem?" Jess said. "*Make New Friends but Keep the Old. The First is Silver and the Second Gold.*"

"That's us all right," I agreed. "24-carat gold. Oh, I wish it wasn't the end of our holiday."

"Plenty more to come," Theo consoled me. "So long as we don't leave it another 32 years this time."

The bottle was empty, the fire flickering towards its finale, and there was a long journey home tomorrow. But Allan's arm was round my shoulders and my two dearest friends in all the world were beside me. If only my son wasn't thousands of miles away in Guyana, I would be content.

"He'll be home soon." Allan demonstrated his disconcerting ability to read my mind. "And we'll have a party to celebrate."

"We'll be there." Jess smiled at us.

The pension might not be gold-plated but God has blessed me in all the ways that truly matter. I have a family who love me and friends who care. And, what's more, I'm fit and healthy, with sturdy cyclist's legs and rock-hard thigh muscles.

I've never mended a puncture, have only the haziest idea what a sprocket is and I still don't fully understand the workings of a bottom bracket. I don't watch the Tour de France and I'm bored to tears in cycle shops. But what else could you expect from someone who can't even ride a bike?

THE END

ACKNOWLEDGEMENTS

Thank you to everyone who has helped me write this book.

Diana Cambridge, for her encouragement, enthusiasm and perceptive suggestions.

My cousin, Simon Pridmore, for his patience and giving me the benefit of his experience as the recently self-published author of *Scuba Confidential.*

My son Jolyon, for taking the cover photographs.

Jim Bruce, for his editing, proofreading and cover design, and for converting my manuscript into book form and formatting for Kindle. *www.ebooklover.co.uk*

My creative writing teacher, author Ian Burton. And the members of 'Ian's Writers', who laughed in all the right places and supplied invaluable feedback, especially James, who came up with the title.

I owe a great deal – in numerous and diverse ways – to my friends who appear in this book, although at times they might struggle to recognise themselves.

Every bike ride took place but total accuracy as to routes cannot be guaranteed and *Life In Tandem* is not intended for use as a guidebook. Some people and incidents encountered along the way have benefitted from my vivid imagination and flawed memory.

And finally, heartfelt thanks to my husband Allan, who features on every page of this book but who hasn't yet read one word of it. I hope he isn't in for too much of a shock and that our marriage survives the experience.

ABOUT THE AUTHOR

Jackie Winter has lived in Dorset all her life and worked for 22 years in Dorset County Libraries. Besides cycling, she enjoys reading, walking and cooking but nothing too complicated or comprised of ingredients she's never heard of. She likes police dramas on TV but her favourite show is *Loose Women*. She enjoys listening to Radio 4 and is an *Archers* addict.

Riding a bike by herself isn't the only thing Jackie can't do. She would love to be able to join in with hymn singing and chant Happy Birthday when the occasion calls for it, but sadly she has a voice like a crow and is reduced to miming anything with a tune.

Jackie became hooked on writing when her son started school and she had more time for herself. Over the last 20 years she's had numerous articles and short stories published in magazines, once winning £1,000 in a writing competition and spending the money on a gold watch and a treadmill. Jackie still enjoys wearing the watch but made no objection when her husband quietly hijacked the treadmill. It was a daft idea, anyway. Her legs ache quite enough from all that pedalling.